THE V&A
ALBUM 3

The Associates of the V&A

Distributed by

De Montfort Publishing Ltd
37/41 Bedford Row, London WC1R 4JH
Telephone: 01-430 2250

UK & European Distribution
by
Special Book Services Ltd
Saxon House
70–72 High Street
Malmesbury
Wiltshire
SN16 9AG
Telephone: (06662) 4332

USA & Canada Distribution
by
Faber & Faber Inc
39 Thompson Street
Winchester, Mass. 01890
USA
Telephone: 617-721-1427

COVER: Detail of the wall-paintings in the Etruscan room, Osterley Park House, with a late eighteenth century Wedgwood vase. (Photograph: Fritz von der Schulenberg.)

FRONTISPIECE: The British Art and Design 1900–1960 Gallery. Designed by Christopher Firmstone. The installation was sponsored by the Baring Foundation and The Associates of the V&A.
(Photograph: Richard Bryant; reproduced by courtesy of *House and Garden*.)

ISBN 0 905209 99 0

Published by The Associates of the V&A
Photographs Crown Copyright unless otherwise stated
Essays © 1984 The Associates of the V&A

Edited by Anna Somers Cocks
Produced by De Montfort Publishing Ltd, 01-430 2250
Designed by Dand Design Associates
Printed in England by Raithby, Lawrence & Company Ltd, Leicester and London

The Associates of the Victoria and Albert Museum

The Associates of the V&A are companies and individuals who take a particular interest in the
Museum and who form its main supporters through the charity called
The Associates of the V&A.

Associates

Arthur Andersen and Company

The Baring Foundation

Bonas and Company

Christie's

Commercial Union Assurance Company

Colnaghi and Company

Charles Letts (Holdings) Limited

Mobil

Oppenheimer Charitable Trust

Rose and Hubble Limited

J Sainsbury plc

Sotheby's

John Swire and Sons Limited

Thames Television

Individual Benefactors and Associates

The Sirdar and Begum Aly Aziz

Sir Duncan Oppenheim

Mrs Basil Samuel

Sponsors

Through The Associates, the following companies and individuals have sponsored Galleries, Exhibitions, Scholarships, Lectures, Concerts and Catalogues at the V&A.

The Acquarius Trust
The Countess Ahlefeldt
Bankers Trust Company
The Baring Foundation
The Countryside Commission
G P and J Baker Limited
The Daily Telegraph
Express Newspapers plc
H J Heinz Charitable Trust
Ilford Limited
Jaeger
Sirge Lifar
Mobil
Pirelli
Mrs Basil Samuel
Trusthouse Forte
United Technologies

The Friends of the Victoria and Albert Museum

Corporate and Individual Friends exist within the framework of The Associates' charity to aid the Museum.

Alan Hutchison Publishing Company Limited
Albert Amor Limited
Antiques Porcelain Company
Artist Cards Limited
Ashstead Decorative and Fine Arts Society
Asprey and Company
Bank of England Arts Society
Bankers Trust Company
Blairman and Sons Limited
British Petroleum
Cobra and Bellamy
Coutts and Co Bankers
Crabtree and Evelyn Limited
Cyril Humphris
Doncaster Institute of Higher Education
Goldsmiths Company
Hotspur Limited
John Keil Limited
Kennedy Brookes plc
Ian Logan Limited
London and Provincial Antique Dealers' Association
Park Lane Antiques Fair
S J Phillips plc
Madame Tussaud's Limited
Marks and Spencer plc
Mendip Decorative and Fine Arts Society
Barbara Minto Limited
W H Patterson Fine Arts Limited
S Pearson and Son
Charles Pfister Inc
Phillips Auctioneers
Pickering and Chatto
RTZ Services Limited
South Molton Antiques Limited
Spink and Son Limited
The Fine Art Society Limited
The Wellcome Foundation
Winifred Williams

TRES RARE ET EXCEPTIONNELLE
SCULPTURE EN BRONZE
PATINE ET BRONZE DORE
REPRESENTANT "L'AMOUR"
EPOQUE DEBUT XVIII° (1720
environ) de la SUITE DE DU
QUESNOY, sculpteur né à
BRUXELLES dit "FATTORE DI
PUTTI"
REPOSANT SUR SON SOCLE EN
MARQUETERIE BOULLE
d'ECAILLE BRUNE ET BRONZE
DORE à l'OR FIN.

HAUTEUR TOTALE: 59 cm.

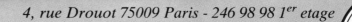

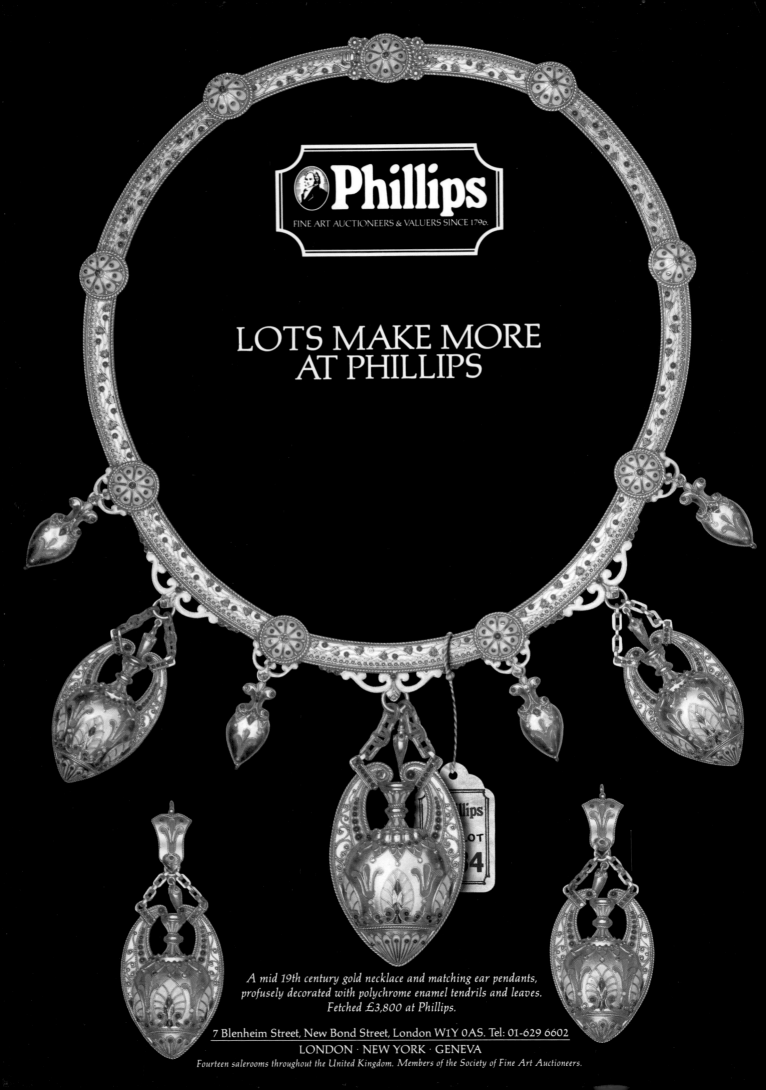

Contents

'TRIUMPHS AND TRIBULATIONS': LORD CARRINGTON, THE CHAIRMAN OF THE TRUSTEES, LOOKS TO THE FUTURE

The Victoria and Albert Museum entered a new phase of its history on 1 April, 1984 when it passed under the governance of a Board of Trustees. This brings the museum into line with our other great collections and severs, after over a century, our role as part of a government department. I realise that during the last decade that relationship put us at an unnecessary disadvantage and we expect under the new system to be treated in exactly the same way as our peers.

How do I see the new form of management affecting the museum? In the first place our role is to build on previous policies and achievements, on what we all recognise to be a remarkable heritage, not only in terms of the quality of the collections, but in those of service to the community. On the other hand our arrival has highlighted the considerable back-log of work that faces the museum. A brave outward face has concealed the grave problems which must now be tackled: a rotting building with leaking roofs, an obsolete heating system, inadequate drainage, vast back-logs of conservation, rampant dry rot, besides miles of hopelessly outmoded gallery installation. In the last few years a start has been made but our aim is to accelerate the pace and to achieve this we must look not only to Government for proper funding but also to the private sector and the visiting public. In other words we are moving into a period when the V&A can no longer be taken for granted.

Already over the last decade much has been done. Three-quarters of our twelve-acre roof has been rebuilt and renewed. The Victorian Cast Court, the Dress Collection and the first phase of the British Primary Galleries are initial phases of a reinstallation programme. The Theatre Museum in Covent Garden is now under construction and the Museum of Childhood at Bethnal Green is well advanced in the comprehensive representation of its collections.

In addition, work has begun and is to stretch over a number of years to rectify all the structural disorders of the main museum. And the cleaning and re-ordering of the entrance hall is a pleasurable symbol of the splendours to come.

But all of this requires financing on a gigantic scale. This is why both the Associates and Friends move to the centre of the stage. The Associates in particular have developed greatly in the last few years and in 1983–84 over £250,000 was raised for the Museum. The role of the Trustees will be to consider the V&A's objectives and how far they can be met in the light of available resources. Their task will be to find out how those resources can be increased. There is no doubt that we shall have difficult decisions to make but they will be made in the light of sustaining and fulfilling this great museum's aims and ideals which are now seriously under threat in the face of diminishing resources.

Illuminated *'Gramota'* (Letters Patent) of Catherine II, Empress of Russia, bestowing on her favourite, Simon Zoritch, then a Major-General in the Russian army, four medals, including those of the Orders of St. George and Alexander Nevsky, together with the estates of Count Buturlin. Zoritch had a great reputation for bravery after the Turkish war of 1770 but his position as favourite of the Empress was short-lived, and he did not challenge the influence of Prince Potemkin in any sustained way. Illuminated documents of this kind follow the same basic design, with a double-headed eagle holding an orb and sceptre surmounting a decorative frame hung with shields of arms. This document is exceptional in having a miniature portrait of the Empress. St. Petersburg, 28 April 1779.
L.31-1983   The National Art Library.

Albert and the Lion. This is a mechanical toy, made largely of natural wood, carved and varnished. The toy represents the climactic incident in Marriott Edgar's verses, 'The Lion and Albert', made popular as a recitation by the late Stanley Holloway. Albert has poked the lion with his stick: the lion is seen eating him. The simple mechanism is visible; it is worked by an electric motor, which starts when a visitor inserts a 10p piece. Albert has earned a lot of money for the museum since he went on show in September 1983. The toy was commissioned from a young designer-craftsman, Michael Howard.
Misc.135-1983   Bethnal Green Museum.

Virgil in his Study by Tom Phillips (born 1937,
British). From the set of nine screen prints
entitled 'Dantes' Inferno'.
1979–1982. Printed by Chris Betambeau.
Published by Waddington Graphics.

The prints were made while Phillips was
producing his own illustrated translation of
Dantes' Inferno from 1976–1983. According to the
artist they 'present major themes in the Inferno of
Dante (for whom nine was a magic number)'. As
with all Phillips' works, the Dante set make strong
literary and art-historical allusions: the brown and
orange castellations to the right are the seven walls
of the castle of Fame, 'Virgil's benign prison in
limbo'; the curious hexagon above it is the light of
inspiration descending; but Virgil has a blank
face, not because he is empty-headed (!), but
because no authoritative image of him exists. He
has his own Aeneid open before him as this was
the principle source for Dantes' Comedy.
E.364-1983   Department of Prints, Drawings,
Photographs and Paintings.

Crucifixion group. Ivory. By Pierre Simon Jaillot
(1633–81). French; signed and dated 1664.

The outstanding masterpiece of 17th century
French ivory carving, this group is very unusual
among baroque ivories in forming a large-scale
ensemble. With its signed and dated crucifix figure
it offers an important fixed point for the study of
one of the most problematic categories of ivory
carving. However, its monumental scale gives it an
importance too as a powerful example of 17th
century French devotional sculpture.
A.1-1984   Sculpture Department.

Mrs Wynne. Terracotta bust. By Aimé-Jules Dalou (1838–1902). Anglo-French; signed and dated 1875.

This impressive portrait was illustrated in Maurice Dreyfous's monograph on Dalou in 1903 where it is described as 'one of the most beautiful works of our time'. By the 1920s, however, it had disappeared from view and was rediscovered in 1983. With its sensitively modelled face and boldly sketch-like quality of the drapery it is among the finest of the works executed by Dalou during his exile in England between 1871 and 1880. During this period he influenced a generation of young English sculptors.
A.2-1984 Sculpture Department.

Baby's Folding Cradle. Toys and other things associated with childhood are usually quickly worn out. Sometimes a child's tragic early death results in things being put away and kept in pristine condition. This was the case with the cradle and its accompanying layette, assembled for Patricia Milson, born in India in 1916. She died at a few days old, and although subsequent children were born to the parents, the cot and layette were sealed away and never used again. They next saw the light of day in 1983, when they were discovered at the family home by Patricia's brother, Professor S.F.C. Milsom, who presented this remarkable 'time capsule' of the nursery to the museum.
Misc.48-1983 Bethnal Green Museum.

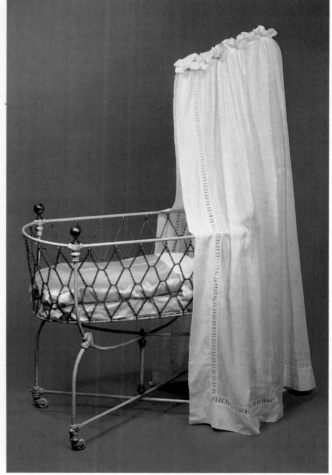

Portrait in oil of Charles Killigrew (1655–1725),
patentee of Drury Lane Theatre, 1680 and Master
of the Revels in that year. He was also Gentleman
of the Privy Chamber to Charles II, James II and
William and Mary, and was the son of Thomas
Killigrew, the dramatist and theatre manager to
whom Charles II granted the first Drury Lane
patent in 1662.

Painted by Sir Peter Lely probably about 1680.
The frame is more recent.
S 540-1983   Theatre Museum.

Design for the drop curtain for the Cave of the
Golden Calf (cabaret theatre club) which opened
in Heddon Street, London, in June 1912 and was
closed by the police in February 1913. In effect
this was London's first night-club, which was
opened and managed by Madame Strindberg.
   Executed in pencil, pen and crayon by
Wyndham Lewis (1882–1957), signed and dated
1912.
S 577-1983   Theatre Museum.

Pair of armchairs, *huanghuali* wood. Chinese; late
17th/early 18th century.

These chairs are from the bequest of seventeen
pieces of classic Chinese hardwood furniture left to
the museum by Sir John Addis, sometime
ambassador in Peking. Together they constitute a
magnificent addition to an already strong
collection, and place the Victoria and Albert
Museum in the forefront of holders of such furniture.
FE.74&A-1983   Far Eastern Department.

Model of a basket of nuts, Yixing stoneware. By
Chen Mingyuan. Chinese; 17th–18th
century.

The kilns of Yixing, some 150 kilometres west
of Shanghai, are famed still for their production of
high-fired stonewares, many of them associated
with the connoisseurship of fine teas. Also popular
with patrons from the educated elite were copies of
objects in other media, or of forms from the
natural world. These pieces, diverting and fun to
handle, satisfy the Chinese delight in fine
craftsmanship.

This model of a basket contains a selection of
nuts and seeds in variously coloured clays. Among
them are a chestnut, water-chestnut, walnut,
water-caltrop, dried lichee and peanuts. The lotus
seed carries the seal *Hecun*, associated with the
potter Chen Mingyuan, who was famous for his
elegant miniatures.
L. 11.5cm.   FE.19-1983   Far Eastern
Department.

Man's nightgown. English, about 1707–08. This
loose-fitting, T-shaped garment is the earliest
informal 'undress' robe to be acquired by the
Museum, unless one counts the miniature versions
belonging to the dolls, Lord and Lady Clapham,
which date from about 1695. The textile is a slight
(lightweight) silk with a 'bizarre' design of a
balustrade and half an arch in yellow on a light
blue ground and with exotic flowers in two shades
of pink. The silk, which from its width and
technical details can be attributed to England, is
dated to 1707–08 by comparison with designs for
those years by James Leman (1688–1745).
T.281-1983   Department of Textiles and Dress.

Tapestry. Nebuchadnezzar releases the youths from the fiery furnace. English, 1670s–80s. Three sets of these *Nebuchadnezzar* tapestries survive in England, at Glamis Castle, Powis Castle and Knole. The last set bears the initials TP for Thomas Poyntz (d.1688). The border on the Museum's Nebuchadnezzar tapestry is of the same design as a detached border in the Museum collection with the name of James Bridges, who seems to have run the workshop of Francis Poyntz after his death in 1685. This tapestry is therefore likely to have come from the workshop of either Francis or Thomas Poyntz.
T.53-1984   Department of Textiles and Dress.

Swinging cot, carved ebony, S. India or Ceylon, under Portuguese influence; 17th century.
   Cots designed to swing on this principle have been known in Europe since at least as early as the 15th century. This one is derived from a Portuguese prototype and was probably commissioned by a Portuguese patron. The carved ornament is drawn from a mixed S. Indian/Sinhalese and European repertoire. The upper framework is intended to support muslin curtains to fend off mosquitoes.
I.S.15-1983   Indian Section.

Opposite: Part (approx. ⅓) of a *chandova* (canopy), probably for a Hindu shrine. Western India (probably Burhanpur), early 19th century.
   Cotton, painted, printed and dyed. The medallions are filled with celestial musicians and dancers, who, with parrots and rosettes, also appear in the spaces between. The alternating large and small medallions in the border contain celestial winged beings.
IM.25-1983   Indian Section.

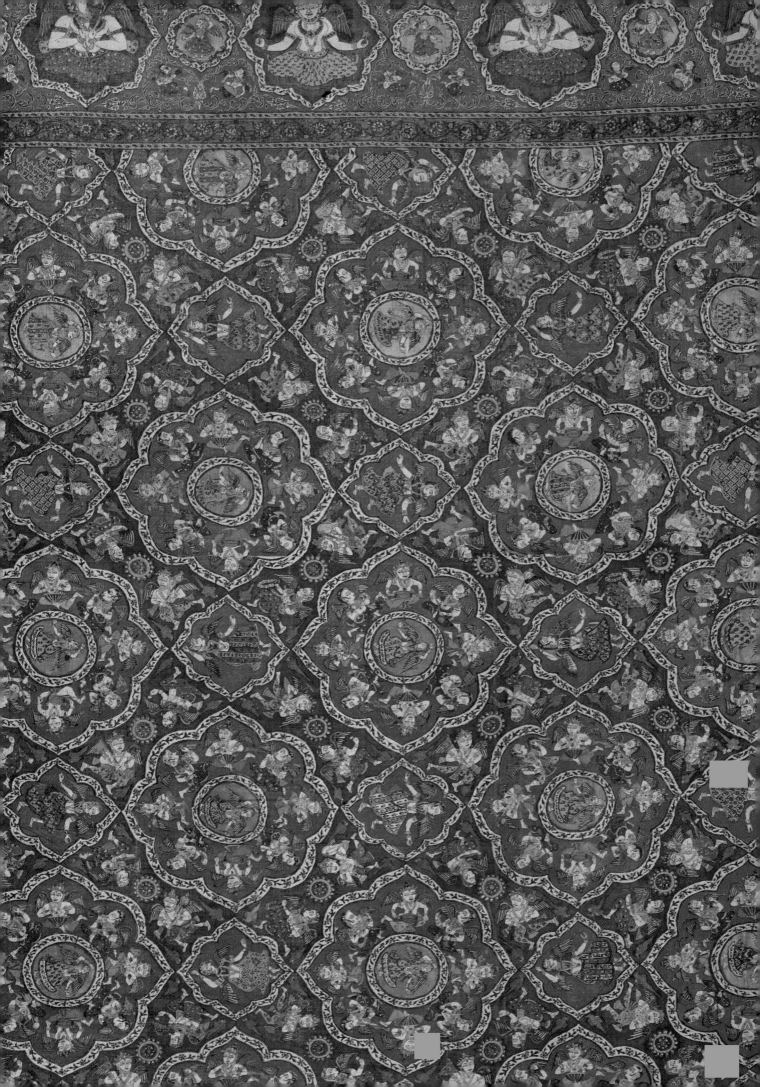

Drug Jar, tin-glazed earthenware, painted with a portrait head and with gothic leaf-scrolls. Italian, about 1475.

This drug-jar belongs to a class for which in recent years an attribution to Naples has been proposed, largely on the basis of pieces with the coats of arms of the Aragonese rulers of that city. It has also been suggested that the heads painted on the jars are portraits, and the word 'SANCZONE' inscribed on the present jar is presumably not the name of the medicine it once contained but the name or nickname of the personage represented.

C.209-1983   Department of Ceramics.

Figure of a Greeting Harlequin. Hard-paste porcelain, enamelled and gilt. German (Meissen), modelled by J.J. Kändler; about 1740.

This figure is from a very important group of Meissen Italian Comedy figures and birds presented shortly before her death by the late Mrs Josa Finney. The collection comprises twenty-seven items of which nine are of birds, mainly parrots, the remaining eighteen are of Comedy figures, all but one being from the Meissen factory. Kändler's harlequins and other Italian Comedy figures are amongst his most prized work today and until this gift was received the Museum had only one of them.

C.12-1984   Department of Ceramics.

The Armada Relics from Belchamp Hall
Snaphance musket, the stock inlaid with engraved
staghorn. English, dated 1588.
Wheel-lock pistol, the stock inlaid with engraved
staghorn, the barrel and mounts damascened in
gold and silver. English, about 1590.

Powder flask, inlaid with engraved staghorn
after designs by Virgil Solis, the iron mounts
damascened in gold and silver.

These were long preserved in the house of the
Raymond family in Essex, and formerly belonged

to Sir William Harris of Shenfield House,
Margaretting, Essex, who married into the
Raymond family in the early 17th century. The
wheel-lock pistol is not only preserved in
exceptionally fine condition, but is also the only
English pistol of this kind to have been identified
so far.

Acquired with the aid of a grant from the
National Heritage Memorial Fund.
M.948-950-1983   Metalwork Department.

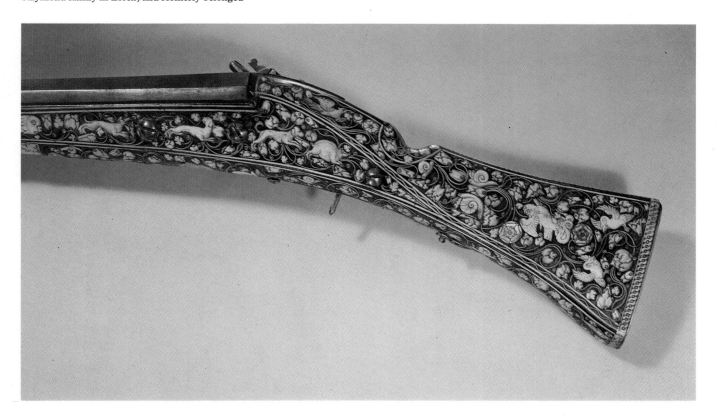

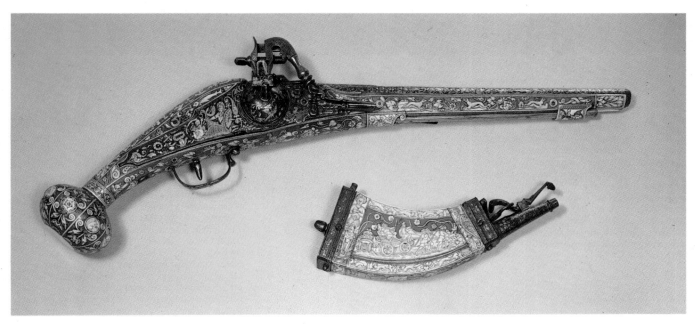

School Furniture. Danish 1983.

The 'Alterna' series of school furnishings was designed by Ib Pors Nielsen and made by Fritz Hansen Eft. A.S., who presented these examples to the Museum.

The 'Alterna' range, which is made in four sizes to suit different age groups, is the product of more than two years research. This included photographing pupils during lessons, and consultations with teachers, pupils and school janitors.

The stacking chairs have a shorter leg at the front so they can be tilted forward to ensure the user's spine is correctly angled for leaning forward to write. The desk top can also be adjusted to form a slope suitable for writing.
W.11&a and 12-1984.

Opposite: A French Royal Cabinet of the 1660s. This small cabinet, veneered in ivory and various woods, was, until its purchase by the Museum, supposed to be Flemish. However, it has now been identified by the distinguished Dutch furniture historian, Professor Lunsingh Scheurleer, with a cabinet described in the 1671 inventory of the Palais Royal, Paris, where it stood in the apartment of Henriette Anne, Duchesse d'Orléans (1644–1670), fifth daughter of Charles I of England, who married Louis XIV's brother, the Duc d'Orléans, in 1661. The cabinet was almost certainly made by Pierre Gole, a distinguished cabinet-maker from Holland who worked for Louis XIV and who played a leading part in the development of floral marquetry.
W.38-1983   Department of Furniture and Wood-work.

25

Rare English and Continental Silver. Miniatures.
Antique Jewels, Fine Snuff-Boxes

A pair of George II silver-gilt octagonal Casters by Paul Crespin, London, 1727.
Height: 8.625 inches
Weight: 52 ounces
From our collection of Early Georgian Silver.

Valuations for Probate,
Insurance and Division

139 New Bond Street London W1A 3DL

TELEPHONE 01-629 6261/2 TELEGRAPHIC ADDRESS: "EUCLASE LONDON W.I."

2a   2b   2c

ENGLISH HUNTING SWORDS

A.R.E. North

Among the most attractive examples of the skill of the sword cutler are the short comparatively light swords known as hangers. References to hangers can be found in English wills and inventories from as early as the mid-fourteenth century. From the brief descriptions which accompany these references it is clear that the word hanger was used to describe a short weapon: one of the entries in the Inventory of Henry VIII's arms taken in 1547 reads, 'One little shorte hanger the crosse locker and chape of copp wt thafte of cristall and the sheathe of vellvet wt a knife and a bodkin' – many hangers seem to have been accompanied by small knives and bodkins which were normally carried in a small pocket set in the top of the scabbard. Other useful sources for contemporary descriptions of the light swords are the advertisements which frequently appear in English newspapers from the latter part of the 17th century appealing for the return of lost or stolen swords. One such in *Mercurius Publicus* for the week 6th to 13th August 1663 appeals for information as to the whereabouts of 'A short hanger, a saw on the back, the handle of black seals skin, twined round with a silver wire, the hilt silvered, with a knife and bodkin in the scabbard suitable'.[1] At

FIG.2a Hanger, the hilt of pierced and chiselled steel plated with silver, the blade inscribed IOHAN KINNDT HOUNSLOE 1634. English (Hounslow) dated 1634. L. 87cm. M.2722-1931.

FIG.2b Hanger, with chiselled steel mounts and buckhorn grip. English, about 1660–70. The blade inscribed INN TI DOMINI (IN TE DOMINE). L. 70.4cm. M.2796-1931.

FIG.2c Hanger, the hilt of blued and chiselled steel overlaid with silver, the grip set with panels of mother-of-pearl and engraved staghorn, the blade inscribed IOHAN KINNDT HOUNSLOE 1634. English (Hounslow) dated 1634. One of the shells forming the guard has been removed. L. 83cm. M.610-1927.

the same period there are several references to 'cuttoes', from the French, 'Couteaux de chasse', i.e. hunting sword, which seems also to have been a form of hanger: in *An Accademie of Armory* published in 1688, Randle Holme describes the 'Cuttow' as 'a small hanger'.

Initially used exclusively for the chase, the lightness and convenient length of these swords soon led them to be carried more generally, especially for travelling. The numerous newspaper adverts of the late seventeenth and early eighteenth centuries which mention swords left behind in coaches would seem to indicate that swords were nearly always worn when on the road.

Because they were usually carried as an essential part of fashionable dress, the decoration of these short swords was often very lavish. It is fortunate, therefore, that the V&A Museum has a good collection to which interesting additions are regularly made. The earliest English hanger in the collection (FIG.1) is more properly described as a hunting-knife. The grip is of iron formed from two plates brazed together, the pommel chiselled and pierced in the form of the head of a bird of prey. The simple guard is decorated with foliage and terminates in rounded knobs. The single-edged blade is very short with a slight curve at the front. There is a curious aperture through the blade adjacent to its hilt, perhaps for a sword-knot, although two projecting knobs on the side of the pommel may have been used to hold the knot. Claude Blair and A.V.B. Norman have convincingly shown that such English hilts date from the period 1610–20.[2] This particular sword has obviously seen hard usage, as the profile of the blade has been considerably altered through repeated sharpenings.

In 1629 a factory for making swords was established in Hounslow, staffed

by German workmen. A speciality of this factory was a type of hanger with a broad short blade. The Museum possesses two Hounslow swords, both dated and inscribed with maker's names. The blades of the swords are virtually identical: broad and double-edged with the maker's name IOHAN KINNDT on one side, and HOUNS-LOE 1634 on the other. The first (FIG.2a) has a pierced and chiselled guard and must have been a weapon of some splendour in its day, for on the hilt are traces of heavy silver plating which, in turn, has been gilded. A hilt of similar design is shown in the portrait of Sir Thomas Southwell dating from about 1630. This depicts Sir Thomas in hunting costume holding a snaphance gun,[3] lending credence to the suggestion that these short broad-bladed hangers were designed for the chase. The second Hounslow sword (FIG.2c) originally had a guard formed of twin shells, one of which was subsequently removed. The decoration consists of silver foliage inlaid into the blued and chiselled steel hilt. The grip is inlaid with engraved mother-of-pearl and staghorn, a technique used on English gun-stocks and furniture of the period. The blade is secured to the hilt by means of a threaded tube which forms the pommel button and is screwed to the blade tang (FIG.3). This would enable any broken or damaged blade to be replaced quickly. The Hounslow factory is also associated with a type of hanger with a cap and scroll pommel and twin shell guard (FIGS.4a, b). As with other Hounslow hilts, the decoration consists of a dot and trellis design in silver. The blades are usually single-edged and curved. This type of hanger seems to have been fashionable in England in the period 1640–50.

In spite of having a factory capable of making sword blades, the majority of hangers were fitted with blades im-

FIG.3 View showing the Hounslow hanger (overleaf) dismantled. The hilt is attached to the blade by a threaded tube enabling the blade to be replaced quickly should it become damaged. On the tang is the unicorn mark used by Clemens Horn of Solingen – probably a forgery.
L. of blade 81.1cm.   M.610-1927.

FIG.1 Hanger, the hilt of chiselled steel. English, about 1615.
L. 49.2cm.   M.946-1983.

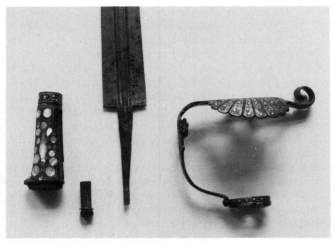

FIG.4a Hanger, the mounts of blued steel overlaid with silver. English (Hounslow) about 1650. The German blade inscribed with the number 1551 and an orb and cross.
L. 84cm.   M.2788-1931.

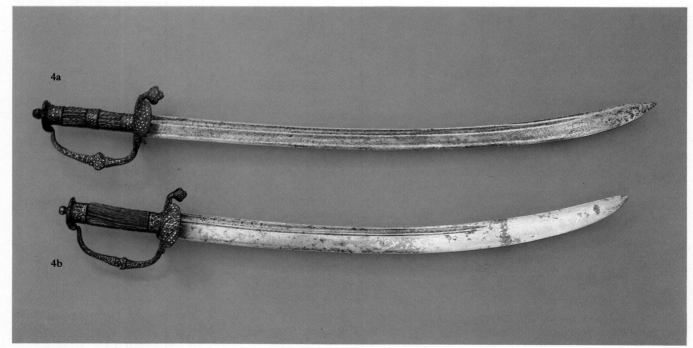

FIG.4b Hanger, the mounts of blued steel overlaid with silver, the blade inscribed ANDRIA FERARA. English (Hounslow) about 1650.
L. 76cm.   M.2797-1931.

FIG.5 Blade from a hanger. German,
(Solingen), dated 1651. Made for the English
market.
L. 54.3cm.   M.1820-1944.

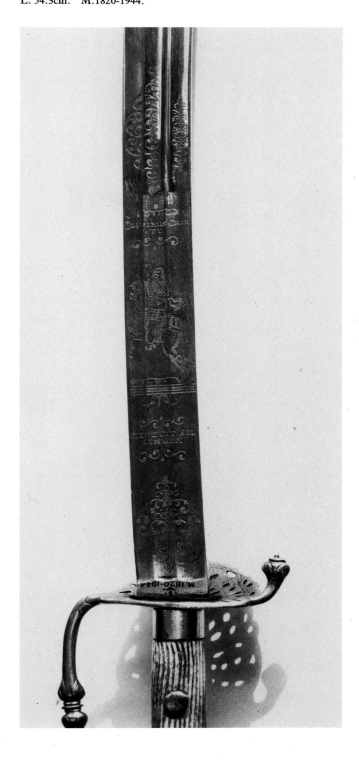
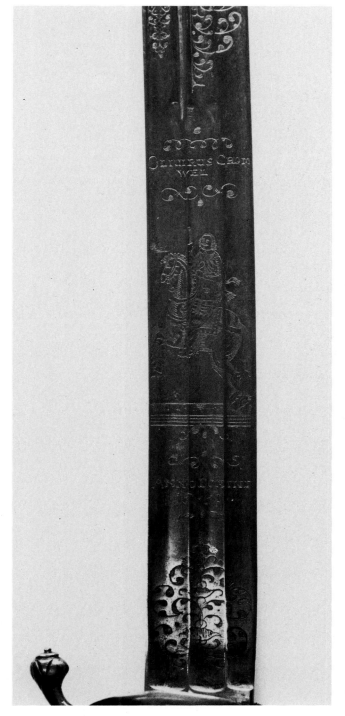

FIG.6a Hanger, the mounts of silver. English (London hall-marks for 1702/3). Maker's mark indecipherable.
L. 63.7cm.   M.152-1922.

FIG.6b Hanger, the mounts of silver the grip of staghorn. English about 1685. Maker's mark GW below a crown (unidentified). The blade with a serrated edge for use as a saw, inlaid with marks used by the Cutlers Co. of London.
L. 62.3cm.   M.38-1983.

FIG.7a Silver-hilted hanger. English about 1675. Maker's mark a crowned T on the blade the mark of the WUNDES family.
L. 60.4cm.   937-1864.

FIG.7b Hanger, the hilt of buckhorn mounted in silver. English, about 1670; on the mounts the owner's initials IF and the maker's mark WS.
L. 64.5cm.   M.76-1939.

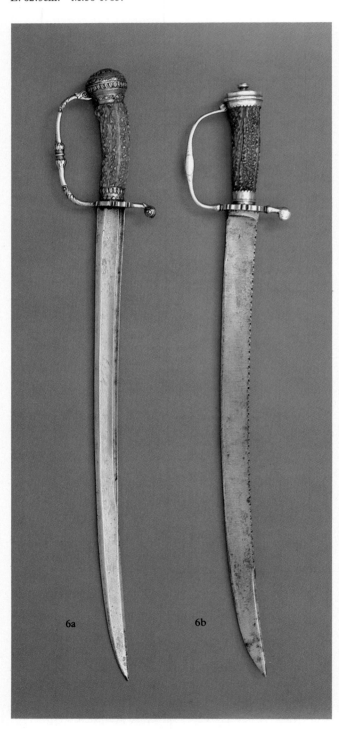

6a   6b

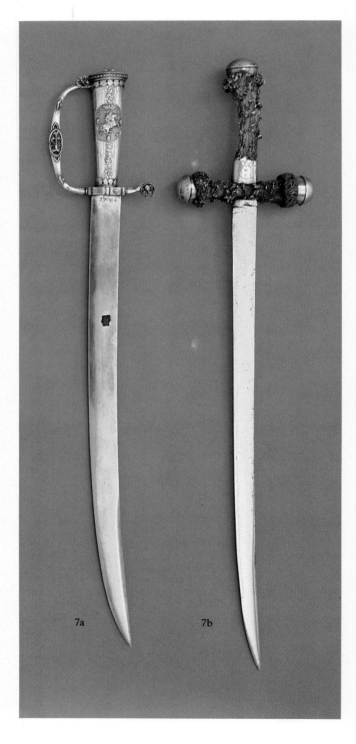

7a   7b

FIG.8 Hanger, the mounts of silver, the grip of
agate. English, about 1700. Maker's mark
TN. Fitted with a German blade of *c*. 1740
engraved with the twelve apostles.
L. 87.8cm.   M.194-1928.

FIG.9 Hanger, the mounts of silver, with
original scabbard. English, date-letter for
1724-5. Maker M.C. The hall-marks are
distorted and may well be contemporary
forgeries.
L. 80.5cm.   M.154-1922.

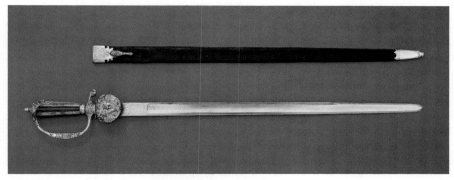

FIG.10b Hanger, the mounts of silver, the grip
of polished horn. English, about 1730.
Maker's mark J.R. (unidentified).
L. 62cm.   M.156-1922.

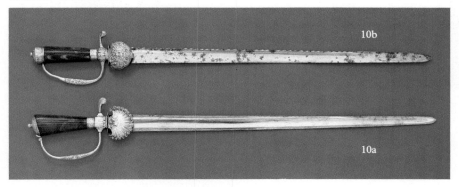

10b

10a

FIG.10a Hanger, the mounts of silver, the grip
of agate. English (London hall-marks for
1739–40).
L. 69cm.   M.155-1922.

ported from Germany. One such blade
in the collection, unfortunately fitted
to a heavily restored hilt, is preserved
in almost perfect condition. The
single-edged curved blade is pierced
with a series of crosses and circles at the
top and is forged with a number of
shallow channels. The surface is decorated with engraved foliate scrolls on
both faces of the blade. On one side is
engraved the name OLIVIRUS
CROMWEL with a figure on a pranc-
ing steed and the date ANNO
DOMINI 1651 below (FIG.5). The
same figure and name appear on the reverse but instead of the date there is the
inscription ME FECIT SOLINGIN.
This refers to the German city of
Solingen which was a major producer
of sword-blades for every market
throughout the period. The figure is
almost certainly intended to be the Earl
of Essex, commander of the Par-
liamentary armies.

The exact chronology of English
hanger hilts during the period directly
after the Civil War has not yet been
properly established. A number exist
which are fitted with guards formed of
single radiating shells, usually of fluted
steel. Some have the large oval pom-
mels associated with the end of the
seventeenth century, but at least one
has a blade bearing the arms and
cypher of Charles II, which suggests
that others date from the period *c*.
1660–70.[4] Certain of these hilts have
very small shell-guards, closely resembling those found on German
rapiers of the 1650–60s. The hanger of
this form in the Museum collection has
this feature (FIG.2b). It would be
difficult to ascribe this particular hilt to
an English workshop were it not for
other features such as the raised cusps
on the guard which are found on
several demonstrably English hilts.

The chronology of English hanger
hilts from the late seventeenth century
onwards is considerably aided by the

FIG.11a Hanger, the mounts of silver, with original scabbard. English, about 1770. Maker's mark WF.
L. 83cm.   846 & a-1905.

FIG.11b Hanger combined with a flintlock pistol, the mounts of engraved steel. English about 1760.
L. 65.7cm.   813-1893.

FIGS.12a, b, c Hunting knives, steel mounted in nickel silver. Designed by Alfred Stevens (1817–75) and made by the cutler George Wolstenholm. English (Sheffield) made for the Great Exhibition of 1851. Wolstenholm Collection.

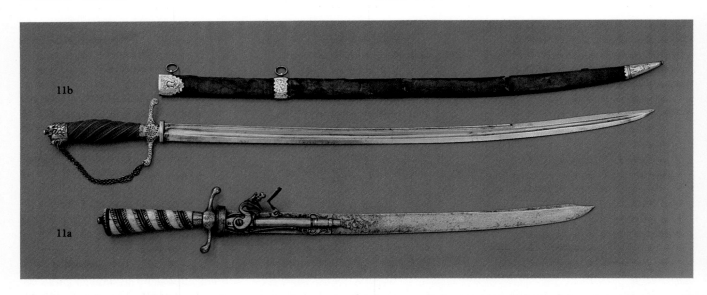

survival of hangers with silver hilts, many of which bear date-letters. The maker's marks that appear on these are generally less than helpful as few have been identified but the actual shape of the maker's stamp can, however, be useful in giving some indication of date.

A few silver hilts dating from the seventeenth century are recorded, with small shell guards linked to the knuckle-bow, although this form is much more common in brass. The majority of silver hilted hangers dating from 1670 to 1700 have very simple hilts consisting of a knuckle-bow extended at the front to form the forequillon (FIG.6a, b). Grips are usually made from buckhorn or staghorn. What is probably the earliest silver-hilted hanger of English origin in the collection (FIG.7a) is unusual in having a silver grip, the knuckle-bow being pierced with figures and foliage. The central motif of the grip consists of a crowned equestrian figure, the plain blade bearing the crowned head mark used by the Wundes family of cutlers of Solingen. This sword dates from about 1675–80. A rather less sophisticated hanger of about the same date (FIG.7b) has a cross-shaped hilt formed of buckhorn with plain silver mounts. An appeal for a lost sword in the *London Gazette* of October 5–8th 1696 described as 'A rough bucks horn handle hanger, tiped with silver having no bow to it' probably refers to one of similar appearance.

Hanger hilts were occasionally mounted with small-sword blades. There is an elegant example with plain silver hilt and agate grip, and a fine

German blade (FIG.8). The shape of the knuckle-bow and small shell suggest a date of about 1700, but the blade is one of a well-known group engraved with figures of the apostles along its length, and dates from about 1740.

In the first quarter of the eighteenth century there was a fashion for hangers with large shell guards mounted parallel to the blade (FIG.9). Some are decorated with masks in relief, rather like those that are found on the butts of silver-mounted English pistols of the period. The rococo style is represented by guards decorated with shell motifs, the museum having some fine examples from the 1740s. In the first half of the eighteenth century there was a tendency to use polished staghorn for the grip (FIG.10a, b), often decorated with a series of parallel flutes.

In the 1770s a type of hanger was fashionable which had a distinctive pommel formed as a lion's-head, and a short guard usually linked by a short chain to the side of the pommel (FIG.11a). The grip is of bone cut in a wrythen pattern and usually stained green. It is generally fitted with a long, slightly curved, single-edged blade, and presents a very elegant appearance. Such hangers appear to have been especially favoured by military and naval officers, to judge from the numbers that are shown in contemporary portraits. Although the lion's-head pommel is generally very stylized the guard usually reflects current fashion. With this example the guard is pierced with scrolls and decorated with the faceted studs also found on small-sword guards of the period.

A few hunting-hangers exist which

are fitted with a flint-lock mechanism and barrel alongside the blade. It has been suggested that these were designed to give the *coup de grâce* to a dying animal, but some may simply have been intended as interesting toys. The example in the Museum collection (FIG.11b) has a folding trigger but the lack of wear on the steel and the insubstantial mainspring would seem to imply that it has not been made for hard use. From the engraved decoration on the guard, and the shape of the grip, this combination sword and pistol dates from the 1760s.

Most of the artists who made these attractive objects remain anonymous; however the Museum is fortunate in having on loan a group of hunting-knives made for the Great Exhibition of 1851 (FIG.12a, b, c). Mounted in nickel silver these were designed by the artist Alfred Stevens (1817–75) and made by the well-known cutler, George Wolstenholm, founder of the Washington works in Sheffield. These elaborate objects are far removed from their plainer and sturdier ancestors. However it should be remembered that Wolstenholm also specialized in the manufacture of a rather more practical product, perhaps the best known style of hunting knife ever made – the Bowie knife.

1   See *Journal of the Arms and Armour Society* VIII No. 6 (Dec. 1976) p. 347 following.

2   A.V.B. Norman, 'Some Hanger Hilts of the Early 17th Century'. in *Blankwaffen* (Zurich 1982) p. 79.

3   H.L. Blackmore, *Hunting Weapons* (London 1971) Plate 91.

4   Wallis & Wallis Sale 192, Lot 1218.

Wartski

ESTABLISHED 1865

14 GRAFTON STREET, LONDON W1

TELEPHONE: 493 1141/2/3

An English eighteenth century, shaped gold box with panels of mother of pearl engraved with wavy lines and applied with chased gold sprays of flowers and butterflies, c. 1740. 6.8 cm.

A Fabergé gold miniature frame in the form of a daisy enamelled shaded white, the aperture set with rose diamonds. 3.5 cm. diameter.

Fabergé spray of lily of the valley, the rose diamond set pearl flowers issuing from chased gold stems with a single reeded nephrite leaf; contained in a crystal vase with *trompe l'oeil* water. 3.5 cm. From the Collection of Queen Helen of Rumania.

An enamelled gold *boîte à mouches*, the inner panels enamelled translucent royal blue over a sunburst *guilloché* ground, further decorated with gold scrolling *paillons*, the *sablé* borders set with half pearls between green enamelled leaves, the interior compartments divided by a sable brush; the lid fitted with the original mirror. By Jean Joseph Barrière, Paris 1787. 6 cm.

A demantoid garnet and diamond set brooch in the form of a lizard with ruby eyes.

An eighteenth century diamond, emerald and ruby set flower brooch.

A jewelled papal cameo by Santarelli of Pope Pius VII, the gold mount profusely set with rose diamonds and the gem set reverse shows the blind heathen in the presence of the light of Christ. Italian c. 1826. 6.3 cm.

K. Henninger-Tavcar
Kunsthandel

Miniatures, fine Snuffboxes, Objects of Vertu etc.

Left: A ring with a miniature painted on ivory, after Guido Reni depicting the portrait of a Lady, inscribed Beatrice Cenci.
Original Chagrin leather étui. Size Oval 2.9 × 2.2cm.

Middle: A four-colour gold sealing wax box, Paris 1760. Size: Height 12.3cm.

Top right: A fine Louis XV gold box with miniatures in the style of *Van Blarenberghe,* depicting a sea-landscape with fishermen. Mark of the Master: Louis Roucel, 1763–87, signed *Orf. du Roi, Paris* 1770–71; stamped: Julien Alaterre, 1768–74.
Size: 7.6 × 5.4cm., height 3.2cm.

Lower right: A fine gold and enamel *à mouches* box with flowers, birds and scrolls. Engraved in the middle with exotic birds. Interior with mirror and green enamel. France, *circa* 1750.

HACHELALLEE 7 · 7530 PFORZHEIM · GERMANY · Telephone: (07231) 31189

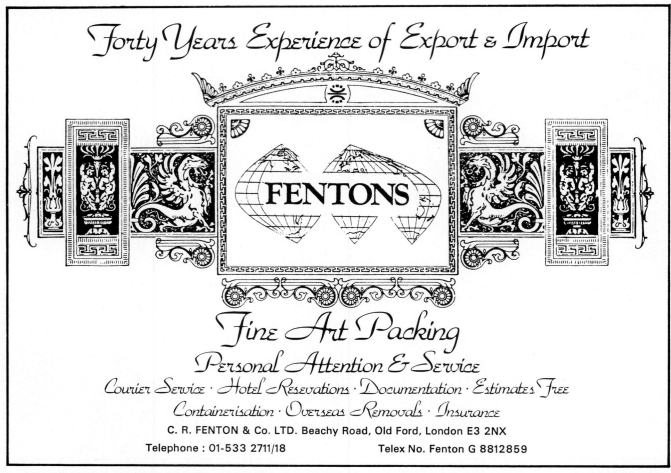

REMEMBERING BILL BRANDT

Mark Haworth-Booth

The great photographer Bill Brandt died on 20 December 1983. He was 79. He was closely associated with the Museum, principally from the period 1974–75 when he selected the exhibition The Land: 20th century landscape photographs. Bill Brandt's Literary Britain *was shown in the Henry Cole Wing (7 March–20 May 1984). He is remembered here by his friend Mark Haworth-Booth, Assistant Keeper of Photographs.*

Some people say they know exactly when they fell in love. I know exactly when I first found photography interesting. I visited Bill Brandt's exhibition of photographs at the Hayward Gallery in 1970. It seems extraordinary that it was only on for a month (30 April–31 May) but fortuitous in that it coincided with Bill's birthday which fell on 2 May. He was the first photographer to be shown at the Hayward Gallery – which was then of course, only two years old and on the crest of its New Brutalist wave – by the Arts Council of Great Britain. He was then sixty-four. The show received many favourable reviews, including those written by art critics who are more or less my contemporaries: Guy Brett on *The Times*, Richard Cork on *The Evening Standard* and William Feaver, then contributing to a paper in the north-east, who saw the exhibition during its tour to twelve galleries outside London. There is no doubt that Bill Brandt appealed to us as an artist – a necessary, surprising, wonderful artist who made pictures of complicated social realities and *also* of shadowed, private reveries. The effect on me was instantaneous. I had taken a pretty dim view (in every sense) of the photographic medium from the age of twelve or fourteen when a kindly uncle had taken me along to a photo-club

evening. Members showed mounted prints to each other. An impression of scores of photos of arches in Spain, done in sepia, remains – no doubt unfairly – twenty-five years later. Photo-appreciation seemed to me an unbeguiling concentrate made up of pretension and mediocrity in equal parts. Bill Brandt's photographs demolished this characteristically English (I regret to say) perception of the art of photography.

I remember little in detail of that show. Even by 1974 when I first met Bill I had forgotten what should have been a memorable feature of the exhibition – the installation was painted *black*.

However, I do recall my first sight of Bill himself. He came to a meeting at the Museum in 1974 to discuss the exhibition *The Land*. He wore a pale grey suit, a collar and tie – rather awkwardly, as if unused to them – his eyes were a pale but bright blue. He seemed to be on his best behaviour. He was shy, his smile was enchanting and those eyes demanded to be looked at. One can find oneself stealing glances at stones in a similar way – sapphires in finger-rings, for example. He was tall, slight of frame, handsome, silver-haired, still debonair. For me it was certainly affection at first sight. We were pleased – and relieved – when he wrote to say he would select *The Land* for us. It meant a lot of going through portfolios of photographs, magazines, books, etc., over a year or so. We met often at the Museum, but also at the Royal College of Art and the Royal Photographic Society. Elizabeth Underhill (now in charge of the modern print collection at the Tate Gallery) and I would assemble likely material for Bill to see; he would then survey the pictures and decide at once what he wanted. He would leave at the end of these sessions – a murmured goodbye, a flash of the marvellous smile –

apparently as fresh as a daisy. Liz and I, in contrast, were drained. . .

Late in the preparations the time came for Bill's own photographs to be chosen. This job he asked me to perform. He provided a box of 10 × 8 inch prints of his best landscapes. These were mainly from his great period of landscape in the 'forties but included examples from a set commissioned by *Vogue* in the 'sixties but never published. I made sure to represent the 'sixties set but my choice of twelve omitted one of Bill's favourites: *Stonehenge under Snow* 1947. 'You are not choosing *this one?* he whispered (but with clear emphasis of his surprise). I think I must have explained that I did not care for the obvious retouching on the stones. The reader may or may not believe what I say next. I *felt* the blood rush to Bill's head. The next day I wrote to him. The exhibition would be like *Hamlet* without the prince if we left out his *Stonehenge under Snow*. Please would he make a print for the exhibition. I am pleased I did this, of course. I still do not *like* the print – the retouching seems both amateurishly obvious and anyway unnecessary – but now I think I know why the photograph meant so much to him.

I saw Bill's photography for the first time in a gallery but had I been fifteen years older I would have been aware of his photographs as important constituents of magazine news and debate. His Stonehenge photograph appeared on the front cover of Tom Hopkinson's *Picture Post* (FIG.2). This was a 'Special Issue on the Crisis' dated 19 April 1947. Sir Tom Hopkinson once spoke in a seminar at the Museum on the work of Don McCullin and said that such a photojournalist was akin to a thoroughbred race-horse and should be handled with great sensitivity by the responsible editor. As Bill Brandt's editor at *Picture Post* (and also simul-

41

FIG.2 *Picture Post* 19 April 1947.
Cover photograph by Bill Brandt.

FIG.3 Sir Roy Strong giving the opening address, *Literary Britain*, 6 March 1984.

FIG.4 Sir Tom Hopkinson speaking at the opening of *Literary Britain*, 6 March 1984. L. to R. Sir Roy Strong, Brian Coe, (Kodak Museum), John Ward (Science Museum), Mark Haworth-Booth, Julie Laird (Secretary, Friends of the V&A).

taneously at *Lilliput*) Hopkinson used another 'thoroughbred' with discernment. Brandt's Stonehenge was a photographic image equal to the crisis of spring 1947 – an economic crisis which was also a crisis of morale – and Bill's feelings about the photograph must have included his memories of its importance in articulating a particular moment in recent history for the million or more readers of *Picture Post*.

Sir Tom Hopkinson spoke movingly of his old friend at the opening of *Literary Britain* at the Museum on 6 March. After Bill's death, friends had talked of holding a memorial service for him. Bill did not belong to any church and did not feel comfortable with any institutional religion and so the nearest we could manage to a memorial service was an occasion at the Museum. He was remembered with eloquence and affection by those who knew and admired him. Sir Roy Strong introduced the evening and spoke of his association with the two twentieth century British photographers he prizes most – both of whom photographed him, by the way (FIG.3) – Sir Cecil Benton and Bill Brandt. Some years ago Sir Roy ensured that the Museum should have the largest and best collection of Bill's work – there are about 250 prints now in the collection, dating from different periods. Sir Tom then reminisced (FIG.4) about Bill's practice as a photographer, how he was prepared to spend days in the darkroom printing the same negative again and again until he had achieved exactly the tonality he wanted. He spoke of Bill's quiet persistence and charm and told us how Bill had gone to Haworth to photograph for a set on the Brontë's for *Lilliput* (1945). An aged custodian at the parsonage had found herself opening ancient cupboards to provide the photographer with the accessories required – here Sir Tom conjured up the sound of keys turning rustily in

FIG.5 Sir Tom Hopkinson and Mrs. Noya Brandt at the V&A, 6 March 1984.

FIG.6 David Bailey and Sue Davies at the V&A, 6 March 1984.

antiquated locks – and lighting candles to illuminate Emily's trunk and the night-dress carefully folded over it. Hadn't Bill ever been threatened by the villains whom he photographed in *A Night in London* (1938), Sir Tom once asked him. No, they were really very helpful, Bill had replied. Sue Davies, Director of the Photographers' Gallery was the third and final speaker. She spoke as representative of the generation which had come to Bill's work with great excitement when he was already over sixty and she reminded us of how much Bill put into good works such as the Gallery, the teaching of students of the Royal College of Art,

and his generosity with his time in seeing visitors to London. When visitors asked Sue how they might contact Bill she said forthrightly 'Why don't you just ring him up!' My advice to visitors was the same – he was far more approachable than those of his eminence sometimes are. It was an evening when we thought happily and tenderly of Bill in company with his family and old friends. A few nights later, on *Kaleidoscope*, Sir Tom had this to say of Bill:

He wasn't interested in anything that didn't lend itself to mystery. The mystery was in Bill, and he projected it on to whatever he photographed.

This is true. Bill did, without being either cold or aloof, preserve a barrier between his personal life and mystery, and such friends as myself. Like perhaps one or two other historians, I made a private pledge some years ago not to write about matters that I had reason to believe would be unwelcome to Bill. For this reason a biographical outline of his early life did not appear until we published *Literary Britain* in a revised catalogue edition in spring 1984. Also in the catalogue is Sir Tom Hopkinson's first essay on Bill Brandt, dated 1942, and a touching retrospect he wrote specially for us soon after Bill's death. Similarly, I was never keen to write of Bill's photography at all analytically while he was alive. It is, actually, a noticeable pattern that the heroic modern photojournalists of his generation have hardly been exposed until lately to standard historical analysis of the kind attracted by even ordinary and unremarkable painters. In Bill's case the academic blade was bid keep to its sheath almost by virtue of some mesmeric influence. 'We murder to dissect': I believe Bill remained 'immune', in the main at least, from academic intrusion because he continued to think in terms of a very large audience (as in the *Picture Post* days). Also, while enjoying thoughtful reviews he disliked mere publicity. Very fortunately he agreed to be interviewed by Peter Adam for a BBC TV programme made in 1982 and as a result a *Picture Post* size audience was able to view his photographs for the first time since the 'forties and to enjoy the charm of his remarkable personality. As visitors to *Literary Britain* will know, the exhibition was a great success. *Punch* remarked: 'We see Haworth parsonage; Aldeburgh with the words of Crabbe; Stonehenge with Hardy; and Berkeley Castle with Marlowe, among many others. We also see the backs of many heads – this is a very popular exhibition so plan the hour of your visit carefully.'

The day the exhibition opened I met Bryn Campbell in the Photo-Gallery. 'But weren't you at the private view?' I asked him. 'Ah, but you can't get too much of a good thing, can you!' Bryn Campbell, photographer, picture editor and author, recently brought back into print Bill's only extended statement on photography. The text in *Camera in London* (1948) is substantially reprinted in Bryn Campbell's *World Photography* (1981). Bill inspired great love, that is one of the fundamentals about him. Bryn told me three very typical and touching little

stories about him that morning, which he has kindly allowed me to pass on. Over twenty years ago, when Bryn Campbell was Picture Editor at *The Observer*, it was decided to run a feature on British landscape. Bryn thought to ring up Bill and ask him for a photograph or two, preferably unpublished. 'Will someone come for them?' inquired Bill's somewhat disembodied voice. Bryn had never met his idol and so he decided to go himself. Driving up to Belsize Park, where Bill then lived, Bryn thought of all the things he'd have the opportunity to say to Bill about his work, his influence, the questions he might be able to put to him, at last, etc. Arriving at the door, the acolyte – brimming with feeling and sense of occasion – rang the bell. The door opened. A lean wrist and hand appeared with a packet of photographs. The door closed. On another occasion, more than ten years later when he had got to know Bill quite well, Bryn felt justifiably excited about some experimental colour work he was doing. One day he took a portfolio of these pictures for Bill to see. He still remembers very clearly how the Master looked attentively at every one and then pushed the pile to one side and looked at Bryn, then out of the window. There was nothing said, except I think, a vague 'Yes'. Later still, and this is another glimpse at Bill's minute truthfulness – he was a person who would not say what he did not mean – he wrote to thank Bryn for some service that he had been able to perform and concluded: 'I look upon you almost as a friend'. The recipient treasured the *almost*. That was Bill, Bryn thought: every sentiment and remark carefully measured to fit his rather rare sense of exactness and truthfulness.

Last year David Bailey presented his vivid and unexpected portrait of Bill Brandt (1967). Not long after *Literary*

Britain opened the Museum received another valuable addition to its Brandt collection. Laelia Goehr will be known to some readers from her exhibition and catalogue *Stravinsky rehearses Stravinsky* organised by the Theatre Museum in 1982. She began photographing at the end of the Second World War and was taught the rudiments of exposure, development and printing by Bill Brandt. Among the best photographs ever taken of Bill Brandt (FIG.1) – perhaps the most evocative and truthful of all – is her picture of 1945. He advised her in arranging the composition, in which he peers over the newly acquired stand camera with which he began his long experiment in nude photography the same year. It is a marvellous portrait of a photographer immersed in and spoken for by his medium. The photograph, rediscovered in 1982 by Terence Pepper of the National Portrait Gallery, was presented to the Museum in memory of Bill Brandt in 1984 by Laelia Goehr.

This is a particularly generous gift because the print, which was made in 1945 and is therefore 'vintage', may well be unique. The portrait was taken at the first of Laelia Goehr's 'lessons' with Bill Brandt. As there was no model she suggested that Bill himself sit down and be the portrait subject. His teaching consisted only of letting her watch him working. He developed his materials in the kitchen of his flat in Belsize Park Mansions. He said very little but she was able to watch him photographing the girls doing the 'Lambeth Walk', a subject which later became among his best known. When she began photographing properly he took her prints to the Hulton Press and her photographs were published for the first time. The episode is typical of Bill's reticence, his kindness, and the lasting love he inspired.

'MOULDING A PHYSIOGNOMY' — A CHINESE PORTRAIT FIGURE

Craig Clunas

How clear a picture of China did early eighteenth century Europeans possess? How well informed were early eighteenth century Chinese about the manners, customs and even the physical appearance of their European contemporaries? If we base our answer upon the art of the two civilisations, we might well come to the conclusion that misconceptions, preconceptions and a deliberate urge to exoticism were of more weight in deciding the West's image of the East and the East's image of the West than were either direct observation or plain representation. It is well known that in late Stuart and early Georgian England the term 'Indian' was used indiscriminately to describe objects manufactured in the craft traditions of China, Japan, or any of the regions of the Indian sub-continent. Indian chintzes, Japanese lacquers and Chinese porcelain were just three of the most important ingredients in the strong cocktail of exotica which enjoyed increased esteem in fashionable circles following the strengthened cultural contacts with the Netherlands after 1688. The representation of 'the East' however was not left to Eastern craftsmen. Textile designers, cabinetmakers, silversmiths and potters all joined in the production of objects with decoration of Asian origin, adapted to a greater or lesser degree, which we would today rather rashly subsume under the blanket term *chinoiseries*.

In China too, the representation of the 'ocean people', as western Europeans were known, was a subject of interest to book illustrators working in the woodblock tradition, as well as to weavers and porcelain painters. Both ends of Eurasia seem to have been more interested in establishing a vision of a fantasy Europe, a fantasy China than they were in ethnographic observation. This at least is the orthodoxy established by studies of chinoiserie and the western taste for things Chinese.

There is, however, an alternative strand in the history of the artistic relations between China and the West, a vein of clear-eyed, almost photographic realism which has been relatively little remarked on. There is no more striking evidence for the existence of this strand than the small number of survivors from what must once have been a much larger group of Chinese portrait figures of western merchants, executed in unfired clay in Canton between about 1700 and about 1800. An example of these figures, possibly the earliest known, has recently entered the collections of the Far Eastern Department, Victoria and Albert Museum, and is the subject of this article (FIG.1). The figure, which stands 29.5cm. high excluding the base (a modern replacement), is modelled in a greyish-white unfired clay over an armature of bamboo, which protrudes through the soles of the shoes. The head, which is removable and simply lifts off the collar, is also modelled round a bamboo core. Though there is some sign of chipping to the paint on the coat, and a few repairs to the base of the wig, and though the posture of the hands sugests the existence of a now vanished walking stick, this remarkably fragile piece of sculpture remains in surprisingly good condition. This must at least partly be due to its possessing a lacquered wood fitted case, painted with floral sprays and with fantastic landscapes. Like the figure, this case was probably made in Canton and, as will be discussed below, is of some importance in establishing the object's date.

Much more important however, and allowing a dating of *c.* 1710–1715 to be fairly confidently adopted, is the figure's clothing. He is wearing the fashionable dress of a northern European gentleman, probably from Britain or the Netherlands. His coat would be of brown superfine wool, the sort of cloth of English manufacture which English merchants of the eighteenth century tried so hard and so unsuccessfully to sell to the Chinese in return for the coveted tea, silk and porcelain. The coat, which has a waistcoat and breeches to match, is decorated on the pockets and cuffs, the tail and the front with embroidery which is now black. This may once have been painted silver, however, to represent the silver-gilt thread which is known from both pictorial sources and from surviving garments to have been extensively used. The presence of lead, or possibly even of real silver in the silver paint would account for its tarnishing to black (FIG.2).

The collections of the Department of Textiles and Dress contain one coat, T.357-1980 and one complete suit, T.327 & A-1982, which are remarkably close in cut and date to the clothes worn by the portrait figure. The suit, made for a child, is in red wool embroidered with silver gilt, but the coat, traditionally the property of Thomas Severne (1644–1737) is in nearly the same shade of brown. These rare garments, both of which are illustrated and discussed in *Four Hundred Years of Fashion*[1] help to fix the date of the figure, just as the figure aids in reconstructing the 'body-language' suitable to the wearers of such clothes, as well as the now vanished accessories of hats, stockings, neckcloths, and wigs. The wig in particular is of interest to the social and costume historian, since paintings relatively rarely afford a 360° view of a figure. It is a full bottomed campaign wig, that is, one with knotted ends, suitable for active rather than high formal occasions (FIG.4).

FIG.1 Portrait Figure of a European Merchant, painted unfired clay CHINESE (Canton); *c.* 1710–1725 and its original lacquered box. Height of figure: 29.5cm.; of box: 42cm. FE.32 & A-1981.

Where was this figure made? To answer such a question it is necessary to consider other known examples of the Chinese portrait figure, as well as the history of Sino-European relations in the early part of the eighteenth century. Several other figures do carry contemporary inscriptions serving to locate their manufacture in the port city of Canton, which after 1710 became almost the only centre of commerce open to westerners. However, the only other example in a British public collection is remarkable not only for its size and its early date, but for the fact of its having been made by a Chinese artist in India. This is the figure, now in the National Portrait Gallery and published by R.J. Charleston[2], of Joseph Collet (1673–1725) who had been administrator of the English trading settlement on the west coast of Sumatra, and who was Governor of Fort St. George, Madras from 1717 to his death. The figure, which is some 76cm. high, descended in the Collet family until given to the Gallery by W.P.G. Collet in 1956.

Two crucial pieces of evidence increase its importance. One is contained in a letter from Collet to his daughter Elizabeth, written from Fort St. George on 14 December 1716:

> I also send by the Governour in requittal for your Pictures a sort of Picture or Image of myself. The lineaments and the Features are Esteem'd very just but the complexion is not quite so well hit; the proportion of my body and my habit is very exact.[3]

The second piece of evidence is the inscription in gold paint or possibly gold lacquer on the base; *Amoy Chinqua fecit 1716.* Amoy, or in the modern transliteration Xiamen, is a port in the southern part of China's Fujian Province much frequented by Western merchants in the opening years of the eighteenth century. The name 'Chinqua' is typical of the type of name employed by Chinese craftsmen and merchants in contact with Europeans, which often carries the suffix *qua*. This has frequently been glossed in Western sources as a derivation of the word *guan*, 'an official', and hence as an honorific, though this etymology may well be unreliable. Whatever its meaning, we have no reason to doubt that Chinqua from Amoy was a real person and the actual modeller in India of Joseph Collet's portrait. He many not necessarily also have written the identifying inscription, which with its fluent European hand seems likely to have been added, perhaps by Collet himself.

Was Chinqua from Amoy, working among the British community in Madras, also the modeller of the Victoria & Albert Museum figure? The two models share similarities not only of date but also of posture. However, Joseph Collet towers over the diminutive, anonymous gentleman in the brown wool coat, and is rather crudely modelled by comparison. The existence also of a fitted case for the V&A example, which is lacquered, however simply, in an east Asian technique seems to put its place of manufacture back on the Chinese mainland.

This wooden case is decorated on the front with a landscape of huts set by the edge of a river or lake, and dominated by towering rocks and huge, distorted pine trees. The scene has undergone a fair amount of restoration in the west. The sides and top show randomly arranged sprigs of flowers and butterflies, painted in gold but also in colours such as pink, blue and white. These colours cannot be achieved by true lacquer painting, and are doubtless a vegetable oil-based paint, probably containing lead oxide as a drying agent. The black background lacquer is of rather poor quality, thin and dull, with no sign of the meticulous preparation of the wooden core or the numerous undercoats necessary for the best surface. (FIG.6).

The colour scheme and the landscape composition on the box represent a rather feeble Chinese attempt to imitate Japanese lacquer. For just as China gave its name to its porcelain, so Japan was viewed by seventeenth and eighteenth century Europe as the source of the best 'japanning', lacquerwares, executed predominantly in the gold on black *maki-e* technique. Throughout the seventeenth century English merchants made several attempts to resume commercial contacts with Japan, viewing trade with China as very much second-best, though their rivals in the Netherlands United East India Company managed to resist any incursions on their monopoly. It was thus only natural that Chinese lacquerers should attempt to fill the gap in demand with imitations of and variations on Japanese types. The city of Canton (*Guangzhou* in Chinese), which increasingly became the focus of Sino-Western trade following the arrival there of the French ship *Amphytrite* in 1698 and the English *Macclesfield* in 1699, already had a tradition of cabinet making and lacquering which dated from at least the mid-sixteenth century. It was only natural that Western clients could be catered for with some ease. As early as the 1720s lacquered furniture was being made to Western patterns in Canton. A chair from the Museum's collection, FE.116-1978, originally one of a set of eight at Warwick Castle, and dating from around 1730, demonstrates the same sort of decoration as our figure's box (FIG.7).

Not only the box, but the existence of a number of figures in Denmark point to Canton as the likely place of manufacture. These are a remarkable series of four seated portrait figures of the principal officers and merchants of the *Kronprins Christian*, which re-

FIGS.2–5 Detail of the figure.

FIG.6 Detail of the box.

FIG.7 Chair, Lacquered wood and leather
CHINESE (Canton), for the English market;
c. 1730. Height: 100cm. FE.116+A-1978.

turned to Copenhagen in 1732 after the first direct royally sponsored trading voyage to Canton. Michael Tønder, Pieter van der Hurk, Peter Mule and Jochim Severin Bonsach are shown seated in miniature wooden armchairs. Two of them wear caps of real cloth. Two of them, rather disconcertingly, have thick heads of real human hair. Mule carries a book inscribed in Danish 'Manufactured in Canton in China Anno 1731'.[4]

The material, scale and modelling of these figures all provide close parallels with those of the figure under discussion. Another piece in Denmark, a life-sized bust of Captain Zacharias Allewelt brought from Canton in 1739, even has a lacquered wood case deco-rated in gold on black in the manner we have already seen.

Canton continued to be a centre of production of clay portrait models throughout the eighteenth century, and the acquisition of one seems to have been a regular part of a visit to the city. The young William Hickey, in Canton in 1769, describes in his *Memoirs* (I p.227) his visit with a companion to 'a China man who took excellent likenesses in clay, which he afterwards coloured...' In the same year, through a series of shipwrecks and unhappy accidents there arrived in London the unfortunate 'Chitqua', a portrait modeller in clay whose adventures were detailed by Aubrey Toppin in *Transactions of the English Ceramic*

Circle (1942) pp.149–152. His brief period of celebrity included an audience with George III and inclusion in Zoffany's *The Life School of the Royal Academy of 1772*. Along with Amoy Chinqua, he is the only Chinese artist in this medium, the fragility of which surely makes surviving examples only a fraction of those originally existing, whose name has survived.

Chinese sources throw remarkably little light on these pieces. Art executed purely for sale to foreigners was of no interest to Chinese authors. However one early nineteenth century source does give a hint of the milieu out of which portrait modelling may have developed. The *Records of Leaning on the Table by Paulonia Bridge* by Gu Lu

FIG.8 Detail of the figure.

published in 1842 describes the craft of *su zhen*, 'modelling a likeness' or *nie xiang* 'moulding a physiognomy' as practised at Suzhou. There, modelling in unfired clay was used not only for portraiture but to produce cheap, colourful images of religious and mythical figures. Some of these figures, for a relatively unsophisticated Chinese market, can be found in Western collections, such as the Royal Danish Kunstkammer and the Chinese Pavilion at Drottningholm near Stockholm. It seems very likely that taking likenesses of Westerners was simply a sideline for modellers whose principal trade was in figures of gods and immortals.

Perhaps the most tantalising problem associated with this example is the sitter's identity. Here we are at a loss, for without a clear history of transmission within a family, and in the absence of an inscription there is no way for research to proceed. Could he be Nathaniel Torriano, Peter Godfrey, Samuel Ward, John Horsmonden, William Foster, or any of the other Englishmen known to have been in Canton in 1721, for example? We simply cannot say. He stands anonymous, a testimony to the entrepreneurial spirit which sustained the early China trade, and to the ability of an equally anonymous craftsman to represent a person from the other side of the world in a manner so lifelike one feels sure one would recognise the sitter were he to come into the room (FIG.8).

1 Ed. N. Rothstein; text by M. Ginsburg, A. Hart and V. Mendes *et al.* (London 1984) p. 55.

2 *Antiques Magazine*, May 1958, p. 459.

3 Quoted from *The Private Letter Books of Joseph Collet* ed. H.H. Dodwell (London 1933) pp. 140–141.

4 J. Hornby 'China' in *Ethnographic Objects in the Royal Danish Kunstkammer* ed. B. Dam-Mikkelsen and T. Lundbaek (Copenhagen 1980) pp. 155–219, 179.

India's Sacred Treasure Beckons You to Temple Art

Male deity. Gupta period (5th century AD). Red terra cotta, height 11¾".

This superb and rare example of an unidentified deity comes from the remains of the terra cotta temple near Hardoi, Uttar Pradesh

CHELSEA.
Circa 1750.
Height: 5¼ inches.
(original wood stand).

Only three other
examples are recorded.

Winifred Williams
Robert Williams

Rare Porcelain
Collections Purchased   Valuations

3 Bury Street
St. James's
London S.W.1
Telephones: 01-930 4732/0729
Cables: Winbury London S W 1

A Wei Dynasty horse and rider. This ming-chi
(tomb-figure) has traces of polychroming.
Northern Wei Dynasty circa 5th Century A.D.
Height 9½ inches, 24¼cm.

E&J FRANKEL Ltd.
ORIENTAL ART

1020 Madison Avenue, New York, New York 10021

Telephone (212) 879-5733

Members of The Art and Antiques Dealers League of America.
The Appraisers Association of America and C.I.N.O.A.

CHINA HOUSE OF ARTS
10TH ANNIVERSARY

Sieur Tzen moved from Paris to New York in 1975. At that time he founded the China House of Arts at 1100 Madison Avenue, one block from the Metropolitan Museum of Art. Coming from a family in the academical field, he had taught in Taiwan for several years as Adjunct Professor of Art in the Nan-Yong Industrial Institute and as Visiting Lecturer in the National Taiwan Normal University. At first Mr. Tzen's knowledge of Chinese antiques, although extensive, was mostly theoretical. Through 10 years of hard work, however, he gradually gained a wealth of first-hand experience. His straightforward relations with both scholars and collectors, coupled with his formal and practical connoisseurship, have earned him a reputation as one of the leading dealers in antique Chinese Art.

In 1981, China House of Arts published a work on 'Chinese Ceramics', including an article written by Tzen on neolithic painted potteries. In 1982 another publication, 'Significant Aspects of Early Chinese Ceramic Arts', contained a number of scholarly and authoritative articles on various subjects: Thermoluminescence Authenticity Test, Tang ceramics, Ding ware, and Yue ware – all with a strong emphasis on research. These two works have since become valuable references for students of Chinese Art.

In recent years, China House of Arts has also organized several exhibitions. 'Ming and Qing Blue and White Porcelain', in 1982, included rare objects from the reign of Yonglo in the early Ming Dynasty to that of Kangxi, in the early Qing. In 1984, 'The Golden Age of Chinese Ceramics' included exceptional pieces from the neolithic period to the Song Dynasty, with an emphasis on Tang Dynasty three-colour glazed sculptures. This exhibit was fully illustrated in another gallery periodical: 'Archives – Ancient Chinese Art'.

Floyd Ratliff, Ph.D.

Marbleized ware bowl of the Song Dynasty (960–1279 AD), height: 12 cm. This bowl, formerly of the Lord Cunliffe Collection, and later in the Mount Trust Collection, was exhibited at the Victoria and Albert Museum, London 1970 Catalogue no. 63.

Through the many publications and exhibitions of the China House of Arts, Sieur Tzen manages to illuminate, in a brilliant, and colourful way, the past ages of one of the most remarkable civilizations in the world.

CHINESE UNDERGLAZE COPPER-RED DISH   DIAMETER: 7¾ inches 14th CENTURY

CARVED AMBERS — BALTIC GOLD: PRUSSIAN SILVER

Marjorie Trusted

In the splendid *Kunstkammer* collections made by rulers and wealthy burghers throughout Europe in the Baroque era, amongst the paintings and bronze statuettes, the ostrich-eggs and coconut-shells, the stuffed armadilloes and tropical birds' feathers, amber works of art almost always figured as highly treasured items. Amber was sought after both for its beauty and its mysterious, even mythical origins. One of the myths about the origins of the material occurs in Ovid's *Metamorphoses*, where we are told of the sorrowing sisters of Phaethon, Apollo's son, who had been struck by Jove's thunderbolt and who had fallen to earth after losing control of the chariot of the sun; his sisters wept for so long that they were metamorphosed into trees and their tears turned into amber. From ancient Roman times, amber was known to be a resin, but not until the late 18th century was it established that it was a fossilised resin, and only in very recent times has its exact age been calculated. Thus throughout the great period of amber carving, the late sixteenth to the early eighteenth century, it was a mysterious substance, but it was also easy to carve, and its glowing colour inspired many new decorative techniques to create works of art peculiar to it.

The type of amber most often used for works of art comes from the Baltic. Baltic amber originated 40 million years ago, when what is now the Baltic Sea was land, and forests of coniferous and deciduous trees grew in that area, in a subtropical climate. For reasons unknown, the trees exuded large amounts of resin, which accumulated, and fossilised to become amber. Some Baltic amber comes direct from the Baltic Sea, having been dredged up in

nets, or washed up on the Baltic beaches, especially during heavy storms, and much is now mined further inland, from a stratum known as Blue Earth, as some of the amber had been carried southwards, to what is now Poland, by rivers and glaciers during the Ice Age. Although Baltic amber is more plentiful and accessible than many other types of amber found elsewhere in the world, it has always been recognized as a rare and precious substance, and was traded from Paleolithic times onwards.

What was amber used to make, and why was it particularly in demand for works of art in the Baroque period? In prehistoric times, amulets were made of it, for it was thought to have magical properties. During the Roman period, many amber statuettes and reliefs were carved; the raw material was taken from the north to Rome, and probably carved in Aquilea in Northern Italy. Pliny the Elder expatiates on its healing qualities, especially for throat-infections, and also comments that an amber figurine, however small, is valued more highly than several able-bodied slaves![1]

Although some amber beads have been found dating from the Dark Ages it was not until the medieval period that amber was again valued as it had been in Roman times, but it was used primarily for rosaries. Guilds of amber-workers known as *Paternoster-macher*, because they made rosaries, or paternosters, were established in Bruges and Lübeck, (by 1302 and before 1360 respectively), and raw amber was exported from Prussia to these cities. The rulers of Prussia from the late thirteenth to the late fifteenth century were the Knights of the Teutonic Order, a Catholic charitable order originally set up during the Crusades, who had settled in Prussia, and maintained a strict monopoly over the supply of amber, forbidding the

Prussian shore-dwellers to keep or sell any themselves. However, during the fifteenth century the power of the Teutonic Order began to decline, and by 1525 the Grand Master of the Order, Albrecht, was converted to Lutheranism, and declared Prussia to be a secular duchy of which he was Duke, although he remained a vassal to Poland, which had helped to undermine the power of the Order. Duke Albrecht of Prussia coined the phrase 'Prussian silver' for amber, for he at once saw the wealth which it could bring to his duchy. The conversion of Prussia to Protestantism decreased the demand for rosaries, and other secular objects began to be made from amber, such as gamesboards, handles for cutlery, goblets, tankards and caskets. In the century or so following Duke Albrecht's conversion, guilds of amber workers were set up all along the Baltic coast, the leading centres being Königsberg, (Kaliningrad), the capital of the Prussian court, and, further west, Danzig, (Gdansk), a city with local autonomy. Perhaps even more important, later still, during the late seventeenth and early eighteenth century, artists at courts, such as Kassel, Dresden and Copenhagen, were appointed to carve and turn amber.

By the late sixteenth century, amber carving was thriving; Königsberg seems at this time to have been the principal centre, mainly because of the presence of the Prussian court, for a guild of amber-workers was not to be established there until 1641. The type of object made in amber at this time has close analogies with other contemporary decorative arts such as goldsmiths' work, and turned ivory. Cutlery handles were especially popular, and such cutlery, made of precious materials and of fine workmanship, was often presented as a wedding-gift, or used for ceremonial occasions. The cutlery illustrated (FIG.1) of the late sixteenth

FIG.7 Altar. Amber on a wooden carcase with ivory reliefs. Danzig, about 1650. Inv. no. 270-1875.

FIG.2 Two knives and their embroidered case,
the handles of amber.
Inv. no. M.12 to B-1950.

century shows the fruitful combination of ivory with amber: small circles of clear amber, placed over gold coloured foil, are embedded in the ivory like precious stones. The vertical amber panels are over foil which has been painted with full-length figures, another popular decorative technique. The two knives with their embroidered case (FIG.2) which are dated 1638, are slightly later, but reflect the techniques practised in the late sixteenth century. Here can be seen the use of amber of different colours: the busts of a man and a woman, carved of white amber, are placed under clear golden-coloured amber panels, the clear amber acting like an orange glass over the figures. Although the colour of pure amber is a golden-yellow, which may darken to a ruby red colour when exposed to the air, impurities can give it darker colours, and it can vary from blue-black to brown, green, red, yellow or opaque white; the white opacity is caused by microscopic water droplets being caught up in the amber, which give it an appearance similar to meerschaum. The knives are dated (FIG.3) and a name is inscribed on foil: 'ANNO–1638 ANNA MICKLE-THWAIT'; the name is probably that of the owner. The method of inscription employs the same technique as seen above: painted metal foil under a clear amber panel. It should be noted that the blades of these knives are English, for the marks are those of the London Cutlers' Company, and the handles may have been carved in London, as occasionally English artists appear to have worked in amber.

Tankards and cups mounted in silver-gilt and enamels were made for many *Kunstkammer* collections. The two-handled cup mounted in gilt metal (FIG.4) is a typical example from the early seventeenth century, and probably comes from Königsberg, perhaps from the workshop of George Schreiber

FIG.3 Detail of FIG.2.

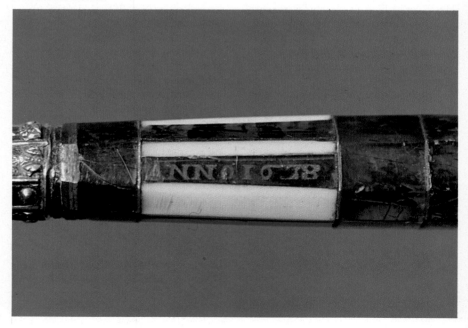

FIG.4 Two-handled cup. Amber mounted in
Königsberg; perhaps the workshop of Georg
Schreiber (active 1617–1642).
Inv. no. 659-1904.

FIG.1 Cutlery handles. Amber and ivory.
Königsberg, late 16th century.
Inv. no. M.920 and a-1926.

(active 1617–1643), who signed some of his works, and who was one of the founder members of the Königsberg guild of amber-workers in 1641. The panels are carved in low relief with animals and birds on trophies of fruit and flowers probably derived from an engraved source; the transparency of the panels allows the design to be viewed from both inside and outside. It is unlikely that such a cup would ever have been used for drinking; alcohol would have reacted with the amber, and the cup, like the many tankards made in the early seventeenth century, would have been prized as a treasure, and regarded as a work of art rather than an object with any utilitarian function. Some works of amber may have been functional, but still figured as treasures in royal collections; as has been seen above, amber could be used to make cutlery handles, and other examples of amber items which were used include games-boards inlaid with amber. One of the courtiers of King Sigismund III Vasa of Poland regularly played chess with the King and gave him an amber chess-board in 1608. This chess-board still exists in Cracow and may well have been used by the King and his courtiers. The games-board in FIG.5 is dated 1620, and is of oak elaborately inlaid with amber, ivory and tortoiseshell. It is hinged, with a chess-board and a nine-men's-morris board on the two outer faces, while on the inner faces is a back-gammon board. The inscription which runs along the centre of the back-gammon board, painted on foil under clear amber (FIG.6) (the same technique seen in the cutlery handles), warns the players of the hazards of gambling: 'Whoever wants to play this board game must have plenty of numbers; in 1620 God gives more in one day than a whole Kingdom has. When I had plenty to give I got along with everyone; now that I no longer have,

FIG.5 Games-board. Oak inlaid with amber,
ivory and tortoiseshell. Königsberg, 1620.
Inv. no. W.15-1910.

FIG.6 Detail of FIG.5.

FIG.8 Altar. Amber on a wooden carcase with
ivory reliefs. Danzig, about 1650.
Inv. no. A.1-1950.

no-one wishes me good day. Good luck
and glass; how soon they break'. It is
written in dialect German, an indication of its provenance, which is once
again Königsberg.

Just as the amber-workers of
Königsberg were patronised by the
Prussian court, Danzig amber-workers
would seem to have been favoured by
the Polish court, and Danzig was a
rival centre to Königsberg in the art of
amber-carving. Following the union of
Prussia and Brandenburg in 1618, the
Elector of Brandenburg ruled Prussia
from his court in Berlin, and Königsberg thus declined in importance as a
royal city, while Danzig continued to
flourish as an important trading centre.
As early as the late sixteenth century
amber had been carved in and around
Danzig; in 1604 the Abbot of the Oliva
Monastery near Danzig presented an
amber statuette of the Madonna and
Child to the Shrine of the Black
Madonna in Jasna Gora, where it still is
today. However, the great period of
amber carving in Danzig came after the
flowering of the art in Königsberg, and
most of the works from Danzig which
survive date from the second half of the
seventeenth century. In Königsberg
some amber works, particularly cups
and tankards, paralleled the works of
Königsberg goldsmiths, but in Danzig
amber was used to make monumental
and more sculptural works. One of the
reasons for this was the introduction of
a construction known as incrustation:
gluing amber panels onto a wooden
framework. Raw amber is generally
found in relatively small fragments,
rarely more than two inches long (the
largest known lump, now in East
Berlin, weighs only just over nine kilo-
grammes), and an amber worker would
often have to wait for years in order to
amass sufficiently large pieces for a
particular work. Although wooden
frameworks had been used for games-
boards in the late sixteenth and early

FIG.9 The Judgement of Paris. Amber relief by Christoph Maucher (b. 1642; d. after 1721?). Danzig, late 17th century. Inv. no. A.61-1925.

seventeenth century, other works of amber, such as tankards and caskets, adorned with metal mounts, had no supporting wooden carcase, in order that the light could shine through the translucent amber panels. The technique of incrustation expanded the repertoire of the amber-workers, although at the same time, arguably, second-rate works were sometimes produced as the skill required was considerably less. Nevertheless some notably fine works were made, such as the altar in FIG.7 which probably dates from about 1650. The form of the altar

reflects contemporary tomb-monuments and architecture in Danzig, and it was almost certainly made there. The amber half-moon on the top once supported a figure of the Madonna and Child, which has subsequently been lost. Small reliefs in pierced ivory set against black horn backings depict scenes from the life of Christ and the Virgin, in accordance with the lost figure of the Madonna and Child at the apex of the altar, which was probably dedicated to the Virgin; the altar's almost certainly Catholic iconography is another indication that it was made

in Catholic Danzig, rather than Protestant Prussia. The combination of ivory reliefs with the richly coloured amber panels is a further characteristic of Danzig works, where the colour contrast between amber and ivory was exploited to the full.

An even more ambitious example of Danzig amber work set on a wooden carcase, also of the mid-seventeenth century, can be seen in FIG.8. This altar is 4 feet high, and is adorned with ivory reliefs of Biblical scenes, while finely sculpted amber figures of the Apostles stand on the base. In the centre of the front of the altar is a scene in low-relief of the Adoration of the Shepherds, made up of a mosaic of different coloured opaque amber pieces. On the back of the altar is a perpetual calendar displaying signs from the Zodiac made in ivory. Pierced ivory reliefs of Old Testament subjects surround the perpetual calendar, complementing the New Testament subjects on the front of the altar.

Small-scale sculpture in amber was a speciality of Danzig, and one of the leading artists was Christoph Maucher (b. 1642; d. after 1721?). Maucher came from a family of ivory-carvers in Southern Germany and was himself trained as one. In about 1670 however, at the age of about twenty-eight, he came to settle in Danzig, and learnt the art of amber carving. Little is known of him, but the few surviving references to him tell of his success as an artist: he was given a series of commissions for amber and ivory works in 1682 by the Great Elector of Brandenburg, Friedrich Wilhelm, and the prestigious commission of carving an ivory monument for Emperor Leopold I of Austria in 1700. However, Maucher was envied and reviled by the members of the guild of amber-workers in Danzig, who made an official complaint about him in 1705, declaring that the commissions he had undertaken had led to

FIG.10 The Judgement of Paris. Amber figure-group on a wooden base with inlaid amber panels and reliefs; previously the crowning group of a casket.
By Christopher Maucher (b.1642; d. after 1721?). Danzig, late 17th century.
Inv. no. 1059-1873.

a decline in the Guild's prosperity, for he was neither a member of the Guild, nor a citizen of Danzig. He appears to have disappeared shortly after this, perhaps fleeing the city, for the next known reference to him is in a book by a Polish Jesuit, published in 1721, where we hear that Maucher found refuge in a 'haven beside the woods and glades'.[2]

Two of Maucher's works in amber are in the Victoria and Albert Museum. The relief of The Judgement of Paris (FIG.9) depicts Paris presenting the apple to Venus: Juno and Minerva look on with Cupid at their feet. The stocky figures and skilful, if crowded, composition are typical of Maucher's work. He invests the classical story with a rustic humour, depicting the disappointment experienced by the two defeated goddesses, and the curiosity of the infant Cupid and the dog. The story of the Judgement of Paris evidently appealed to Maucher, for the other amber by him in the Museum is also a depiction of The Judgement of Paris and there is a third in Berlin. The figure-group (FIG.10) is one of the finest examples of Maucher's art, and shows even more clearly his narrative strengths. This was probably the crowning figure-group of a casket; several caskets from Danzig retain an amber figure group on the top, and holes drilled into the base of this group indicate how it was originally intended to be displayed, although it can be appreciated as free-standing sculpture, the sloping top of the casket now acting as a socle for the figure-group. Neither of these ambers is signed or documented, and they are attributed to Maucher on the basis of stylistic parallels with his one signed and documented work, the ivory monument made for Emperor Leopold I of Austria in 1700. The faces are particularly characteristic of Maucher: the full cheeks, the eyes turning downward at the outer edges, and the half-open mouths. The down-to-earth quality of the ambers is also typical of Maucher: the figures are chunky and peasant-like; in FIG.10 Paris sits with his feet firmly on the ground and Mercury pushes his way between Minerva and Juno, so that he can see more clearly. The animals around the figures, the dog, owl and peacock, correspondingly inquisitive, peer curiously at the scene taking place.

Maucher's works demonstrate an important development in the art of amber carving, the way in which it could rival boxwood and ivory as a material for sculpture. Amber also continued to be employed for making decorative objects, such as caskets and cabinets, into the 18th century, but gradually it came to be used for fashionable courtly items, such as cane-tops, snuff or perfume-bottles, and, having become fashionable, it inevitably eventually went out of fashion, so that by the mid-eighteenth century, amber-carving was seldom practised, and the Guilds along the Baltic coast, Königsberg and Danzig among them, petered out. However, if we are now less interested in any magical or healing powers amber may possess, we may still admire the great works of art made of amber in the Baroque period.

1 Pliny, *Natural History,* Book XXXVII, Chapter 12.

2 G. Rzaczynski *Historia Naturalis Curiosa Regni Poloniae* Sandomira, 1721, p. 184.

QUALITY OF OLD, ANTIQUE AND RARE

69

Sabattini
al Victoria and Albert

RICAS

sabattini

Sabattini Argenteria s.p.a. via Don Capiaghi 2, 22070 Bregnano (Como) tel. (031) 771019
Show-room: via della Spiga 2, 20121 Milano tel. (02) 798449

J. CHRISTIE

ANTIQUE SILVER, ANIMALIER BRONZES & OBJECT D'ART
26 Burlington Arcade, Piccadilly, London W1. Tel: 01-629 3070

Pierre Jules Mêne 1810–1879
Arab Mare ('Nedjibé') with gun
and saddle at her feet
Dated 1855

George IV Silver Tea Tray
Made by William Bruce,
London 1829, Weight 205ozs.
Centre armorials of Wickam
Impalling Lawrence, Co.
Lancaster

Pair of Victorian Silver Gilt
mounted, cut glass Claret Jugs.
Made by H. Walker & Co.,
Birmingham 1874-1881

A Word to the Collector

MEMBER

ART AND ANTIQUE DEALERS LEAGUE OF AMERICA, INC.

Organized 1926

OMNIA VINCIT VERITAS

Protect your investment.
Beware the Instant Experts with
their impersonal mass sales techniques...
Look for the emblem of
The Art and Antique Dealers League of America.
A membership of established experts
dedicated to the preservation of quality,
authenticity and professionalism
in the World of Art & Antiques.

Art and Antique Dealers League of America, Inc.

Headquarters: 353 EAST 53rd STREET, NEW YORK, N.Y. 10022 (212) 355-0175

"Walking Lion"

Very fine N.Italian Bronze, c.1490, light brown patina with traces of lacquer, on original marble base.
Height: 8.4 cm. (without base), length: 16 cm., height of base: 6.7 cm. Ex-collection: Robert Strauss
Sculpture derives from the Antique, Rubens made a drawing after this Bronze. A similar example is in
the Herzog Anton Museum, in Braunschweig, in the Untermyer collection, and in the Kunstgewerbe
Museum, Berlin.
Literature: Hind IV. Platte 437 "North East Italy", c.1490 Y. Hackenbroch "Bronzes in the Irwin
Untermyer Collection" 1962 Figure. 32. K. Pechstein "Bronzes and Placques", 1968, Nr. 85.

KUNST- UND ANTIQUITÄTENMESS HANNOVER-
HERRENHAUSEN GALERIEGEBÄUDE, STAND 31,
MESSETELEFON: 05 11/71 21/22

GEMÄLDE17.-19. JH   ERLESENE ANTIQUITÄTEN   ALTER SCHMUCK

3 HANNOVER · BECKMANNHAUS · GEORGSTRASSE 48 · TELEFON 0511/323074
GECENÜBER DER OPER

Ständige Parkmöglichkeiten auf geschäftseigenem Grundstück.

FIG.1 Stratford Canning, first Viscount
Stratford de Redcliffe (1786–1880). Chalk
drawing by George Richmond, 1853. National
Portrait Gallery.

FIG.2 Charles Robert Cockerell (1788–1863).
Watercolour attributed to A. A. Chalon.
National Portrait Gallery.

STRATFORD CANNING'S PICTURES OF TURKEY

Charles Newton

A puzzle that had lain unsolved for many years was recently unravelled in the Prints & Drawings Department of the V&A. A series of intriguing pictures of Turkish life, architecture, and costume, which had been in the collections since 1895, has been identified as part of a set once belonging to Stratford Canning, first Viscount Stratford de Redcliffe (1786–1880) (FIG.1), and sold to the Museum by his daughter [1]. Canning was the ambassador to Turkey whose skilful negotiations with the Turks in arranging a peace between them and the Russians was a decisive factor in the war against Napoleon [2].

When the young Canning was sent out to Constantinople as first secretary to Robert Adair in June 1808, he was going to a country of which popular misconceptions abounded. He was soon aware of these misconceptions however, for in a letter to George Canning, his cousin (and Foreign Secretary), he wrote, 'Very false notions are entertained in England of the Turkish Nation. I am myself a daily witness of the personal qualities of the inhabitants . . .' [3]. At first there was very little to do after the initial negotiation of a peace treaty between England and Turkey in January 1809. The Turks, in this case, lived up to their reputation for delay so Canning was able to amuse himself with riding, with the small number of European 'society', and with observing the inhabitants. He was established in the British Embassy, 'a hired house in the main street of Pera' (the European quarter across the Golden Horn). From there he wrote, 'We had already slaked our curiosity not only by visiting such objects and places of resort as every itinerant author has described, but also by attending official ceremonies and those occasional sports at which the Sultan presided in public, as well as for his own diversion as for the gratification of his many-coloured and

many-creeded subjects.' The events ranged from the formal audience and the magnificent processions of the Sultan and his officers, to the more homely diversion of watching wrestling in the presence of veiled ladies. Canning was obviously deeply impressed by the scenes of everyday life around him; the exotic ceremonial and gorgeous male costumes of exquisitely figured silk must have contrasted with his memory of the gloomy days of his youth in Hackney and the relative sobriety of the playing fields of Eton. Again, he commented, 'The splendid old costume at once so appropriate and so diversified, shone out with Oriental brilliancy. The usage of centuries in dress and manners, associated with history and typical of the unchanging East, occupied even to rapture both sight and mind.' What was more natural than that he should commission an artist who was on the spot to record the buildings, costumes and ceremonies? That he did this we know from an account by the young architect C.R. Cockerell (1788–1863) (FIG.2), who had just embarked on his travels to Greece and Asia Minor to study ancient architecture and antiquities. He had arrived in Constantinople in June 1810, and the lyrical description of his arrival echoes the feeling of many travellers on seeing that most beautiful city. 'We approached Constantinople as the sun rose, and as it shone on its glorious piles of mosques and minarets, golden points and crescents, painted houses, kiosks and gardens, our Turks pulled harder at their oars, shouting 'Stamboul, guzel azem Stamboul!' [Istanbul, beautiful and great]. The scene grew more and more brilliant as we drew nearer, till it became overwhelming as we entered the crowded port. Nothing but the despatches under my arm recalled me from a sense of being in a dream . . . I had jumped from sombre London to

this fantastic paradise' [4]. Cockerell first refers to the pictures now in our collection when writing of his host: 'Mr Canning, of whose kindness on all occasions I cannot speak too highly, has obliged me exceedingly in lending me a large collection of fairly faithful drawings of the interiors of mosques, some of them never drawn before, as well as other curious buildings here, made by a Greek of this place. In copying them I have been closely employed, as when Mr Adair leaves, which shall be shortly, they will be sent off to England.' Some of Cockerell's copies of these drawings are now preserved in the Department of Classical Antiquities of the British Museum. The Greek artist's originals are highly coloured watercolour and gouache, whereas Cockerell's copies are in pencil. Cockerell, a superb draughtsman, has improved on the originals: his drawing of the figures in particular is more elegant, although the Greek artist's handling of the architecture is workmanlike. The Greek artist, whose name is still unknown, seems to have been torn between the Turkish style of manuscript illustration and a desire to follow European models. He handles the gouache and metallic paint in a similar way to other anonymous Turkish artists who produced books of costume and ceremonial at that period, but the treatment of the architecture and the figures shows knowledge of European art, possibly because he had seen French or English prints of architectural antiquities. The Greek may have been in the employ of the Sultan, which would have given him privileged access to many things denied to Europeans. Cockerell said of him, 'I have made several useful friends. One is a brother artist, the Greek who did the mosques for Canning. We have paid each other several visits, and have become fairly intimate by dint of Dragoman [interpreter], mutual ad-

FIG.3 The Bab-i-Hümayun, the Imperial Gate to the Sultan's Palace, Topkapı Saray, Constantinople, with the fountain of Ahmet III. To the right of the Gate is a rubbish heap where the corpses of malefactors were thrown. 1809–1810. D.142–1895.

miration, and what was a superb present from me, a little indian ink and two English pencils. He has been specially attentive in his visits here, hoping as he confessed, to find out some secret in the art from such a connoisseur as myself.' As is plain from this passage the Greek had no knowledge of the English or French languages but did desire to learn from European models.

Canning's exact reasons for commissioning the drawings are not known; nor is it known why Cockerell was eager to copy them, but it is likely that Canning intended them as a visual record, possibly to complement the dispatches he sent to England. In the early days of his tenure the British Government had given Canning little instruction and he had to use his own initiative, triumphantly as it turned out.

While Cockerell was visiting the Embassy, he met another Englishman, none other than Lord Byron who was touring in Greece and Turkey with John Cam Hobhouse and staying for the moment at the Embassy. (Canning had last seen Byron when he was playing against him in an Eton and Harrow cricket match, with another boy running for Byron when he struck the ball.) Hobhouse's and Byron's adventures in Albania, Greece and Turkey were recorded in Hobhouse's *A Journey through Albania and other provinces of Turkey in Europe and Asia, to Constantinople during the years 1809 and 1810,* published in 1813. There is a close correspondence between the scenes of life in Constantinople described in the book and the Greek artist's images. Most of them could be slotted in as illustrations to the text, and one indeed was: the Greek artist's view of the Bab-i-Hümayun, the main gate of the Sultan's palace, Topkapı Saray (FIG.3).[5] It appears there as an aquatint, reproduced not from the

original, nor indeed from a version by Cockerell, but from a watercolour copy by yet another artist.

This copy, from which the aquatint illustration published by James Cawthorn was made, is now in the Searight collection. Rodney Searight recognised some years ago that not only was his picture the original of the illustration but that the V&A had another version. The Greek artist's drawings were so important as a primary source that other artists besides Cockerell made copies of his work: in the Searight collection there are further versions of his pictures, including some made in the 1820s by Mrs Turner, wife of William Turner (1792–1867), the diplomat.

Canning, Cockerell, Byron and Hobhouse tried to see as much as they could of the places normally forbidden or difficult of access to Europeans, and there were stories of being smuggled in to see palaces belonging to the Sultan's family, mosques and other places. Canning writes, 'We had ourselves figured conspicuous in the official

audiences to which the Embassy had been admitted . . . We also had been present under the rose [secretly], at some purely Turkish festivities whether of a religious or of a civil character.' Cockerell also mentions going into forbidden places. 'In arriving here just in time to take advantage of Mr Adair's firman [permit] to see the Mosques I was most fortunate. It is a favour granted to ambassadors only once, and Mr Adair thinks himself lucky to get it before going away.' Cockerell also bribed a gardener in order to see a royal palace. Somehow the Greek artist had managed not only to gain admission but also to sketch the interiors of the Seraglio, of Aya Sofya, and of the mosque, Fatih Camii. To do this he may have disguised himself as a Turk, but, alternatively, he may have been a member of the Sultan's household as suggested earlier.

This world that was recorded at Canning's behest by the Greek artist was about to change forever. Sultan Selim III (1789–1807) had begun some

FIG.4 The inner court of the palace, Topkapı
Saray, Constantinople. The ceremony of
paying the Janissaries by making them race to
collect the money for their Officers. View
taken from the Hall of Audience, with the
kitchens to the right of the picture. 1809–
1810. D.143–1895.

FIG.5 A wrestling match, apparently in the
grounds of the Sultan's Palace, with a view
across the mouth of the Golden Horn, an
audience of veiled women, and the Sultan in
his kiosk. 1809–1810. D.115–1895.

FIG.6 Sultan Mahmud II in procession,
escorted by his senior officers and officials,
leaving a gate of the palace. 1809–1810.
D. 123–1895.

FIG.7 A Tekke or convent of Dervishes being
visited by a European, red-hot skewers being
swallowed by the participants in the
ceremony. 1809–1810. D.140–1895.

FIG.8 A European (probably Stratford Canning or Robert Adair) dining with the Kaymakam or Governor of Constantinople, in the presence of a dragoman or interpreter. 1809–1810. D.124–1895.

reforms, but these had been interrupted by the hostility of the Janissaries, who had deposed and then murdered him, terrified by the prospect of having their privileges curtailed and their customs changed. Selim, who had been very pro-French, allegedly under the influence of Aimée Dubucq de Rivery, cousin to the Empress Josephine, and the mother of the future Sultan Mahmud II, had tried to introduce new uniforms and tactics on the Napoleonic model, but these were swept away in a wave of reaction at his death. Sultan Mahmud II, who ascended the throne in 1808 after the brief reign of Mustapha, wanted to proceed with changes but he had to wait until he finally managed to destroy the Janissaries in 1826 before anything significant could be done.

Thus the Turkey that Canning saw when he arrived in 1808 was hovering on the brink of the modern world of English steam engines, French fashions and German militarism, but outwardly had not yet changed very much. The costume, the customs, the

processions and the uniforms were frozen in time; they evolved no further but were to be replaced eventually by European models, often hideously incongruous, like the 'Stambouline' or European frock coat which looked very odd on the Sultan's officials, particularly the Eunuchs.

The Greek artist's pictures, which show eighty-six single figure costume subjects, ranging from the Sultan and his officers down to a knife-grinder, and thirty-nine images of manners, customs, architecture and topography, are important because they are a last glimpse of a Turkey barely influenced by Western ways; little did Canning know that he was recording the end of true Oriental splendour unalloyed with the drab West.

Some of the views are ones that every tourist saw, but others are unique or not yet identified (FIG.4). There are no contemporary inscriptions, in fact no information at all on the pictures, but careful reading of books like Hobhouse's *Albania* . . . enables many of the subjects to be identified. Here

there is a description of an audience with the Kaymakam, or Governor of Constantinople, during which a remarkable custom of the Janissaries was witnessed by the English notables. Purses of money were set down in the inner court of the Seraglio and each section or 'Oda' of the Janissaries ran forward in turn to pick up the purses and give them to their officers, tumbling over each other in their haste. Each man, according to Hobhouse, received one piastre from the officer if he was fast and strong enough to get there first. Hobhouse was not impressed: 'We were heartily fatigued before the conclusion of the ceremony, which according to an established usage, was, however, designed to captivate and astonish us by a display of Ottoman wealth.'[6] The drawing by the Greek artist appears to be the only known visual record of this custom; it must have been an impressive sight as the soldiers in full robes and head-dresses ran forward at tremendous speed towards the enormous sums of money laid out in yellow bags. The picture shows the elaborate architecture of the palace and the senior officers of the Sultan in the foreground, including a colonel of the Janissaries watching his men.

Some of the pictures have unexpected subjects. There is a curious picture of a wrestling match which seems to be taking place in the Seraglio gardens in the presence of veiled ladies, with the Sultan himself in his kiosk watching the action from above (FIG.5). This may be a flight of fancy by the Greek artist, but it may also be one of the sports which the Sultan enjoyed and Canning attended.

There is a splendid picture of Sultan Mahmud leaving the palace in procession on his way to Friday prayers (FIG.6), surrounded by the plumed head-dresses of the Soulaks, his bodyguard, and some of his chief officers;

FIG.9 An eating house or shish-kebab shop at the back of the Valide Köşkü near the Yeni Cami, with a view of Galata in the background across the Golden Horn. 1809–1810. D.119–1895.

FIG.10 The Sandal Bedestini, or silk market, Constantinople. 1809–1810. D.138–1895.

FIG.11 A view of a street outside the French Embassy in Pera, Constantinople, with a patrol of watchmen filing past. 1809–1810. D.136–1895.

FIG.12 Janissaries with soup-kettles and the ceremonial spoon. 1809–1810. D.117–1895.

the chief white Eunuch can clearly be seen just in front of the horse. Individual studies of these officers are included in the first group of Canning's pictures, but many are now difficult to identify precisely, because of the lack of titles and the unreliability of comparative European material. When this group of costume studies is eventually fully identified, it will be a most important source of information on the subject, for the Greek artist seems to have been very accurate in distinguishing between the tiny details which indicated rank.

Another aspect of Turkish life was the variety of religious sects: one picture shows a European visiting a Tekke or convent of dervishes (FIG.7). Unusually, the group shown here is not the Mevlavî or whirling ones, but probably the Rufai, or 'howling dervishes', as the Westerners called them. They stand in a circle, in a trance-like state induced by chanting the name of God continuously and then, when moved, swallow red hot skewers. The assistant is heating them at the hearth at the right and the leader or Shaikh of the order is seen standing in front of the niche. One of the participants is shown being revived after his ordeal.

The same European who visited the dervishes (Canning or Adair?) is shown taking refreshment with the Kaymakam, wrapped, as was customary at such meals, in an elaborate shawl (FIG.8). A dragoman [interpreter], in the distinctive robes of his office, stands conveying pleasantries between them. Humbler, but no less interesting meals are being prepared in a picture of an eating house (FIG.9), a shish-kebab shop at the back of the Valide Köşkü near the Yeni Cami, next to the docks. Soup is being served, (perhaps tripe soup which was reputedly good for hangovers); merchant ships and the waters of the Golden Horn can be seen in the background.

Commerce is also shown in a view of the interior of the Sandal Bedesteni, or silk market (FIG.10): the merchants sit patiently on the counters, standing up to reach for and display their goods at the request of the customer; the massive structure of the spacious market hall is clearly depicted.

Architecture which has subsequently completely disappeared is shown in a view of a street (FIG.11), outside what may be the French Embassy in Pera. The European is walking past the gates, while a patrol of watchmen is filing past in the other direction, each armed with his distinctive knotted club, with which he beat the ground to give warning of the frequent fires in

Constantinople. It may well have been a fire which swept away these quaint buildings, for no trace of them now remains.

The last picture reproduced here (FIG.12) shows a group of Janissaries carrying small soup kettles under the watchful eye of a senior officer. Soup had a special meaning for these soldiers; for example, the overturning and drumming on the soup cauldrons signalled mutiny, and one of their standards in battle was the giant spoon whose loss was as serious as the loss of the Eagles to a Roman legion. The officer who is leading the procession in the picture is carrying the ceremonial spoon of honour. Each Janissary carried his own spoon in his head-dress when on parade.

There are twenty-nine other drawings of Turkish scenes, apart from the large number of costume studies, all of them filled with interesting details which will justify much more research. All these pictures by the Greek artist could well illustrate a new work on the vanished customs and manners of the Turks, thus fulfilling what may indeed have been Canning's original intention when he commissioned them one hundred and seventy years ago.

I am deeply indebted to Bryony Llewellyn who first drew my attention to these pictures, and helped and advised me throughout. I am especially grateful to Godfrey Goodwin who identified many of the places and buildings depicted. Among many others who have helped in different ways are Patricia Baker, Rosemary Crill, Rodney Searight, Michael Warr and David Watkin.

1 Museum records state only that this series was bought from 'Miss Canning'. This was Charlotte Louisa Canning (d. 1902) who was the only one of the Cannings' three daughters (all unmarried) still alive in 1895. There is no reference at all to Stratford Canning in the minimal cataloguing, nor any indication of whom the artist might be. Almost none of the pictures was identified properly. With the series was a group of three small sketches by D. R. Morier, colleague and close friend of Canning at the Embassy.

2 The Treaty of Bucharest released the Russian Army on the Danube to attack the French during the retreat from Moscow in 1812. This disaster proved that Napoleon was not invincible.

3 This, and all subsequent quotations from Canning are taken from S. Lane-Poole, *Life of Lord Stratford de Redcliffe*, 1888.

4 This, and all subsequent quotations from Cockerell are taken from S. P. Cockerell, *Travels in Southern Europe and the Levant 1810–1817. The Journal of C. R. Cockerell R.A.*, 1903.

5 J.C. Hobhouse, *Albania* . . . p. 992.

6 *Ibid.* p. 994–5.

National Museum of Wales

French Art from the Davies Bequest
Celf Ffrengig o Gasgliad Davies
Französische Kunst aus dem Davies Vermächtnis
L'art français du legs Davies

84pp., 30 colour plates, 56 monochrome illustrations.
This picture book by Peter Hughes, published separately in 3 translations, illustrates all the French works in the Museum's internationally-famous collection, including important Impressionist and Post Impressionist paintings. Among the 39 artists represented are Daumier, Millet, Corot, Renoir, Manet, Pissarro, Monet, Cézanne and Van Gogh.

Price: hard cover £6.50 (£7.50 by post)
soft cover £3.25 (£3.80 by post)

For full details of nearly 200 Museum titles in print write for the free *Catalogue of Publications* to the Publications Officer, National Museum of Wales, Cathays Park, Cardiff CF1 3NP.

French Art
from the
Davies Bequest

National Museum of Wales

Detail of La Parisienne *by Renoir*

Grave Stele.
Attic (from Athens), last
decade of fifth century B.C.
Pentelic marble, 102.5
x 44.5 x 17.5 cm (40⅜" x
17½" x 6⅞"). 83.AA.378.

A deceased warrior in full
battle armor takes leave
of his wife. The couple's
names, Philoxenos and
Philomene, are inscribed
upon the architrave above
their heads. The stele's·
date and marble suggest
that Philoxenos most
probably died in the
Peloponnesian War.

THE
J. PAUL
GETTY
MUSEUM

17985 Pacific Coast Hwy.
Malibu, California
90265 USA
Telephone: (213) 459-7611
Telex: 82 0268

BLUMKA GALLERY
949 PARK AVENUE, NEW YORK CITY, N.Y. 10028
212-734-3222

PLEASE NOTE
AS OF JANUARY 1, 1985
NEW ADDRESS:
101 EAST 81st STREET
NEW YORK, N.Y. 10028

Twelve very fine Limoges Enamel Panels depicting the Stations of the Cross.
French, 16th century. (Panels 9cm. by 10cm.)

N. M. Rothschild & Sons Limited

Merchants and Bankers

William IX, Elector of Hesse, entrusting valuables to the care of Mayer Amschel Rothschild.
Frankfurt, 1807

New Court, St Swithin's Lane, London EC4P 4DU
Telephone: 01-280 5000   Telex: 888031

FIG.1 *Towards Glaramara from Watendlath Path:* '25 Sepr 1806 – Borrowdale – a fine clouday day tone very mellow like – the mildest of Gaspar Poussin and Sir G[eorge] B[eaumont] & on the whole deeper toned than this drawing –' R.74.

JOHN CONSTABLE IN THE LAKE DISTRICT, SEPTEMBER—OCTOBER 1806

John Murdoch

'Pity that he did not prolong his stay in this beautiful country, i.e., that we might have had its features reflected by his pencil': thus Wordsworth thanked Constable's daughter for the gift of Leslie's Life of their father in a letter dated 6 June 1844 from Rydal Mount[1]. Leslie had written that Constable's mind was formed for the enjoyment of a different class of landscape: 'I have heard him say that the solitude of mountains oppressed his spirits. His nature was particularly social and could not feel satisfied with scenery, however grand in itself, that did not abound in human associations. He required villages, churches, farmhouses, and cottages . . .'[2] To Wordsworth, as to others, Leslie's statement rang true: Constable himself, significantly, did not include a Lake District subject among the English Landscape mezzotints by which he epitomized his achievement. Wordsworth[3] as an acute and well-informed judge of the visual arts, knew that the mature Constable had developed an imagery of sublime and emblematic landscape from material very different from that typically found in the Lake District. But Constable's daughters, had they replied to Wordsworth's note, could have told him that their father had in fact produced many pictures including an important series of watercolours which was still intact, on his Lake District Tour; and that the watercolours were quite unlike most of his finished work in the medium, belonging primarily to a large private repertoire of studies in oil, watercolour and graphite, distinct from the major public statements of his finished pictures and from the English Landscape mezzotints[4].

At its simplest, the series of drawings is a partial record of the tour. Many of the sheets are inscribed with dates and topographical notes, and most of them are concerned with the high mountain landscapes of the Borrowdale area. There is little or nothing to record the earlier social part of the tour, no image of boating or sketching parties on Windermere or on the navigable Brathay, nor even any graphite studies[5] of the music parties, given by John Harden, his host at Brathay Hall or by Mr Worgan at Storrs. Clearly the Constable of 1806 was very sociable, but when confronted with a choice of subjects, the gentry and the genre of Arcadian Windermere, or the sublime solitude of Borrowdale, he actually concentrated on the latter.

For the next three years, Lake District pictures made up virtually all of his contributions to the London exhibitions – at the R.A. in 1807 all three subjects were from his tour: View in Westmorland (52), Keswick Lake (98), and Bow Fell (150); in 1808 at the British Institution, one, A Mountain Scene in Westmorland (380), out of two; and at the R.A. again all three, Winandermere (sic.) Lake (52), A Scene in Cumberland (100), and Borrowdale (103); in 1809 three out of four at the B.I., Windermere Lake (248), Borrowdale (260), and Keswick Lake (282). His 1809 picture for the Academy, a five-foot treatment of Borrowdale, was abandoned when Farington advised him against sending it in on the grounds that it was 'in appearance, only like a preparation for finishing' – wanting 'variety of colour and effect'.[6] None of these pictures is now known, but in 1809 they formed the greater part of Constable's public achievement, thoroughly in step with the interests of other young professionals, if not of the market, and evidently, if we accept Farington's sense of the big Borrowdale, boldly executed in the spirit of the Burkeian Sublime, with some apt 'privation of colour'. In the absence of the paintings, especially without the Borrowdale, which was clearly the most ambitious picture he attempted before the later series of six-footers, the record of this first period of Constable's active professional life, the period in which he began to use landscape to illuminate great movements in the human consciousness, lies necessarily in the watercolours.

It is sometimes said that Constable's main discovery in the Lake District was that weather mattered, and that it was during this tour that he first began making systematic notes recording it.[7] The whole question of Constable's attitude to the weather has recently been reviewed, especially of course in relation to the cloud studies of 1820–21, and the long-standing suggestion that he was responding in those studies directly to Luke Howard's work on the climate of London has been largely abandoned.[8] A fortiori, the suggestion that Constable's attitude to the Lake District weather was in any way systematic should founder, since an examination of the inscriptions on the drawings themselves certainly does not suggest even a day-to-day record of rain or shine, nor wind direction, type or density of cloud let alone any 'scientific' terminology. Constable, from his hostess Jessy Harden's account,[9] sensibly enough seems to have gone out only when the rain was not pouring down, though he did, on the evidence of sheets such as Helvellyn (R.73), occasionally get caught. There is no doubt about his commitment to his work, but what took him out was not the wish to record the changes in the weather for their own sake. Why and how, therefore was he interested in the weather, in the time of day and the quality of the light?

The basic explanation is that he was responding to ideas that existed already in the culture of painters and of others interested in landscape. Thus he would have been aware perhaps that Gainsborough's Show-box[10] studied and presented the changes in atmosphere and effect through the times of day, and that, more profoundly, the stately sequence of morning, noon, and evening were fundamental to the sense of harmony that ruled the old master tradition of landscape painting. This was required study for the ambitious young painter, and he referred specifically to it in two of the drawings – 'very mellow like – the mildest of Gaspar Poussin'; (FIG.1) the effect exceeding terrific – and much like the beautiful Gaspar I saw in Margaret St.'[11] (FIG.2). The centre of his interest here is obviously pictorial and not at all meteorological, the weather being merely the cause of the effect that interests him.

From the tourist literature would have come an additional impulse. It may have been chance that Constable approached the Lake District by nearly the same route as William Gilpin, and there is no hard evidence that Constable had actually read his family copy of the *Observations . . . on . . . the Mountains, and Lakes of Cumberland, and Westmorland* by the time he set out.[12] It does seem likely, however, that he would have read something, at least what was close to hand, and Gilpin was the only guide that we know to have been in his library. There seems not to have been a copy of Thomas West's *Guide to the Lakes . . .* (1778), which was the standard text for visitors to the Lake District, and indeed, there is no similarity between West's recommendations for viewing the scenery and the views that Constable actually took. On the other hand, there are suggestive similarities, not only topographical, but in the whole approach to the landscape, between Constable and Gilpin. Thus Gilpin, the traveller, who is almost always moving through scenes and is intensely aware of their unfolding around him, is vividly aware also of the time of day and the presence of cloud.

If he did indeed read Gilpin's descriptions of the Borrowdale area, Constable's imagination must have been stimulated by passages such as this: 'The clouds which were gathering upon the mountains, and sweeping along the vallies, began to interrupt our view. Everything was wrapped in obscurity . . . The whole valley of Gascadale [Keskerdale] smoked like a boiling cauldron; and we got our ideas of it only by catches, as the volumes of clouds dispersed, at intervals, into purer air . . . Among the beautiful appearances of fogs, and mists, their *gradually going off* may be observed. A landscape takes a variety of pleasing hues, as it passes, in a retiring fog, through the different degrees of obscurity into full splendour.'[13]

Gilpin's sense of landscape was intensely theatrical, and Constable too would have been aware of the relevant theatrical tradition, pioneered by Garrick and de Loutherbourg at Drury Lane and Covent Garden between 1772 and 1785, which brought about the most spectacular and dynamic effects of stage scenery seen in England since the masques of Jonson and Inigo Jones. Loutherbourg made his reputation as a painter by his work as a set designer, and his employment at Drury Lane duly culminated in his election as a full Academician in 1781. The Eidophusikon, which he opened the same year, formally separated scenery from drama, asserting the sufficiency of the spectacle alone to arouse response. Employing all the resources of theatricality, it focused the attention of the audience on landscape, not as the background to a drama primarily of human passions (though some of the scenes that Loutherbourg inserted were historical or mythological), but as the theatre of Nature's far more dramatic cycles. Reynolds praised it highly, recommending it to students as 'a school of the wonderful

effect of nature'.[14] The times of day changed from dawn to sunset to moonlight, storms raged and the sublime landscape of Hell appeared, lit by gloomy fires. What Loutherbourg was doing was to employ the Burkeian Beautiful and Sublime, which comprehended the highest perceptions and aspirations of men, and portray them within a dynamic vision of natural landscape. The theatrical tradition thus taught that landscape, perceived especially as a changing spectacle, could be the area of pictorial art in which the most serious statements about the world, at its grandest superhuman level, could be made.

Any reference to Nature in connection with Constable deserves in fact as much sceptical care as references to his later interests in meteorology and science. The famous passage of his letter to John Dunthorne of 1802 – 'however one's mind may be elevated and kept up to what is excellent, by the works of the Great Masters – still Nature is the fountain's head, the source from which all originally must spring – and should an artist continue his practice without referring to nature he must soon form a *manner* . . .'[15] – should not be taken as a declaration of independence from the received traditions of the old masters, but it does announce Constable's commitment to the sort of Naturalism which, sanctioned by Reynold's Discourses, was current among professional artists at this time. The trip to the Lake District was surely, in the sense meant in the letter to Dunthorne a trip to the 'fountain's head'. Accordingly, most of the Lake District drawings have no inscribed reference to the Old Masters, nor any obviously imitative quality. They are indeed usually so accurate in the portraiture of places that, even without inscriptions, their location can be recognized. In terms of date, in topographical precision, in their in-

FIG.2 *Looking into Borrowdale Narrows from the South:* 'Borrowdale 4 Oct 1806 – Dark Autumnal day at noon – tone more blooming [than] this . . . the effect exceeding terrific – and much like the beautiful Gaspar I saw in Margaret St.' R.80.

FIG.3 *Borrowdale from Rosthwaite, looking North, Castle Crag on the left;* inscribed on the back: 'Borrowdale 4 Octr 1806 Noon Clouds breaking away after Rain'. R.79.

FIG.4 Robert Hills, *Derwentwater from Sprinkling Tarn;* Birmingham City Museum and Art Gallery.

FIG.5 *Newlands towards Skiddaw (?)*, perhaps Monday 22 September. R.89a.

scriptions, their immediate analogy is with the work of Robert Hills and Joshua Cristall on their tours of 1803 and 1805. Cristall especially has a turn of phrase as vivid as Constable's, noting for example at Lodore on 25 July 1805 that 'reflections of foam frequently fall on the rocks'. Yet it is by comparison with their work that the special quality of Constable's Lake District drawings emerges most clearly. Cristall examines minutely, and is indeed typically fascinated by such small evanescent effects as the foam, and Hills studies boulders covered with moss in a stream bed. Constable, on the other hand, never lowers his eyes to what is at his feet. Typically he sees 'Clouds breaking away after Rain'[16] (FIG.3), and even in fine weather, notices the mellowness that mediates vision (see FIG.1). Hills and Cristall are interested in seeing clearly, perhaps preferably in close-up, whereas Constable is classically concerned with tone and distance.

Even when Hills is drawing a line of distant peaks,[17] (FIG.4), he annihilates the intervening air with the long penetrative focus of telescopic sight, leaving the foreground and periphery in the blank margins of perception. Constable, on the other hand, similarly high up and in fine weather, fills his sheet with hazy mountain forms[18] (FIG.5).

He was not, then, an 'optical naturalist' in the sense that Cristall and Hills were, nor was he interested in the nascent cult of random or natural composition. His art was, however, powerfully specific, and it is arguable that his readiness to paint the actual effect of atmosphere was itself the most telling aspect of his naturalism. Naturalism, in that sense, may be added to the other motives behind the drawings, the more potent because of its consistency with the academic doctrines of aerial perspective which stressed the importance

FIG.6 'Helvellin 21st Sepr 1806 – evening stormy with slight rain'. R.73.

FIG.7 'Sty Head Tearn – Borrowdale – Sunday Octr 12 1806 – Noon Great End – Scorfell – Longmell –' R.83.

FIG.8 *Upper Borrowdale, with Gt. Gable in the distance:* 'Borrowdale 2nd [Oct] 1806 morning previous to a fine day' R.76.

of atmosphere in pictorial design and for properly organized recession of planes within the painting. Most of the Lake District drawings are accordingly conventional in design, receding both by linear and aerial perspective, sometimes led by a winding stream or road (*Helvellyn* R.73, FIG.6) or equipped ready with a figure as foreground motif or point of emphasis at a change of direction in recession (*Sty Head Tarn* R. 83, FIG.7). Their ready convertibility onto a larger scale or into finished pictures is indicated by those that are squared for transfer (*River Brathay with Figures,* Christie's 20 March 1984 lot 88). As drawings, they should be classified as 'composition studies', not 'studies from nature': to be used not as the material for a picture, but the schematic picture itself.

As a summary critical point about Constable one might say that throughout his career his central interest was in the architecture of painting, the construction of grandly articulated and eloquent tableaux on a plane of noble utterance. It was in that pursuit that he poured out his energy in sketches, a greater proportion of his most impressive achievement being contained in 'exercises' than for any other academically successful painter. The sketches are, in a sense that Gilpin would perhaps have understood, Observations: a study of the surroundings undertaken with extraordinary persistence and passion, as with the great series of oil sketches of 1808–11 of Dedham, East Bergholt and Flatford, which had him circling round the familiar scenes like a surveyor, establishing their lines, bearings and general relations. In the Lake District two years earlier Constable was just beginning to work in this way, not so systematically, but with a similarly strong grasping for the local particularity of the scenes he found. The Rosthwaite drawings, in which he crosses and re-

FIG.9 *Gt. Gable, Kirk Fell and Pillar* 'from the top of Onister Craig – Oct 1806 – noon'. R.77.

FIG.10 *A Bridge near Rosthwaite:* 'Oct 2 1806 – twylight after a very fine day'. R.78.

crosses the valley, laying out his lines towards Glaramara and Gt Gable, and back to the Narrows, over and over again at different times and in different conditions, are nearly as systematic as the East Anglian sketches and lead on to them, but their prior analogy is with the systematic, ordered and decorous observations of Gilpin in the same part of the valley: 'As we stood *under* the beetling cliffs on each side, they were too near for inspection: their harsh features wanted softening; but we had noble views of them all in order, both in *prospect*, and *retrospect*. Not only the design, and composition, but the very strokes of nature's pencil might be traced through the whole scene; every fractured rock, and every hanging shrub which adorned it, was brought within the compass of the eye: each touch so careless, and yet so determined: so wildly irregular; yet all conducting to one whole'.[19]

What Constable has beyond this, in addition to the vitality of his hand, is the ability to infuse drama authentically into the scene, so that the dark cliffs of Borrowdale can be sublime by an observed circumstance of gloom and obscurity rather than by exaggeration of their size. The sequences of 6 October when he surveyed Lodore and Derwent, on 13 October when he worked on Rosthwaite, and especially when he walked up to Esk Hause on the 12, imply the presence of the artist as witness. They exploit the narrative implications of movement, the sense of starting and finishing as the artist climbs over passes and surveys mysterious valleys. Clouds constantly moving across the hills, like the masks of comedy and tragedy, have a literal significance of security or fear as they pass across the protean face of nature. Some days he went out after dark, witnessing the *Doppelgänger* world of moonlight. On 2 October he was out from early morning, climbing high

into the Honister Pass, marking his return at evening with the elegiac composition of the woman carrying a pitcher over the bridge at Rosthwaite in the twilight (FIGS.8, 9, 10). Like the meditative shepherd at Sty Head Tarn (FIG.7), she is an explicitly classicizing element in the picture, borrowed from the sculptural repertoire to express with an added associational richness the sweet sadness of the fine autumn evening.[20]

In these cases, as in the drawings which study the effects which remind him of Poussin, classicism interests him because of its power to excite emotion – 'the effect exceeding terrific',[21] (see FIG.2). For Constable, the drive to connect his art, an art of personal observation and 'ordinary' subjects, with that of the past, came from his recognition that the language of important communication lay in the formality and decorum of the classic tradition. As he put it, struggling painfully with words, crossing and recrossing the subject in the laboured drafts for the introduction to *English Landscape*: 'It is surely to be regretted that the scenes with which we are surrounded – abounding as they do in Grandeur, and every description of pastoral beauty, and endeared as they are to us by the most powerful associations – should be either overlooked, or else rejected as unsuited to the Classical Style. But why should not subjects purely English be made the vehicle of General Landscape? – and, when embodied by its highest principles, be so rendered, as to become legitimate, and at the same time original – and consequently classical art.'[22]

1 *John Constable's Correspondence*, ed. R.B. Beckett, V,78 Suffolk Records Society XI.
  Charles Rhyne's forthcoming catalogue of the Constable oeuvre up to 1816 will deal comprehensively with the Lake District watercolours, and with the difficult questions that surround the few oil sketches and apparently finished pictures that have from time to time been attributed to Constable's Lake District tour. I am greatly indebted to Charles's generosity in

sending me notes and xeroxes on these and other problems, and I hope that this short piece, together with a longer account in a forthcoming book on the Lake District, may seem like some acknowledgement.
2 C.R. Leslie, *Memoirs of John Constable*, 1843; ed. J.H. Mayne 1951, 18–19.
3 – to whom Constable had sent a set of *English Landscape*.
4 The greater part of the Lake District series is in the V&A, having come with the rest of Isabella Constable's selection of her father's work to the Museum in 1888. The drawings are described in detail in Graham Reynolds, *Catalogue of the Constable Collection*, 1960, 2nd ed. 1973, nos. 72–94, arranged in roughly chronological order and topographical grouping. It is conventional to refer to V&A Constable drawings by their authoritative Reynolds numbers, rather than by their random museum inventory numbers.
5 – such as he had made earlier in the summer while staying at Ipswich and Tottenham. See L. Parris and I. Fleming-Williams' note in *Constable*, (exhibition catalogue) Tate Gallery 1976, no. 66.
6 3 April 1809; quoted from *Constable op. cit.* no. 69.
7 The claim is made popularly; but more weightily by L.C.W. Bonacina 'John Constable's Centenary: His Position as a Painter of Weather', *Royal Meteorological Society Quarterly Journal*, (1937), LXIII, 483–490.
8 The new and much more subtle position is outlined by John Thornes, 'Constable Clouds', *Burlington Magazine*, CXXI, 1979, 697–704.
9 See the quotations from her journal-letters in *John Constable's Correspondence*, ed. R.B. Beckett, V, 2–6, Suffolk Record Society XI.
10 Constructed *c.* 1781–1; now in the V&A; J.H. Mayne, 'Thomas Gainsborough's Exhibition Box'. *V&A Bulletin*, I, no. 3, July 1965, 17–24; John Hayes, *Gainsborough's Landscape Painting*, 1981, no. 132.
11 R.74 and R.80 respectively.
12 The Constables owned the third edition of 1792. The first volume only survived in the family collection. *Further Documents and Correspondence*, ed. I. Fleming-Williams, 1975, 31; Suffolk Record Society XVIII.
13 *Observations . . .*, I, 227–8;.
14 R.D. Altick, *The Shows of London*, Harvard 1978, 125.
15 29 May 1802; Beckett, *John Constable's Correspondence*, II, 32; Suffolk Records Society, VI.
16 R.79a.
17 Birmingham 230'70.
18 R.89a.
19 *Observations . . .*, I, 219; Gilpin's italics.
20 Constable, Louis Hawes has shown, was deeply interested in Archibald Alison's work on the value of association in aesthetic sentiment; *John Constable's Writings on Art*, PhD dissertation, Princeton 1963, University Microfilms, Ann Arbour, Michigan, Reprint 1964, esp. ch. IV. For Constable's other reading in aesthetics, see also *Further Documents and Correspondence, op. cit.*
21 R.80.
22 R.B. Beckett, *John Constable's Discourses*, Suffolk Record Society, 1970, XIV, 83.

Galerie Bellefontaine

Jean FUSARO Nature morte bleue à l'atelier oil on canvas 89 × 116 cm

FINE XXth. CENTURY PAINTINGS

Lebasque — Loiseau — Maufra — Le Sidaner

Aujame — Brianchon — Planson — Terechkovitch — Savin

Boncompain — Brasilier — Cottavoz — Fusaro — Maly — Menghini — Roudneff

Upton Lodge Galleries

Avening House, Avening, Tetbury, Gloucestershire GL8 8NH
Telephone: Nailsworth (045 383) 4048

The Drinking Trough
Signed and dated 1912

by Stanhope Alexander Forbes, R.A.
1857-1947

Oil on canvas
56 in by 46 in

Stanhope Forbes studied at the Royal Academy Schools and in Paris before settling in Cornwall, where he became leader of the Newlyn School and from about 1885 was a major influence in British art.

101

GET ACQUAINTED WITH
RICHARD A. BOURNE CO., INC.
America's Great Small Auction House

Oil on canvas by Fritz Thaulow. Sold on January 8, 1983, for $55,000 — a world auction record.

Paintings, furniture, silver, rare glass, oriental rugs, marine memorabilia, decoys, clocks, prints, dolls and toys, rare antique & collectible weapons and great Estate Auctions.

We do NOT have reserves
We do NOT charge a 10% buyer's premium

We DO guarantee what we sell
We DO publish excellent, well-illustrated catalogs

RICHARD A.
BOURNE CO. INC
Estate Auctioneers and Appraisers
PO Box 141VA
Hyannis Port, MA 02647
U.S.A.

102

ALEXANDER & BERENDT LTD.

*Fine 17th and 18th Century French and
Continental Furniture and Works of Art.*

1a Davies Street, Berkeley Square,
London W1Y 1LL
Telephone 01-499 4775.

**AN EQUESTRIAN STATUETTE OF
LOUIS XIII (1601–1643)**
FRENCH (Paris), 1635–1643
Bronze, hollow-cast by 'cire perdue', with
translucent reddish-gold lacquer.
Height, 25″ (63.5cm), Length 25″ (63.5cm).
Attributed to SIMON GUILLAIN (1581–1658).
Literature: Dr. Charles Avery, The Burlington
Magazine, September 1984, pages 553–554:
'An equestrian statuette of Louis XIII attributed
to Simon Guillain (1581–1658).'

105

DESERT ISLAND OBJECTS

Stephen Bayley

It is said that one of the painters of The School of Paris had a friend whose interest in art jostled for possession of his soul with his indomitable kleptomania.

'I'm just going to The Louvre' he would say. 'Is there anything you want?'

There can be few people associated with museums who have not fantasised about what they would like to take home were they let into a museum with a *nihil obstat* on the one hand and an empty furniture van on the other.

For this year's V&A Yearbook Sir Terence Conran, one of the Museum's Trustees, was given this opportunity to indulge himself . . . although it was only make-believe. Sir Terence had to do without the furniture van and actually nothing left the premises, but for two hours one spring morning the Museum's Departments collaborated on this fantastic voyage of would-be acquisition. It was a session of sophisticated voyeurism for one particularly discriminating eye as the Departments made available some of their familiar and unfamiliar treasures to a man whose own tastes – both his admirers and critics agree – have changed the face of Britain since his first Habitat shop opened twenty years ago.

There was a sort of inevitability about Sir Terence becoming a Trustee of the V&A. Not only does he belong to that generation of art students who once actually used the Museum's collections for inspiration, but the whole design ethic which makes Habitat stores different from the other High Street shops can actually trace its origins back to lessons once taught by Henry Cole and his colleagues when they established the V&A's precursor on this same site in then rural Brompton. Cole had a High Victorian

FIG.10 Chinese Chippendale bedstead. Perhaps designed by Thomas Chippendale. English, *c.* 1755.

want of squeamishness in using his Museum as a starting point for commercial design; Conran is the same. His subtle and refined eclecticism has created a synthesis that is entirely novel.

Only those with curiously blunt perceptions – usually art and design critics – see Habitat as suburban Bauhaus or stripped pine. It is, in fact, neither, but it was amusing to see the Departments, forewarned of Sir Terence's discriminating progress through the Museum, assemble for inspection items almost exclusively from the twentieth century that anticipated the journalists' prejudice that Conran's point-of-view was a wholly contemporary one. For my part, I went along as a sort of poor man's Boswell. The experience must have reminded Sir Terence of one of his regular Habitat merchandise meetings when eager buyers present findings from their international trawls for the judgement of his eye and his thumb . . . only this time it was Museum Keepers.

We began with the Twentieth Century Study Collection. Our hostess, Anna Somers Cocks of the Metalwork Department, presented some modern silver with an air of cautious optimism.

'Nothing there that I'd buy' was said in passing and a famous silversmith's work was dismissed as 'excruciatingly vulgar'; a rumpled look of dismay went like a passing cloud as we put some of Gordon Russell's 'Utility' furniture behind us. Gio Ponti's celebrated 'Superleggera' chair (the one Enzo Apicella made famous in Mario and Franco's Italian restaurants) was admired with reserve, Sir Terence remarking that he in fact preferred the original, vernacular rush seated chairs from Chiavari which Ponti had copied. New-found proprietorial concern was shown when we came to a Heal's cabinet of the late 'twenties:

'That was not one of Heal's best

periods and anyway, I hate macassar ebony.'

The furniture of the Wiener Werkstätte was looked on with affection, but Sir Terence's choice from the Twentieth Century Study Collection was unequivocal. It was two chairs, Hans Coray's aluminium 'Landi' of 1938 (FIG.1), a timeless classic of the Machine Age, and Yrjo Kukkapuro's 'Karuselli 412' fibreglass armchair of 1965 (FIG.2). The elegant minimalism of Coray's chair and the austere, thoughtful luxury of Kukkapuro's commended themselves as the first objects to be selected for this desert island Habitat . . . (although in the second instance personal association made Sir Terence's recollections particularly warm: he first saw the chair, and its designer, when the latter was lying dead drunk in a bank of snow in Finland, glass of vodka in hand. Sir Terence was too reserved to enlarge on this incident or to remark that his own company had long ago manufactured this very chair . . .).

We moved on to Metalwork. Simple church plate was enjoyed hugely, the general rule here being the less busy the better.

'Jewellery I find very difficult indeed. It's hard to judge as an object-in-itself . . . **particularly when displayed on slubbed rayon.**'

Our hostess was only briefly nonplussed before Sir Terence, widely understood as being Britain's most influential *modern* designer, declared a marked preference for the metalwares of the Middle Ages, in particular a highly functional fifteenth century visored sallet (FIG.3) on display in a case of armour. Any direct Christian reference, he said, disturbed him with miserable reminiscences of a Catholic childhood, but this affiliation having now lapsed, a Pre-Columbian nasal decoration could cause innocent delight. Overall, in the Metalwork

107

FIG.2 'Karuselli 412' armchair. Designed by
Yrjo Kukkapuro. Finnish, 1965. Circ.375-
1970.

FIG.1 'Landi' stacking chair. Designed by
Hans Coray. Swiss, 1938. Circ.16-1970.

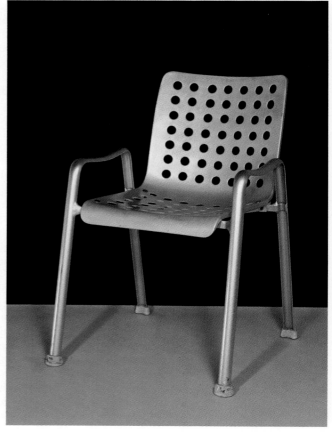

FIG.5 Cotton kimono with design of pines, cranes and chrysanthemums. Japanese, eighteenth century. T.18-1963.

FIG.6 Dish, Ash-glazed stoneware. Japanese, by Takeuchi Kimiaki (b.1948). FE.14-1984.

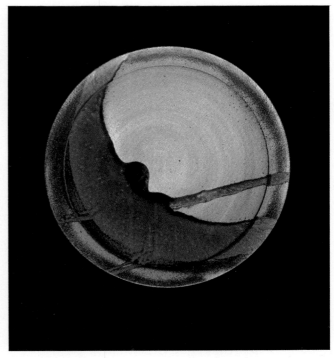

FIG.3 Sallet with visor. English, late fifteenth
century. M.580-1927.

FIG.4 Tea service. Designed by Jean
Puiforcat, but made in England, 1936.
Circ.521 to 524-1974.

FIG.7 Clear glass goblet. English, early
eighteenth century. C.539-1936.

FIG.8 Staffordshire mug, salt-glazed
stoneware. Made by William Ball, 1747.
Schreiber 79.

Department famous-name designers did not do well, Sir Terence's somewhat puritanical and zealous taste for the understated moving him to prefer items of honest workmanship: 'I'd be very happy with that whole case of spoons', for instance, rather than self-conscious *tours-de-force*, except that is in the case of a metal tea service (FIG.4) designed by Jean Puiforcat in the mid-'thirties: 'I **love** that', adding miserably, the functionalist's conscience to the fore, 'But I don't suppose it pours very well . . .'

Our progress brought us to the Far Eastern Department where curatorial staff eagerly unveiled a superb lacquer water bucket by Suzuki. They met the Functionalist with a genial irreverence for the bogus who asked the properly professional young Deputy Keeper, handling the exquisite vessel with cotton gloves, why an apparently utilitarian item such as a bucket needed to be treated with reverential care. Further nonplussing occurred at this stage.

But there were two Oriental items which touched a very fundamental part of Sir Terence's taste. The first was a superb eighteenth century kimono (FIG.5), stencilled and resist-dyed, from the Japanese Ryuku Islands. He said, 'You can understand why contemporary Japanese fashion designers are so successful when you look at the tradition they come from . . .'

The tact, commitment, restraint of Japanese design is very deeply admired by Sir Terence, although when a learned member of the curatorial staff informed us that, before fabricating a samurai sword the Shinto priests charged with the task abstain from sex and meat for an entire month, Sir Terence said he was surprised they didn't rush the job. The same humorous unity of vision made him remark,

as we left the Keeper's office, 'I rather like things that are bashed up a bit . . . that come into the Museum after a testing period.' And a second item which was certainly bashed-up, if untested, came into his eye on the dusty top of the Keeper's cupboard. A vernacular, plastic sake barrel was enthusiastically admired in an irreverent moment for its fresh and vigorous calligraphy, but on more mature reflection an ash-glazed stoneware bowl (FIG.6) was, perhaps, decided to be more representative of traditional Japanese skills.

Remembering that he has gone on record with stong views about the more sensational manifestations of the Crafts Revival, calling the chairs of one celebrated exponent, 'tortured rubbish', it was with some concern that we passed onto the Ceramics Department. Sir Terence explained his views: 'It's things that *pretend* you can put peanuts into them that annoy me . . .', but this hard line view of the Crafts Revival only briefly disguises what is a very basic love of glass and pottery.

It was in the upper reaches of the Museum, where there is a magnificent cornucopia of glass and ceramics, that the most vivid expression of sensuous delight passed over the tycoon's face. Perhaps it brought to mind the happy news that Habitat has become the country's biggest retailer of glassware. At one moment in the Glass Gallery he shrugged, a look of amused and satisfied despair possessing a face that can glower ferociously, and said, 'I'd choose everything. Here is everything I like best in the whole world.'

Sir Terence finds glass aesthetically exciting because it has a special tactile quality and it is one type of consumer good represented very extensively in the Museum's collection which has genuine use in real life. A good glass

can help you enjoy a good wine by transmitting light in agreeable refractions and that is a sensation of unity of form and content often sought by contemporary designers, but rarely achieved.

In the end three items were selected: two were anonymous, one autograph. The first of the two anonymous desert island objects was an English goblet of the early eighteenth century (FIG.7), the second was a salt-glazed Staffordshire mug made in 1747 (FIG.8) which Sir Terence liked as, 'A practical, sculptural object'. The one autograph piece was a William De Morgan earthenware tile (FIG.9), originally made for a Norman Shaw house.

Leaving the Museum one last item recommended itself to our discriminating eye. We saw an extraordinary Chinese Chippendale bed (FIG.10), made about 1755. The strong grid pattern behind the Rococo excess was admired, so was the humour and the stylishness. The bed is coming to the desert island too.

What does this eclectic choice of ten apparently unrelated objects tell you about Sir Terence Conran's taste? Well, it betrays an admiration for things that meet a need rather than those which externalise an ego, things which cause delight through simple quality rather than through extravagant and indulgent excess, but it's the last choice of the bed which gives the lie to the whole operation. There was a crooked smile when the decision was made. There are many elements which comprise the complex edifice of this man's taste, but there's one uniting idea which the bed gave away: the **pleasure principle**.

Then Sir Terence left to get back to a meeting in The City.

FIG.9 Earthenware tile. Designed by William
de Morgan. English, late nineteenth century.
Circ.35 B-1970.

THE FRIENDS OF THE V&A

AIMS

To help in the work and activities of the Victoria and Albert Museum and in particular:

To purchase works of art

To maintain a lively exhibition programme

To expand the Museum's training schemes and research projects

To contribute towards the cost of refurbishing the galleries

PRIVILEGES

1. Free and immediate entry to all paying exhibitions at the Museum and to Ham House, Osterley Park, and Apsley House (Bethnal Green has no entry charges).
   The membership normally admits husband/wife or other guest and Friend's children under 16.

2. Special Evening Private Views

3. Advance information on Museum activities.

4. Discounts on selected catalogues and other publications, and purchases in the Craft Shop.

5. Visits abroad and in this country, accompanied by staff from departments of the Museum.

6. Social occasions at the Museum, Ham House, Apsley House and Osterley Park.

MEMBERSHIP

Membership Fee
£15 annually

Special Fee
£10 annually
(for pensioners and those working full time in UK museums)

Corporate Fee
£100 or more annually
(with transferable membership cards)

Benefactor
£1,000 annually
A Benefactor may specify which department or project of the Museum should receive his gift

For further details and application form, please apply to:
Friends' Office
Victoria and Albert Museum
South Kensington
London SW7 2RL
01-589 4040

FIG.1 Wood-engraving of a toyshop, an illustration in *Cobwebs to catch flies* [by Lady Fenn], London: J. Marshall, [1783]. Library: 1509-1895.

FIG.2 Four wood-engravings, illustrations in *The toy-shop*, Swaffham: F. Skill, 1830. Library: L.5583-1961.

ON TOY-SHOPS AND TOY-SELLERS

Anthony Burton

Fashions change in museum work, as in everything. Sometimes, even in an art museum, it seems right to be a scientist, pinning down specimens in logical order; sometimes, to be an aesthete, setting out nonpareil pieces with exquisite refinement. Just now, the fashion for jumble is regaining scholarly esteem, as museums everywhere recreate the 'cabinet of curiosities' – that Renaissance clutter (which caught the eye because strange or sparkling, but signified to the inner eye of the humanist that all knowledge hung together) from which true museums developed.

Glamorous as they may seem now, such cabinets in their time often appeared foolish. They were derided as mere toys. Sir Hans Sloane's cabinet became the British Museum in 1759; 'But what in oddness can be more sublime,' sneered Edward Young, 'Than Sloane, the foremost toyman of his time?'. And Young went on to ridicule 'Ashmole's baby-house' (i.e. doll's house): the Ashmolean Museum at Oxford, England's first public museum, opened in 1683. Earlier, in a poem describing the curious collections to be seen in London, Henry Peacham jeered at those who rushed 'To gaze on trifles, and toyes not worthy the viewing'. And in 1592 Thomas Nashe scoffed at antiquarians:

A thousand guegawes and toyes haue they in their chambers, which they heape vp together, with infinite expence, and are made beleeue of them that sell them, that they are rare and pretious thinges...[1]

So some of the most respectable museums may be said to have started life as toyshops; a comforting thought for the staff of the Bethnal Green Museum of Childhood if ever that outpost of the V&A is disparaged (which, to be sure, it rarely is) in relation to the great museum at South Kensington.

More to the point, perhaps, is the fact (which the reader will have detected from the quotations above) that the word 'toy' has been less certain in its meaning in the past than it is now. Today, as a noun, 'toy' means 'children's plaything', almost exclusively. As a verb, however – 'to trifle with' – it retains something of the sense that the noun also kept until the late eighteenth century, 'a thing of little or no value or importance, a trifle... an ornament or curiosity' (N.E.D.). It derives, probably, from the Dutch or German words for children's toys, and doubtless entered the English language (during the sixteenth century) as the things themselves began to be imported into England – for the toy industry started in Germany and exported along the Rhine through Holland. Among the various metaphorical senses of the word, male chauvinist overtones may sometimes be detected: in *Paradise Lost* (ix, 1034) Adam 'forebore not glance or toy, Of amorous intent, well understood Of Eve'. A pejorative application of the word to woman or her propensities comes out the more clearly, when the sense of the word as 'a thing of little value' lies near the surface. It is there in Pope's resonant lines in *The Rape of the Lock* (1714) on the fickleness of women:

With varying vanities, from ev'ry part,
They shift the moving toyshop of their heart. (i, 99)

This brings us to the problem which prompts this article. Pope was obviously not referring here to a shop which sold children's playthings. So when does a toyshop become a real toyshop as we understand the word? In 1714, a toyshop meant a fancy goods shop. Addison (quoted N.E.D.) wrote in 1712 of a toyshop as more or less synonymous with a mercer's, and referred to 'ribbons, brocades, embroidery' such as would have been sold at a mercer's or draper's. It would

have been the more trivial items in a mercer's shop that were called toys, so perhaps a closer synonym for toyshop would have been 'haberdasher of small wares' – the sort of shop that 'included every kind of small manufacture too unimportant to have a specialist shop of its own'.[2] Such small wares, as we shall see, would have been made not only of cloth, but of metal, wood, leather, or anything else.

Throughout the eighteenth century, it was usual to refer to a tradesman by his trade rather than his premises, so 'toyman' is actually the word we must look for, rather than 'toyshop'. Studying the history of manufacture and retailing is all in a day's work for curators in a decorative arts museum, but little enough has been written on the subjects, particularly the latter; and while big and restrictively organized trades have left behind plenty of records as sources for the historian, there is no such accessible information for small, fly-by-night trades like toy-selling. Still, some well-tried sources can be consulted, in pursuit of 'toymen'.

A pleasingly picturesque source, for the eighteenth century, is the 'trade-card', a kind of pictorial advertising handbill. Trade-cards survive randomly, but evidently existed for quite a variety of trades. No doubt, however, it was the richer tradesmen who were inclined to produce them; so most toymen, or fancy goods dealers, who appear on trade-cards turn out to be connected with the expensive jewellery or silversmithing trades.

Thomas Clark, for instance, at the Golden-Head, Arundel Street 'selleth all Sorts of Plate, Jewels, & Jewellers Work... and all Sorts of Toys in Gold, Silver, & other Metals', and in the border of his card many such knick-knacks are represented.

On Joseph Creswell's card such bibelots cascade from a cartouche. Many tradesmen are described by the triple designation 'jeweller, goldsmith & toyman': Thos. Harrache, at the Golden Ball & Pearl in Pall-Mall ('Sells all sorts of Rich Gold Toys'); Morris, in St. James's, Hay-Market, and Henry Morris, in Salisbury Court, Fleet Street; Pantin, in Fleet Street.[3] Trade-cards are especially useful because they often give copious lists, and sometimes illustrations, of a tradesman's stock. So it is clear that many toymen dealt chiefly in such things as curiosities of amber, tortoiseshell and mother-of-pearl, toothpick cases, pocket books, cutlery, coffee-mills, garters. But some did sell 'all sorts of Childrens Toys': we read this phrase among the twenty or so items on John Sotro's card.[4] And the aptly named Coles Child, on London Bridge, includes among over a hundred different kinds of goods listed on his card (from knitting needles to dog collars) 'all sorts of English and Dutch toys Pill Boxes Nest Boxes Babies Marbles Alleys Pitch Gold Childrens Trumpets Ball Counters Brass Pewter Lead & Wood Toys of all sorts'.[5]

Trade cards, then, offer some fleeting glimpses of toymen. It is possible to make a more sweeping survey by consulting trade directories, which aim to be comprehensive and try to categorize the listed tradesmen, though in the briefest possible way rather than by describing their wares at length. Perhaps the earliest usable London directory (and London is, of course, much better covered by such publications than any provincial town) is the *Intelligencer or Merchants Assistant* of 1738, which does, indeed, include as toymen William Deard (of whom more below) and Francis Deveer. But it is only from the 1750s that directories begin to be useful, Kent's being the most informative, but Mortimer's of 1763 being the first to have a list classified by trades. What is found in these

FIG.3 Hand-coloured wood-engraving, an illustration in *Wonders of a toy-shop*, London: Dean, [*c*.1852]. Library: L.5297-1968.

volumes confirms the impression derived from trade cards: 'toyman' is often combined with other trades such as jeweller or goldsmith; watchmaker; cutler; pewterer; dealer in hardware. In the early nineteenth century (when we can consult Pigot's directories, which have classified lists, and Robson's, which do not), 'toyman' drops out of use, but 'toy dealers' often prove to be the same as 'turners' or makers of 'Tonbridge ware', i.e. small woodworkers. Some still double as pocket book or dressing case makers, and several as perfumers. Doll makers and rocking horse makers are normally listed separately, so some specialisms were evidently established. But directories do not help us, any more than trade cards, to disinter from historical

oblivion a genuine children's toyshop.

As so often, visual evidence supplies the best clues: hence the illustrations to this article. One of the earliest depictions of a London toyshop is a satirical print of 1751, showing the premises in Cockspur Street of Mrs Chenevix, who was the daughter of William Deard, mentioned above. Horace Walpole bought the lease of Strawberry Hill, Twickenham, from her in 1747 and described the cottage on the site as 'a little play-thing that I got out of Mrs Chenevix's shop'. Unfortunately the items in Mrs Chenevix's window visible in the print do not look much like children's toys, more like adult knick-knacks.[6]

A more fruitful source for our purposes is children's books. Lady Fenn's

FIG.4 Detail of a toy theatre sheet, Scene 13
no. 14, for *Harlequin Red Riding Hood*,
published by W. Webb, 1858. Theatre
Museum: Hinkins Collection.

Cobwebs to Catch Flies: or, dialogues in short sentences, adapted to children from the age of three to eight years first appeared in 1783, with little wood-engravings accompanying dialogues on 'The Doll (In words of Four Letters)', 'The Baby-House (In words of Six Letters)', and 'The Toy-Shop (In words of Five Letters)'. The latter (FIG.1) begins in an engaging real-life way. 'BOY: I will have a gun. No, I will have this dog. May I not have both?' The illustrated toyshop is recognizably a shop specializing in children's playthings, though with a rather limited stock. It must have seemed credible, since not only was the illustration reprinted in many later editions, but new blocks were made without much alteration for later editions in 1825 and *c*. 1852.

What is depicted here is the classic English toyshop of the late eighteenth century and the first half of the nineteenth. FIG.2 (a-d) provides some more views. These are illustrations to *The Toy-Shop*, a children's book first published by John Newbery in 1787. The first edition was illustrated, but I have not seen it, and these illustrations are from an edition published in Swaffham in 1830, by F. Skill (an illustration shows his name over the shop doorway). This is a well-stocked toyshop. Although, oddly, it does not seem to have dolls, it has most of the other toys typical of the period: jumping-jack, rocking horse, horse and cart, stuffed or carved animals, boat, windmill, drum, trumpet, fiddle, gun, sword, bow and arrow, kite, hoop, skittles, top, cricket bat, mask.

The story-line is rather tiresome. It is based on a short play by Robert Dodsley, 'The Toy-Shop', of 1735. Dodsley's toy shop is a fancy goods shop and various fancy adults make purchases which give the moralizing shopkeeper an opportunity to take them down a peg. One customer says:

FIG.5 Toy theatre sheet, Scene 13 no. 15, for *Harlequin St George*, published by J. Green, 1847. Theatre Museum: Stone Collection.

'Why, Sir, methinks you are a new kind of satirical parson; your shop is your scripture, and every piece of goods a different text, from which you expose the vices and follies of mankind in a very fine allegorical sermon'. In Newbury's children's version, the toyman likewise 'reads lessons of morality and virtue' on the children's playthings he sells.

But his shop looks convincing. Its interior resembles another, illustrated in *Youth's Best Friend*, a reading primer published at Deal in 1828; while its exterior, with toys fitting neatly behind the small panes of a typical Georgian shop window, can be compared with the toyshop on a children's lottery ticket by George Cruikshank.[7] The same sort of shop appears in *Grandmamma Easy's Wonders of A Toy-Shop*, a Dean's Toy Book of *c*.

1852. The toyman here is an altogether more agreeable character than the earlier moralizer: he just makes bad jokes about his wares. The first illustration (FIG.3) shows his shopfront: the rest depict interiors in which his stock is displayed.

Another source of illustrations of toyshops is scenery for toy theatres. Among the many plays published in the form of small 'penny-plain-two-pence-coloured' sheets for cutting out and manipulating in miniature theatres, pantomines (usually called 'Harlequin' this or that) bulked large. Generally they included some scenes set in the streets of London, which gave the artists an opportunity to draw typical shopfronts. FIG.4 shows the shop of Mr Kite, the Toyman (obviously named on the 'Happy Families' principle), a detail from

FIG.6 Detail of a watercolour 'Crooked Lane 1830' by George Scharf. (By courtesy of the Guildhall Library).

Harlequin Red Riding Hood, scene 13 no. 14, published by W. Webb in 1858. A well-stocked interior is shown in scene 13, no. 15 of *Harlequin St. George*, published by J.K. Green in 1847 (FIG.5).

All these illustrations show imaginary shops, and while they must have been intended to be convincing, they cannot be regarded as absolutely true. But their accuracy seems to be borne out by a toyshop recorded in a watercolour by the topographical draughtsman George Scharf in 1830 (FIG.6). Wright's Toys is clearly a proper children's toyshop. Scharf depicted it in a drawing of Crooked Lane, London,[8] at the time when many buildings were being demolished to make way for King William Street, the approach to Rennie's new London Bridge. Some of the other shops shown in the drawing can be verified in Robson's 1830 directory, but, tantalizingly, Wright's toyshop is not listed. The shop was a poky little building, crammed in below the church at a street corner; probably it would attract only a short-stay small business.

Still, this documentary illustration, backed up by the imaginary illustrations in children's books, gives us a picture of the kind of children's toyshops that could have been seen in London between about 1780 and 1850; the sort of toyshop that might have been patronized by, say, the young Lamb, Grimaldi, Turner, Disraeli, Newman, Dickens, Rossetti. Behind its small window panes, they would have seen toys such as these (in an order of popularity based – shakily – on all the illustrations reproduced or alluded to in this article). Most often:

doll, pull-along horse, drum, kite, jumping-jack, gun, carved or stuffed animal, boat, doll's house, cart, hoop. Quite often: sword, fiddle, bow and arrow, rocking horse, cricket bat, battledore, mask, windmill. And sometimes: horse and cart, soldiers, Noah's Ark, peepshow or theatre, skittles, top, whip, skipping ropes, trumpet.

From the 1840s plate glass windows began to transform the appearance of London's shopping streets. Previously all shop windows had small panes which tended to impose limitations on the display behind them. Toys, however, suited such windows rather well, and the childish eye must have become used to the chequered pattern. Bigger windows symbolized the bigger scale of retailing in the second half of the century. Some of the big and famous Victorian toyshops were flourishing by the '60s: Cremer of New Bond Street, Morrell of the Burlington Arcade, Hamley of High Holborn. Later in the century the newly arising department stores installed bountiful toy bazaars. And henceforth there is plenty of evidence for the historian. So let us leave this main stream of development, and look aside, and back, at other toy sellers.

Toy-making was a small-scale activity, and, in early days, rather seasonal. So there were few toyshops even in places where the toy industry had its home. A Victorian Englishman might naturally salute Nuremberg as 'immortal Mother of Toys';[9] but he would, consequently be 'surprised... at the small number of toys visible in the town. A single London street would make a greater display than the whole city.'[10]

The traditional way of selling toys in Germany was at a market, particularly at a Christmas market like those in Nuremberg, Dresden, Frankfurt. One of the earliest representations of a mar-

FIG.7 Engraving of a toy stall, an illustration
for Jacob Cats, *Spiegel van den ouden en
nieuwen tyt*, 1632, here reproduced from J.
Cats, *Alle de werken*, Amsterdam: Ratelband,
1726. Library: unnumbered (press mark
67.D.133).

FIG.8 Engraving of a market, after a drawing
by Daniel Chodowiecki, detail of plate xxx in
*Kupfersammlung zu J.B. Basedows
Elementarwerk*, Berlin, 1774. Library: 269-
1879.

ket toy-stall (FIG.7) is of Dutch origin, but represents German practice well enough. It illustrates a moralizing poem by Jacob Cats (1577–1660) in his emblem book *Spiegel van den Ouden en nieuwen Tyt,* first published in 1632 and frequently reprinted. The point of it is to warn against the specious, superficial attractions of the world, but (as often with emblem books) we are entitled to assume that it gives a convincing picture of that world. Dolls, hobby-horses, drums, trumpets, bows, a horse-and-rider, and some kind of theatre or peepshow are on sale.

A similar, later, stall can be seen among those of a market in a modest German village, illustrated in an engraving after Daniel Chodowiecki (FIG.8) for a sort of children's encyclopaedia, *Das Elementarwerk,* published in 1770–4 by the pedagogue J.B. Basedow (1724–90). Here again are dolls, hobby-horse, horse-and-rider, and drum; and, in addition, fiddle, horse and cart, and child's cart. FIG.9 is from a set of mid-nineteenth century German genre scenes. Here is a more modern market stall, selling (besides dolls, drum, trumpet, fiddle and horse-and-rider, such as we have already seen) guns, swords, soldiers, jumping-jacks, windmill and boat.

Markets existed in Britain, and likewise fairs. And at most, toys were sold; witness the many references to toys sold at Bartholomew Fair. In the mid-nineteenth century, however, the equivalent in London to the German fairs were the indoor bazaars. FIG.10, an illustration by Hablot K. Browne to *The Doll and her Friends* (1854), shows a scene in the Pantheon Bazaar (which was on the site on the easternmost Marks and Spencer's in Oxford Street, operating from 1834 to '67). George Augustus Sala also illustrates it, in his *Twice Round the Clock* (1858), his sketch showing more clearly the lines

of the building. He shows much the same range of toys as Browne, but dilates interestingly in the text on 'ugly toys', the kind that gave a child the creeps. Other permanent bazaars where toys and dolls were sold were the Soho Bazaar (1816–85) in Soho Square, the Crystal Palace Bazaar in Oxford Street (1858–89), and, especially, from the late 1850s, the German Fair, or German Bazaar, or Portland Bazaar, in Langham Place, on the site later (from 1867) occupied by St George's Hall.[11] George Godwin, in *Town Swamps and Social Bridges* (1859), praises the imported toys at the German Fair, but notes at the Soho Bazaar a home-grown philanthropic experiment, a toy-stall organized 'by an earnest woman to employ and improve a few girls' (p. 45) working in a garret in Percy Street.

It is clear that toy stalls appeared not only at these commercial bazaars, but regularly at the charitable bazaars organized by aristocratic ladies. F. Nash's watercolour of a bazaar for the British Orphan Asylum at the Mansion House in 1832 (in the Guildhall Library) shows a toy stall; and the atmosphere of these occasions is well enough conveyed by the board game 'The Fancy Bazaar or Aristocratic Traders' with Baroness Goodchild's toy stall (FIG.11).

The supreme London toy bazaar was the Lowther Arcade, though it was not really a bazaar. The Arcade, on the site of what is now Coutts's bank opposite Charing Cross station, was built in 1831. Two rows of small lock-up shops faced each other across a covered way. By the 1860s almost all were taken by toy dealers, and their wares overflowed the shops into stalls along the covered street, making a wonderland for children, fondly recalled in many memoirs of Victorian childhood, but closed in 1902.

Selling toys was, as we have seen, a

small-scale, fairly precarious business. Although recognizable toyshops existed by the end of eighteenth century, a small tradesman, then as now, might retail toys as only one line in a variety of fancy goods. Or he might take a stall in a market or bazaar. Or he might simply put his wares on his back and take to the road.

'Among so many obscurities and uncertainties in the history of retail trade,' writes its principal historian, 'nothing is so obscure and uncertain as the role of the pedlar.'[12] Most pedlars worked in an utterly casual and improvisatory way. But there were some specialists, especially in the toy-making regions of Germany. In bringing toys from remote villages in the Alps or the Erzgebirge to wider markets, the pedlar played an important part in the seventeenth, eighteenth and nineteenth centuries. He might sometimes be himself a toymaker who (if he had time) took his own wares to sell. Or he might be an agent for a wholesaler. The German pedlars devised a cantilevered wooden frame to carry on their backs. It would be stacked with the characteristic oval wooden cartons that contained small toys, and hung about with larger stump dolls and jumping-jacks.[13] At the fairs, especially Christmas fairs like the Dresden Striezelmarkt, children could be seen hawking toys from trays hung around their necks. They themselves were reproduced as seasonal toys, which can still be bought today (FIG.12).

Although rural pedlars tend to have been undiscoverably insignificant, urban pedlars have left a fleeting trace in records of street cries.[14] Few English street cries, to be sure, relate to toys. But in this country, as elsewhere, hobby-horses and windmills were hawked in the streets. Laroon (1711) depicts a seller of the former, with his shout of 'Troope every one', but by 1885 Andrew Tuer noted that he had

FIG.9 Hand-coloured lithograph of a German
market, *c.* 1850. Department of Prints and
Drawings: E.2652-1953.

FIG. 10 Hand-coloured wood-engraving of the
Pantheon Bazaar, after a drawing by H.K.
Browne, an illustration in *The Doll and her
friends*, London: Grant and Griffith, 1854.
Library: L.6284-1961.

THE BAZAAR.—*Page* 16.

FIG.11 *The Fancy Bazaar or Aristocratic Traders*, board game published by E. & M.A. Ogilvy, *c*. 1855. Bethnal Green Museum of Childhood: E.1792-1954.

FIG.12 Wooden dolls representing child toy-sellers at a Christmas market. German, 1983. Bethnal Green Museum of Childhood: Misc. 277-1984.

'long since disappeared'.[15] J.T. Smith etched a jaunty windmill seller in 1815 (while a woman windmill seller was a stock figure in French cries).[16]

Particular to Britain were the sellers of toy lambs, still around up to the turn of this century. Their cry became a nursery rhyme,[17] and so they have often been the subject of imaginary illustration; and one, William Liston, was written up and illustrated by William Hone in *The Table Book* (1827). Liston and his family themselves made their lambs (out of cotton wool, tin and paste); and it would seem that the sellers of dolls' bedsteads, who (oddly enough) crop up repeatedly in English street cry collections, were also offering their own products. For W.H. Cremer, an early and expert toy historian (because he was a toy seller), comments in 1873 on 'the penny Jacks-in-the-box, mangles, bedsteads, stoves and windmills which are hawked about the streets by their makers, or their makers' wives and children'.[18]

Traders who sold any wares they could get hold of included, as Henry Mayhew observed in 1851, the 'swag-barrowmen', whose tight-packed miscellanies of small goods might find room for 'children's wooden swords, whips, climbing monkeys, and tumblers, jointed snakes twisting to the wind from the top of a stick...'. And at an even lower level the 'lot-sellers', who sold penny batches of tiny articles, would include a few toys among their wares. At the lowest level were the child street-sellers. But they, Mayhew tells us, did not sell toys.

Dolls were sold in the streets; not by their makers, however, but by freelance women traders. Mayhew interviewed some, and one revealingly remarked: 'If the vendor can only attract the notice of children – and more especially in a private suburban residence, where children are not used to the sight of dolls on stalls or barrows, or in shops – and can shower a few blessing and compliments... a sale is almost certain.'[19]

The more one looks into the past, the more elusive seems the real toyshop. Although a visit to a toyshop is regarded as an archetypal experience for a child, few children before 1750 could have seen a toyshop, and for another century only the child of the big town would have been able to visit one, as the doll seller's remark just quoted suggests.

After 1850, however, the scene begins to change. A writer on toys in the *Englishwoman's Domestic Magazine* of 1 September 1870 (p. 157), after surveying some of the terrain we have just investigated, from street sellers to toy shops, from Germany to England, commented:

> The manufacture of children's toys has become one of the useful arts of life, if not, indeed, one of the fine arts.... A modern toy-shop has become as much an exhibition of taste, talent, skill, and curious industry, as any mere trading depot can be so designated.

By now, we observe, toys were beginning to arouse the kind of informed interest that the decorative arts attracted by virtue of the advocacy of, among other bodies, the South Kensington Museum. In due course toys would earn their own museum. And the word 'toyshop' would gain overtones of delight and fascination that would raise it far above its early use as a slur to discredit the foibles of antiquarians. Indeed, the toyshop would itself evoke the antiquarian enthusiasm which produces essays such as this.

1 All quoted in Richard D. Altick, *The Shows of London*, Harvard , 1978, pp. 16, 7, 9.

2 Dorothy Davis, *A history of shopping*, London, 1966, p. 111.

3 Creswell's card was shown in the English Rococo exhibition at the V&A, 1984, catalogue I6. For the others see Ambrose Heal, *The London goldsmiths 1200–1800*, Cambridge, 1935, plates xv, xxxvi, xlix, li, lv.

4 *Ibid.*, plate lxvi.

5 Ambrose Heal, 'Old London Bridge tradesmen's cards' in Gordon Home, *Old London Bridge*, London, 1931, pp. 323–4.

6 See Hugh Phillips, *Mid-Georgian London*, London 1964, pp. 94–95 and fig. 116.

7 Redrawn in 1873 after the original of 1804; reproduced in *Connoisseur*, v (1903), 193.

8 The complete drawing is reproduced in *The London Encyclopaedia*, ed. Ben Weinreb and Christopher Hibbert, London, 1983, p. 749.

9 *Art Journal*, 1851, p. 231.

10 *Once a Week*, 22 Dec. 1860, p. 719.

11 See *Once a Week*, 24 Dec. 1859, pp. 532–5.

12 Davis, *op. cit.*, p. 236.

13 See Torkild Hinrichsen, *Battenberg Antiquitäten-Kataloge: Spielzeug*, Munich, 1980, p. 29; K.E. Fritsch and M. Bachmann, *An illustrated history of toys*, London, 1966, plate 1.

14 See Karen F. Beall, *Kaufrufe und Strassenhändler/ Cries and itinerant trades: Eine Bibliographie/A bibliography*, Hamburg, 1975.

15 Beall, E.10. Andrew Tuer, *Old London street cries*, London, 1885, p. 12.

16 Beall, E.35; cf. F.15, F.20, F.49, F.54.

17 Iona and Peter Opie, *The Oxford dictionary of nursery rhymes*, Oxford, 1951, p. 264.

18 W.H. Cremer, *The toys of the little folks of all ages and countries*, London [1873], p. 45.

19 Henry Mayhew, *London labour and the London poor*, vol. I, 1851, pp. 447, 472, 445.

and then, after luncheon, I took my basket down to the Rose Garden. They really are simply heavenly, and their scent was everywhere, suffusing even the drawing-room with their delicious pot-pourri.

Until Tuesday,

Your own and ever loving,

Rose

the Perfect match-

Our Two International Legends –
Dewees Cochran and Su'ben Laning.

A commitment to quality, handcrafted
perfect elegance, and unique art that
will remain classic for years to come.
Select a Dewees Cochran doll . . . when
only the best will do.

Unmistakable – Su'ben Laning's
Edition of Dewees Cochran's Grow-ups:
Susan Stormalong . . . "Stormie,,
radiates the brillance of a thousand
lights. Her blue-green eyes are
as changeable as the sea, her
complexion like the inside of a
seashell, her human hair a
devastating auburn and she
has real eye lashes. Hickory
Jewelers, Tenn. has
customed designed her 14K
gold jewellery. Her
engagement ring is a three
point full diamond and her
14K gold earrings are set
with one point full
diamonds.

Helen Barrett Hansen – a designer who
captures a magnificent elegance – a
perfection if you will – and spins it into
fashion of singular grace, of inestimable
value . . . of timeless beauty. Helen has
spun another favourite theme for this
season's bridal gown. Stormie's bridal
gown – the delicacy of a baby's
christening dress, with French
re-embroidered Alencon lace, seed
pearls and tiny aurora-borealis
rhinestones. Her fully lined cream-
coloured gown is trimmed with white
mink, with a magical lace applique,
trimmed with pearls and gems, fitted
down the front. Turn any of Stormie's
garments and see Helen's handcrafted
tender visions of enchantment.
Limited edition – 100 worldwide.

Margaret R PHOTOGRAPHY

Ultimate Quality . . . since 1934
Among the world's most talked about dolls and accessories – in one singular collection – OURS

Dewees Cochran Dolls, Inc.

RFD, 1 Royce Hill Road, Orwell, Vermont, USA

Write for details

Dealer inquiries invited

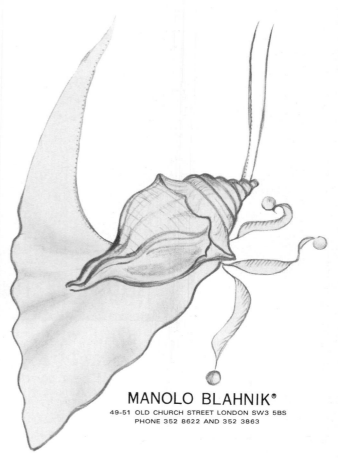

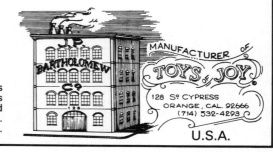

The Waterloo Gallery
Joseph Nash, 1852

'Visitors next enter the wing added by the Duke – passing from his series of not spacious old drawing-rooms into the great Waterloo Gallery, which, however open to architectural criticism, has a palatial character. The saloon extends about ninety feet – the entire western side of the house – but, though crammed with pictures, is better fitted for state-receptions than art-exhibition. The stinted rays of a London sun struggle through an over-pannelled so-called sky-light; and, it is to be regretted that the Duke, who had so much powder at his command, did not, on some darkish day, direct it to be blown off – "hoist by his own petard". The lower and proper windows are plated with iron shutters outside, and inside with mirrors. The general style is that of Louis XIV gone crazy: gilding and yellow damask have done their best for pomp and their worst for art. The paintings either blush unseen, or look like black spots huddled on the gaudy background. It is impossible not to regret this – but the truth is that objects which in every other gallery are the principals must submit to be ranked as secondary ones *here*: – at all events most certainly the absorbing interest strikingly marked on the countenances of the stream of spectators that poured in, was the scene of the *banquet*, and the idea of the *man*, the hero of the day, the first and foremost in the fight, yet spared to preside *here* over so many anniversaries of its glory.'

Richard Ford,
Quarterly Review, 1853

The Waterloo Gallery is now in 1984 shown as a picture gallery. The second Duke of Wellington replaced his father's yellow damask with red but there are plans to revert to the yellow. The windows are now open, the mirrored shutters being slid aside. The hanging of the paintings reflects the Duke's arrangement, and although there are fewer present than in his day, many are in their original positions.

APSLEY HOUSE IN 1853

Simon Jervis

On 14 September 1852 the Great Duke of Wellington died at Walmer Castle. His magnificent state funeral took place on 18 November 1852, the coffin being drawn from Horse Guards to St Paul's on a great triumphal car designed at the Government School of Design under the supervision of Henry Cole, the first director of this museum. In January 1853 the Duke's son, the second Duke of Wellington, consented to open Apsley House to the public on three days a week, tickets to be applied for in writing from John Mitchell of Bond Street. This proved a popular privilege and a short guide book to the house was issued by Mitchell: a later edition included as a preface a report from *The Times* of 7 January 1853 on the house. In 1982 the V&A was given a letter from the second duke to Mitchell concerning this guide book; it is dated from Stratfield Saye, 30 January 1853:

'Dear Sir,

I think your principle is now understood that the house has been opened exclusively in consequence of the interest felt in it on account of the late occupant, and that there is not the same objection to the sale of catalogues now as a month ago.

Catalogues are a decided inconvenience, and are inconsistent with the view of showing the interesting house to the greatest number, but, as Catalogues are introduced in spite of us you may sell yours at the umbrella stand, but not, even when there is rain, within the house; it would cause indecorous pushing which ought to be avoided.

I forsee that Mr Clarke will attack me for it, but I have my answer ready.

I send you a list; will you have the kindness to send them tickets.'

A poetical guide by Charles Augustus Cole also appeared, but such ephemera were eclipsed by *Apsley House and Walmer Castle*, published in early 1853 by Mitchell and Paul and Dominic Colnaghi, with ten coloured lithographs, and a text by Richard Ford (1796–1858). The new full colour guide-book published in 1984, thanks to sponsorship by Mobil, is its latest successor. The watercolours from which the lithographs in *Apsley House and Walmer Castle* were executed were by Frank Dillon (1823–1909), a pupil of James Holland, who later specialised in views of Egypt, Thomas Colman Dibdin (1810–1893), a landscapist who claimed to have invented chromolithography, Thomas Shotter Boys (1803–1874) and Joseph Nash (1808–1874).

In 1982 the preparatory watercolour for *Apsley House and Walmer Castle* were sold at Sotheby's and the V&A was able to secure the five which represented the interiors in its care. These are now, two years later, on view in the appropriate rooms. Four of them, only two of which were finally lithographed, are by Boys, and the fifth is by Nash. Shotter Boys was born in London, the son of a salesman. In 1823 after being apprenticed to the celebrated engraver George Cooke he moved to Paris where he became closely associated with Richard Bonington. He returned to England in 1837 and established his own claim to be the founder of chromo-lithography with *Picturesque Architecture* (1839): a volume of hand-coloured lithographs, *London as it is*, followed in 1842. After that date Shotter Boys experienced a sad financial decline which led to a death in poverty. He is now recognised as one of the greatest watercolourists of his age. Joseph Nash was altogether a contrast. The son of a clergyman and schoolmaster in Great Marlow, Buckinghamshire, he trained as a topographic artist under A.C. Pugin, and later enjoyed sustained success with *Mansions of England of the Olden Time* (1839–1849) and similar works. His more modern *Views of Windsor Castle* (1848) must have been the direct prototype for *Apsley House and Walmer Castle*.

The author of the introduction, Richard Ford, was one of the most engaging figures of his age. A gentleman, he spent the years from 1830 to 1833 in Spain, and subsequently established himself as the unrivalled authority on Spanish art and architecture, especially Velasquez: his *Hand-Book for Spain* (1845) is one of the few immortal guide-books. Ford was a Tory, and knew and admired the Great Duke, whose house in Spain, Casa Real, Soto de Roma, near Granada, he sketched in 1831. In 1852 he had published a *Guide to the Diorama of the Campaigns of the Duke of Wellington*. Ford collected paintings, drawings, prints and majolica and had a wide artistic acquaintance including David Roberts and, no doubt, Shotter Boys and Nash. He was also a practised and prolific journalist, and on all counts the ideal choice for this assignment.

In March 1853 the *Quarterly Review* contained a review by Ford of *Apsley House and Walmer Castle* which incorporated a much longer version of his own introduction. Whether the extra elements had been cut from the book or were added for the review is difficult to judge: one suspects the former, as the *Quarterly Review* article contains critical and humorous ingredients perhaps inappropriate in a commemorative album. But, either way, the fuller Ford text, with its echoes of Thackeray and Dickens, provides an admirable commentary to the illustrations of the watercolours which are the real purpose of this article.

Also in 1853, the *Art Journal* concluded a visit to Apsley House in these words: 'Well it is something to have visited Apsley House, and to have seen these things; and it will be something for our children and theirs too to have the same privilege, as we trust they may have: there are memories that should ever be kept green, and the dwelling place of WELLINGTON ought to be one of the first among them: it will be more fondly cherished than the proudest monument Art can erect to his honour.' When the seventh Duke of Wellington gave Apsley House to the nation in 1947 such hopes were secured and, although much remains to be done, the recent programme of restoration has brought Apsley House yet closer to its appearance under the Great Duke, who was himself one of the great sights of London, 'the observed of all observers', commemorated in Lord Ellesmere's charming verses on the day of his funeral, quoted by Richard Ford:

. . .'And child or man who cross'd
   his pass was proud at eve to tell,
'We met him on his homeward ride.
   The Duke was looking well.
We pass'd him close, we saw him
   near, and we were seen by him –
Our hats were off – he touch'd his
   own, one finger to the brim'.
That sight the loiterer's pace could
   mend, from careworn brows erased
The lines of thought, and busy men
   grew idlers while they gazed.'

The Waterseller of Seville
Diego Velasquez, about 1620
'The *Aguador* or Water-carrier of Seville, one of his earliest known works, was probably painted in the studio of his bold but coarse master, Herrera – the first to adopt in Spain the *naturalistic* style, which Caravaggio was making so fashionable in cognate Naples. This was the reaction of Rafaelle – when an over-banqueting on the ideal and elevated led to a craving for the contrary, as lust when sated in a celestial bed will prey on garbage: *le dégoût du beau amène le goût du singulier*. This specimen of the democracy of art – of humanity in rags – is a true transcript of the low life at Seville, and is treated with the broadest touch and admirable imitation of texture and material.'
Richard Ford
Quarterly Review, 1853

The Waterseller now hangs in the very position in the Waterloo Gallery where the Duke had it, and must then, as now, have suffered from the glare from the windows. With the possible exception of Correggio's Agony in the Garden, the Duke's favourite, the Waterseller is the most famous of the paintings from the Spanish Royal Collection captured in Joseph Bonaparte's coach after his defeat at the battle of Vitoria on 21 June 1813, and subsequently given to the Duke by a grateful King of Spain. In 1701 it was hanging in the Buen Retiro palace outside Madrid and in 1772 in the magnificent new Palacio Real in Madrid.

The Striped Drawing-Room, Apsley House
Thomas Shotter Boys, 1852
'The selection of pictures for the next, the *Striped Drawing-Room*, is vividly characteristic of the Duke. Here he has delighted to group together the members of his family and the comrades of his arms – his adopted brothers and children. The prize of beauty is justly assigned to Lady Douro, whose "high Dama brow" has inspired Swinton to one of his happiest efforts. Around the fair are arranged the brave, who best deserve them. These walls are decorated with not a few countenances that failed never at the anniversaries of the 18th of June, and which, as it were, illustrate the Waterloo Gazette: the Duke himself forms the exception. Often as he sat for others, no likeness of him graces a place and company where it would so naturally be expected – the central luminary about which satellites so bright and many clustered, alone is wanting. Possibly he may have thought that there was little need in-doors of an image which he could not stir out-of-doors without seeing stare at him from every shop-window: at all events no Gerard painted him in ducal robes, stars and garters; no Horace Vernet blazoned his battles on acres of canvass.'
Richard Ford
Quarterly Review, 1853
    The Striped Drawing-Room in 1984 no longer contains a portrait of Lady Douro, while a magnificent Lawrence of the Duke hangs over the mantlepiece. The carpet has gone as have the skirts to the ottomans, but both will be restored. However the rest of the paintings are very much as the Duke had them – mainly portraits of his comrades-in-arms.

The Dining Room, Apsley House
Thomas Shotter Boys, 1852
'The usual dining-room of Apsley House was built by the Duke, and communicates with this room (the Striped Drawing Room) in which his comrades are quartered. It has a royal look from the full-length portraits of the Allied Sovereigns, given by themselves. In company with the originals, it must be allowed that our Prince Regent always looked like the highest of the high: and no less among these pictured figures stands forth that of George IV, in the "garb of old Gaul" worn by him at Holyrood – that picturesque costume of wild mountaineers, the adoption of which in that place by his Majesty – his only precedent, it was said, being Prince Charles in 1745 – gave no less offence to the refined Lowlanders of modern Athens, than the caricature copy by the unwieldly Alderman Curtis did to the portly Monarch himself. It is a vigorous and effective work of Wilkie's – perhaps the best portrait he ever did: the head admirable, and the costume excellently cast and coloured. Opposite hangs the wizen and worn Francis I, of Austria, huddling his spare form in a military great coat, and so much to the life itself that the Duke, who superintended the unpacking, kept exclaiming: "Poor man, very good – poor man, very like".'
Richard Ford
Quarterly Review 1853
    The Dining Room is in 1984 almost exactly as it was in 1853. The paintings are the same, and in their original positions. The only major new ingredient is the Portuguese centre-piece, which is shown in the Plate and China Room in Shotter Boys's watercolour of 1852, and in the Waterloo Gallery in Nash's watercolour of the same year, but which must have often been used in the Dining Room before the Waterloo Banquet moved to the Waterloo Gallery in 1830.

The Plate & China Room
Thomas Shotter Boys, 1852
'Most people, Whig or Tory, will rejoice to pass to the more lively contents of the *Great China Room*. This Eldorado glitters with porcelain, silver, and gold, the offerings of grateful kings and nations. In examining these infinite services of China – French, Austrian, Prussian, and Saxon – it strikes one as strange that a substance so fragile should have been so much selected as an enduring memorial to the Iron Duke. But Diamonds, Orders, and Batons had been exhausted; and these specimens of the ceramic art, the best in form, material, and taste of the period, did good service at the great anniversary banquets. The silver plateau was presented by the Regent of Portugal, as a long inscription records.'
Richard Ford
Quarterly Review 1853

The Plate & China Room was moved to its present position by the second Duke of Wellington. However, as the watercolours by Shotter Boys demonstrate, the original room was similar in scale, character and decoration. Now, in 1984, the Portuguese centre-piece is shown upstairs in the Dining Room, but the Plate & China Room still 'glitters with porcelain, silver and gold'.

The Waterloo Shield
Benjamin Smith, 1822
'The delicate silver tones of this Portuguese gift contrast with the golden splendour of those from the august Corporation of London in 1823 – a fit peace atonement to one, of whom, in the very Talavera tug of war, they recorded discontent and clamoured for dismissal. Where then, but for him, ye sapient cits, would your ducats have been "collected", and by whom your fat turtles consumed? The shield was designed by Mr. Stothard – and, although it cannot rank with that of Achilles in the Iliad, the military conception does honour to the Cellinis east of Temple Bar. Fitter for Guildhall or the Mess-room than the Museum, a fricassee of figures, horse and foot, project in high relief, and gather around the central Duke. The cost was 10,000*l.*; and, whatever the differences about mould and make, the many are satisfied with the material. The candelabras spring from columnar bases, where sentinels, arms, and implements of glorious war are grouped – so excellently modelled and executed, and so pleasing to a soldier's eye, that an honourable acquittal was certain when tried by the courts-martial summoned on the 18th of June.'
Richard Ford
Quarterly Review, 1853

The Waterloo Shield, together with the two candelabra described by Ford, is still shown in the Plate & China Room in the handsome rosewood showcase made for the Duke. This is fitted with a mechanism which allows shield and candelabra to be rotated by turning a handle, so that the spectator can inspect every detail with ease. A number of the original designs for the Waterloo Shield by Thomas Stothard are in the V&A's Department of Prints & Drawings.

The Battle of Waterloo
Sir William Allan, 1842

'Of his dozens of victories one only – the last, the "crowning mercy" – is to be found here (in the Striped Drawing Room) – and in that the point of view and honour is given to his antagonist. The field is depicted as seen from the position occupied by Napoleon: the two captains, pitted against each other for the first and last time, are within range of shot and sight of each other. It must have been under such circumstances that an artillery officer, desiring to direct some round shot at the Imperial group, was checked by the Duke's reply: "Commanders of armies have other things to think of than firing on each other". How differently the Emperor felt and acted at Dresden, when Moreau was slain, we all know well. The Duke, who never missed the Royal Academy dinner, was, during a preliminary lounge, struck with this picture – the work of one who had, among other incidents of an adventurous youth, seen what battles are – the late Sir William Allan – pronounced it "Good, not too much smoke" – inquired for the artist, and secured it on the spot – which, we dare say, did not diminish Allan's enjoyment of that day's turtle and champagne.'
Richard Ford
Quarterly Review 1853

Allan's Battle of Waterloo still in 1984 hangs in the Striped Drawing Room exactly where the Duke had it. The picture represents the position at half-past seven in the evening of 18 June 1815, when Napoleon made a last desperate attempt to force the left centre of the allied army and turn their position. Allan later painted a companion painting now in the Royal Military Academy, Sandhurst.

Trompe L'oeil mural decoration by Richard Shirley Smith

LANDSEER PROPERTY CORPORATION

Distinctive Property Development & Design

24 Bruton Street Mayfair London W1X 7DA
Telephone 01 629 2805   Telex LANDS 25188

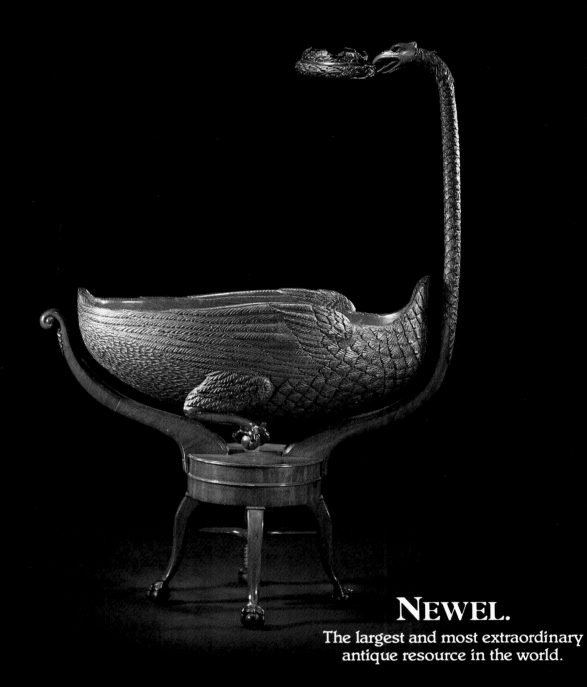

Let our bird cradle your baby.

NEWEL.

The largest and most extraordinary antique resource in the world.

143

TREASURE CARE

Treasure Care is a unique restoration, conservation and interior design service formed by Clement Newman, a member of the Guild of Master Craftsmen.

In forming Treasure Care, Clement Newman has bought together not only his wide experience in the techniques of restoration and conservation but also a great knowledge of the people within that world.

Treasure Care provides individually tailored teams of experts, selected from an amalgam of some of the country's finest design craftsmen and restorers known by Clement Newman, to undertake all aspects and sizes of work ranging from repairing a single decorative saucer to the complete internal conservation and re-styling of stately homes.

All commissions are personally supervised by Clement Newman under his philosophy of "co-operation and co-ordination of expertise" making Treasure Care a totally integrated professional interior design and restoration organisation.

Clement Newman's knowledge of conservation and restoration is complemented with the interior design skills of his colleague Clive Hunt, who directs "interior design services".

Clive Hunt FSIAD, FBID, is a leading commercial, industrial domestic interior and furniture designer with significant worldwide commissions to his name.

Treasure Care's specialist services comprise the following main areas:

Ceramics — European and Oriental
Advanced, continually updated techniques and materials are employed in all areas and methods of restoration. Specialised skills are available for armorial, maiolica pieces and porcelain figures.

Antique Furniture
Treasure Care is able to undertake all forms of furniture restoration including caning and upholstery. The services of a sculptor in wood can be commissioned to design and make specific pieces of sculpture, furniture or carved panels.

Textiles
The creation of large textile wall hangings can be undertaken by a highly talented artist with an appreciation of colour and the facility to utilise it to full effect. A range of textiles, including carpeting, curtains and furnishing fabrics are also supplied.

Precious Metals
A team of goldsmiths and silversmiths can undertake repairs to articles made of precious metals. Gold, silver and copper plating, and the treatment of verdigris on brass, including polishing and lacquering, is carried out by expert craftsmen. Antique and modern gold and silver articles can also be supplied. Repairs to, and the design of art metal objects d'art, including brass fenders with leather upholstered seats, are available from this department.

Fine Art
Fine Art consultants and artists can be commissioned to create original works of art, to evaluate or restore oils, watercolours and prints. Antique and modern picture frames can be supplied.

Marble
Marble fireplaces and statues can be created by commission, and existing marble surfaces can be cleaned and restored.

Glass
Although it is often impossible to conceal glass repairs, Treasure Care's experienced craftsmen perform intricate tasks which achieve an effective end result. For example, replicas can be produced from damaged crystal bowls. Simple repairs to rims of glasses, decanters, liners for silver containers and the restoration of chandeliers are all within the range of skills of this department. Curved glass and antique glass for mirrors can be made to Specification, and stained glass windows designed or restored.

Clocks and Musical Boxes
The skills and expert craftsmanship available to Treasure Care in this area are the result of many years of research into clock and musical box technology.

Renaissance Style Interior Decorating
A highly skilled artist who can create tonal washes on walls and ceilings, and paint botanical freizes and stylised armorial designs.

Further information is available from Clement Newman, Treasure Care, 10 Upper Berkeley Street, Portman Square, London, W1H 7PE. Tel: 01-723 1680. Telex: LONFAC-G 27578.

Stuart
interiors & furniture makers

The specialist designers and makers recreating the rich splendours of 16th & 17th century England. Commissioned furniture from the period as well as oak panelled rooms, staircases, doors and mantels. Antique buying service available.
Consultant: Victor Chinnery.

Send for our colour brochure:
Stuart Interiors, *South Petherton, Somerset. Tel: (0460) 40349.*

LE LOUVRE
DES ANTIQUAIRES

250 Art Dealers

open

from Tuesday to Sunday

11 a.m. to 7 p.m.

2, Place du Palais-Royal, 75001 Paris. Tel. : (331) 297.27.00

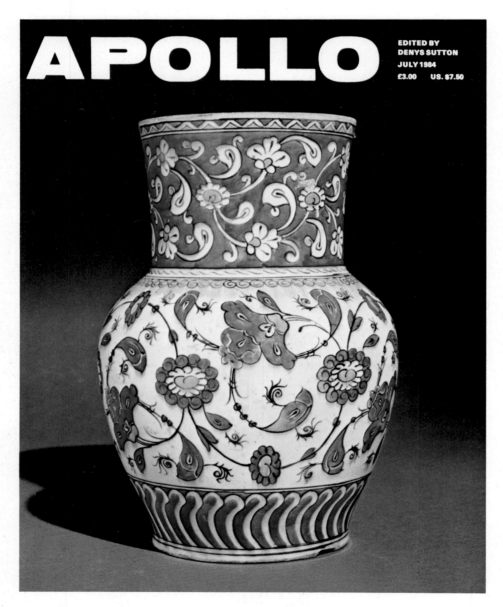

HUMPHRIES WEAVING COMPANY
at PALLU & LAKE

Early 19th Century Jacquard Handloom

HUMPHRIES WEAVING COMPANY
HAND WEAVERS OF FIGURED SILK FABRICS, PLAINS
AND HAND-CUT VELVETS.
SPECIALISTS IN REPRODUCTION OF HISTORIC TEXTILES
MARKETING & TRADE SALES THROUGH PALLU & LAKE

18 Newman Street, London W1P 4AR 01-636 3743

OSTERLY PARK HOUSE: A TEMPLE OF FLORA

J. Hardy

Osterley Park House is a magnificent example of the neo-classical style: its interior architecture is intact, and all its furniture, designed simultaneously with the building, survives to this day. It has been arranged with great care according to eighteenth century practice, but the house still fails to find favour with the average visitor: its measured perfection and formality strike a chill in him and he hurries through and out into the park again.

This is sad, because when Francis Child (1735–68) began his transformation of the old mansion and its estate in the 1750s, he was building for himself a villa dedicated to pleasure and the enjoyment of the countryside. His brother, Robert Child (1739–82) continued in the same vein from 1763 onwards; so why is it that the delight of the place escapes us today?

There are two reasons, the first being that, however perfectly preserved in its essentials, the place does lack the extraordinary abundance of plants and flowers which once furnished it; the second reason is that we do not have an eighteenth century education and viewpoint, which would at once have understood the pattern of allusions in the ornament of the house, summoning up echoes of classical Arcadia and the bucolic poets. This article is an attempt to view the house through eighteenth century eyes and explain what they would have seen.

To begin with the exterior and the park: the first architect and landscape designer was William Chambers (1723–96), who simultaneously was engaged in creating the pleasure garden and ornamental buildings for Princess Augusta at Kew. When he was appointed architect to George III in 1761, his work at Osterley was con-

FIG.1 'A Triumph of Ceres', painted in grisaille above the hall mantelpiece. (Photograph: Ken Jackson).

tinued over the next twenty years by Robert Adam (1728–92). The great square house with its corner towers was given a 'temple' character by the addition of a giant pediment set above an entrance colonnade of Grecian columns which Horace Walpole (1717–97) considered 'as noble as the Propyleum of Athens'.[1] This became the principal feature of the park with its ancient oaks, woods and 'islands' of trees, through which a series of lakes flowed in a great sweep like a tributary of the Thames. There is a walled garden to the north-west of the house and, further away, another huge walled area, the kitchen garden, whose upkeep alone was reputed to cost £1,400 a year in the eighteenth century. In this corner of the park the Childs created a pleasure garden of evergreen trees and serpentine gravel walks with herbaceous borders filled with flowers, fruit trees and evergreen shrubs, such as the newly imported and much prized American rhododendron. Here Chambers built a Doric garden temple, which was dedicated to Pan, the God of flocks and herds, who rule over Arcadia, the pastoral paradise of poets. This is where elegantly informal meals were eaten. Nearby, Adam built a huge greenhouse with a giant pediment supported by Grecian Doric columns, and an elegant semi-circular hot-house, which, according to the 1782 inventory, contained forty-five orange and lemon trees, four flower boxes and six green garden seats. The family's passionate interest in horticulture and exotic plants is reflected in the catalogue of the collection of 'Scarce and valuable Stove, Green House and Hardy plants', made in 1794.

GREEN-HOUSE PLANTS IN POTS

1 Camilla *japonica*, and 12 others, different sorts.
1 Fuchsia, and 12 others, different sorts.
2 Daphne *indica* and 26 others, different sorts.
4 Catalonian Jasmines and 42 others, different sorts.
1 Aristolochia *sempervirens*, and 13 others, different sorts.
2 Oleander, and 25 others, different sorts.
2 Camilla *japonica*, and 31 others, different sorts.
1 Quesa, and 11 others, different sorts.
1 Erica *arborea* and 17 others, different sorts.
2 Olive Trees and 28 others, different sorts.
1 Malabar Nut Tree and 11 others, different sorts.
1 Azorian Jasmine, and 14 others, different sorts.

STOVE PLANTS IN POTS

3 Coal Trees of different species.
1 Herbaceous Coral and 6 others, different sorts.
1 Cotton Tree.
1 large Tamarind Tree.
1 Solandra.
1 Nerium *antidysentericum* and 5 others, different sorts.
1 Ixora *coccinea*.
1 Plumbago *salonica* and 5 others, different sorts.
1 Plumbago *rosea*.
1 Catesbea *spinosa* and 5 others, different sorts.
1 Schotica *speciosa*.
1 Lantana *involucratia*.
1 Hydrangea *hortensia* and 13 others, different sorts.
1 Begonia.
6 Double Nyctanthes and 10 others, different sorts.
1 Gardenia *spinosa*.
1 Cyrilla and 5 others, different sorts.
1 Hura *crepitans*.
1 Dracena *ferra* and 4 others, different sorts.
1 Saphora *hirta*.
1 Mimosa *latus-siliqua* and 5 others, different sorts.
1 large Crassula *perfoliata*.
3 large different Euphorbias.
2 Hibiscus *mutabilis*.
1 Gardenia *nova*.
1 Xylophylla.
1 Cactus *Grandiflora*.
1 Grassula *perfoliata*.
1 Capparis *spinosa*.
1 Mimosa and 5 others, different sorts.
1 Lantana *aculeata*.
1 Double China Rose and 5 others, different sorts.
1 large Sponge Tree and 5 others, different sorts.
1 Sapindus *edilis*.
1 Limodorum *tankervillea* and 6 others, different sorts.

FIG.2 The gallery fireplace decked out with a
Chinese vase and rhododendrons.
(Photograph: Ken Jackson).

FIG.3 'Vertumnus and Pomona', woven at the Gobelins in 1775 after a design by François Boucher. (Photograph: Ken Jackson).

FIG.4 'L'enfant jardinière'; Gobelins tapestry chair back, c. 1775. (Photograph: Ken Jackson).

FIG.5 The pier glass crest with its garlands of flowers, designed by Robert Adam, *c*. 1775. (Photograph: Ken Jackson).

1 Plumbago *rosea* and 7 others, different sorts.
1 large Crinum, and 11 others bulbous plants.
1 Broad Leaf Crinum and 11 others, different sorts.
1 large Pimento Tree.
1 Euphorbia *punica*.
9 Cape Jasmines.
1 large Palm Tree.
2 large Partridge Breast Aloes and 13 others, different sorts.
3 Stapelia *variegata*.
1 Creeping Cereus and 9 others, different sorts.
1 Crotula *punctata*.
2 Aloes retusa and 10 others, different sorts.
1 large Melocactus.
1 large Aspiring Cactus.

AMERICAN HARDY PLANTS IN POTS
87 Rhododendron *ponticum* and 86 other plants, various.
45 Rhododendron *maximum* and 3 other plants, various.
2 Rhododendron *feruginea*.
1 Rhododendron *hirtusa*.

BOTANY BAY PLANTS OF VARIOUS KINDS
137 Botany Bay Plants of different sorts.

ERICAS AND DIVERS OTHER SORTS OF PLANTS
1 Erica *tubiflora* and 59 others, different sorts.
1 Erica *Urceolatis*.
1 Erica *conspicua*.
1 Erica *margaritacia*.
1 Erica *pilulifera*.
1 Erica *simplicifolia*.
2 Erica *concinna*.
2 Erica *triflora*.
1 Erica *cerinthoides*.
1 Erica *parviflora*.
1 Erica *nudiflora*.
1 Erica *monsoniana*.
2 Protea *argentea* and 6 others, different sorts.
1 large Lentiscus.
1 Asparagus Tree.
2 Myrtle.
1 large Carob Tree and 2 others, different sorts.
1 large Camphire Tree.
1 variegated Orange Tree.
1 large willow leav'd bloach'd Orange Tree.
23 Orange Trees.
1 large bloach'd Orange Tree.
2 Shaddocks.
A quantity of Rose Trees in Pots.
Several Pots of Carnations.
Various sorts of Pinks in Pots.

On entering the hall the visitor is greeted by Ceres, goddess of agricul-ture, who extends a welcome to the family hearth with an offering of food: a marble statue of her stands at one end next to an overmantel grisaille painting of some peasants bearing food and corn to this goddess, who, according to classical poets, assisted man after his fall from the Golden Age by teaching him to make a plough so that he could till the earth (FIG.1). The wine god Bacchus, who taught man to cultivate the vine, is portrayed in another triumphal procession at the opposite end of the hall. Both these gods, the symbols of genial abundance, recur in the dining room where his thyrsus rod and scrolling vines ornament the ceil-ing, and the overmantel painting de-picts festive figures sacrificing beneath a statue of Ceres, who this time is shown as the goddess of plenty with an overflowing cornucopia.

The pleasing paradox is that, whereas picturesque buildings adorn the gardens, garden ornament pro-vides the decorative theme for the in-terior, where the classical decoration is

FIG.6 A floral basket woven on the tapestry room carpet, designed by Robert Adam, and woven by Thomas Moore, Spitalfields. (Photograph: Ken Jackson).

theme is 'The Garden of Love'. The drawing room is hung with crimson Gobelins tapestries with, *en trompe l'oeil,* François Boucher's paintings of the Loves of the Gods. Vertumnus, god of Spring, can be found beside a garden fountain wooing Pomona, Goddess of fruit, trees and orchards. He is disguised as an old lady so that he can sing his own praises to the goddess (FIG.3). Together they represent the element Earth. All the wall hangings with their pink foliage background are decked out for a festival, with garlands and great vases of flowers. Two vases are perched on platforms above the doors, while another, in the centre of the principal wall, is accompanied by putti bearing a bacchic thyrsus and a rose-entwined stick. Below them a young shepherd woos a shepherdess on the back of the sofa, while her companion is occupied with making a floral wreath. Amongst 'Les Amours Pastorales' on the chair backs a gardener doffs his cap at the adjoining chair where a garden maid leans coyly on her rake (FIG.4). Flowers are strewn on the chair seats, and the pier glass crest, designed to correspond with the tapestries, is carved with garlands held by putti and nymphs who stand beside a tazza of flowers placed on a pedestal (FIG.5). In addition, four large baskets of flowers, linked by entwined vines, are woven on the carpet (FIG.6).

In the next room, the 'garden', the walls were once lined with green velvet hangings. The state bed still has green hangings bordered with flowers embroidered in coloured silks; the valances are ornamented with gilt poppies, emblems of sleep, and the headboard is painted with more vases of flowers. The domed canopy, supported on eight columns, is garlanded with silk swags of flowers, and, perched at the corners are sphinxes, which according to the classical writers were the guardians of Arcadia. The ar-

partly engulfed by the 'natural' ornament of foliage and flowers. In the long gallery, or saloon, which looks out over the park on the west front, and which used to contain landscape paintings by Salvator Rosa and Claude Lorrain, the 'Roman' acanthus leaf is rampant. Its foliage scrolls around the plaster frieze of the room, where it supports baskets of flowers; it appears on the damask upholstery, on the frames of the mirrors and girandoles, and on the friezes of the marble mantelpieces, where it supports wreaths of oak leaves. The female herms of the mantelpieces would doubtless have been crowned by

baskets of real flowers placed on the shelf above their heads, and in the summer months large bough pots or oriental bowls were also placed in front of the hearth and filled with plants or flowers (FIG.2). In the window bays there stood plain mahogany tables with raised rims whose function was to display a mass of pot plants.

Flowers are also the principal ornament of the state apartment, which Adam created for Robert Child in the 1770s. It consists of a drawing room, bedroom, and dressing room, which are designed respectively as a bower, a garden and a loggia, and its unifying

FIG.7 Interior of the state bed designed by
Robert Adam in 1776.

FIG.8 Medallion painted with nymphs garlanding a herm in the Etruscan dressing room, c. 1776. (Photograph: Ken Jackson).

FIG.9 Pembroke table, painted in the 'Etruscan' style. (Photograph: Fritz von der Schulenberg).

FIG.10 Plant stand painted with terracotta ornament. (Photograph: Ken Jackson).

FIG.11 An 18th century Chinese bowl with a rose bush. (Photograph: Ken Jackson).

FIG.12 A flower container painted by Mrs Sarah Child, *c.* 1775, and filled with silk flowers. (Photograph: Ken Jackson).

chitecture of the bed was inspired by the Temple of the Sun at Baalbek, and part of its ornament was taken from the Grecian temples of Lysicrates and Thrysallus,[3] but it was conceived of as a Temple of Venus, with nymphs garlanding a medallion of the goddess of love and fertility carved on the headboard, together with her attributes of cupids astride dolphins (FIG.7). One of Venus's attendants, the Grace Aglaia, who presides over the budding of plant life and the ripening of fruits, is painted asleep beneath a laurel tree on the ceiling above the bed. In one of the corner medallions of the ceiling there is a scene from the sixteenth century epic, Tasso's *Gerusalemme Liberata:* a shepherd is telling the Princess Erminia about the joys of the pastoral life.

The adjoining dressing room is painted like an open loggia of terracotta-coloured 'Etruscan' grotesque arcading against sky blue walls. Above, there are baskets of fruit suspended from ribbons along the plaster frieze. Festive scenes appear in the painted medallions and bas reliefs, which hang from the arcading, and

below them, nymphs hold floral festoons beside urns set on tripod stands. More nymphs garland a garden herm in the medallion over the mantelpiece, and in the bas relief above, there are playing putti, celebrating the rites of love during the feast of Venus. The painted mantelpiece garniture consists of 'Etruscan' vases and nymphs seated beside a tripod on which there is a bowl of roses, the flower of Venus and an emblem of love (see Front cover). Amongst the furniture, which is painted to correspond with the wall decoration, there is a breakfast table (FIG.9) decorated with a scene in the garden of the Hesperides and inspired by one of William Hamilton's 'Etruscan' vases.[4]

Flowers were probably placed on the painted plant stands set in the window bays, (FIG.10) and more flowers and plants in pots stood on the floor between the chairs, which were set against the walls (FIG.11). Oriental bowls were used as *câche-pots*, or else the plants were left in terracotta pots, which were sometimes ornamented with paper or chalk. We know that Mrs Child herself painted some of the de-

corative flower containers and *câchepots*, and these were made of paper pasted on to the wooden frame which concealed a metal liner (FIG.12). In winter the vases would be filled with dried flowers or artificial flowers made of silk etc.

On special occasions the house might have been even more of a bower, with vast quantities of trees, plants and flowers brought inside from the gardens and hot houses. For instance, Mrs Delany describes a 'rustic' event in February 1752, when a ball-room was decorated to represent a wood with real trees with artificial leaves; there was a 'Jessamine' bower and a grotto set off with ivy, moss and icicles. It was lit by green candles set in baskets of flowers and the musicians were dressed as Arcadian shepherds and shepherdesses.[5] It is hardly surprising therefore, that after all this elevated dallying with the pastoral, when Robert Child's daughter, Sarah Ann, was painted by Daniel Gardner (d. 1805), she chose to be portrayed as a shepherdess.

Today the National Trust and Royal Parks are making great efforts to restore the outlines of the Chambers and Adam landscape, chopping down some trees, planting others and dredging the lakes. This is important and exciting work – after architectural restoration, landscape restoration. But how desirable it would also be to fill the house with the flowers which once stood on every table, mantelpiece and commode and helped to soften the austerity of neo-classicism.

1 Letter to Lady Ossory, 21 June 1773; quoted in M. Tomlin, *Osterley Park*, 1972, p. 53.

2 Robert Wood, *Ruins of Baalbec*, 1757, pl. 4a.

3 Illustrated in James Stuart *The Antiquities of Athens*, 1762, vol I.

4 Pierre François D'Hancarville, *Collection of Etruscan . . . Antiquities . . . of the Honourable William Hamilton*, 1766–67, vol. II, pl. 127.

5 Ruth Hayden, *Mrs Delany, Her Life and her Flowers*, 1980, p. 79.

ART APPLIED TO THE HOME: THE HOUSEHOLD TASTE OF HENRY COLE AND HIS CIRCLE

Elizabeth Bonython

The first two illustrations to this article are paintings executed within a year of each other and they demonstrate two very different styles of English middle-class interior decoration in the middle of the last century. The first (FIG.1) is of a room in a villa in St John's Wood, furnished for letting to a young man for his mistress. Though the muddle of patterns and gilt frames is typical of the new rich middle classes in the 1850s, Holman Hunt intended the viewer to recognise the raffishness of a less-than-regular household in the debased rococo style of the room. (It was over twenty years earlier that the rococo had been in full swing, when such rooms as the Grand Reception Room at Windsor Castle were installed.) The other painting (FIG.2) is of Henry Cole's drawing room in Kensington High Street (FIG.3), and is decorated with a coolness that seems modern. Indeed, it has a simplicity that was only seen, at that time, in the houses of people with artistic leanings and pretensions. Cole's circle of friends included several artists Richard Redgrave, Daniel Maclise, William Mulready, Charles Cope and the engraver John Thompson and his family. Some of them taught at the Government Schools of Design and were dissatisfied with the way they were run. Cole, who already had experience of running a publicity campaign, had joined them in their attempts to get reforms. We have no idea of what the insides of the friends' houses looked like except that of the surgeon and etcher, Francis Seymour Haden.[2] The music room of his house in Sloane Street was painted by his brother-in-law James McNeill Whistler[3] (FIG.4). In this painting, a scheme very like Cole's can be seen: the same

pale stone-coloured walls and similar chintz curtains sweeping the floor and held back by ties. As in Cole's room, there are no lace or net curtains. Haden has a plain shelf under the looking glass to the left, instead of a more usual gilt table. Cole, in his own room, has placed white parian-ware figures resting on brackets between the windows. These are objects from his 'Felix Summerly's Art-Manufactures', a small business that he had been running for about six years which sold ornaments and small pieces of furniture designed by the well-known painters who were his friends.[4] It never made any money, but examples were exhibited at the Society of Arts and were bought by the Royal Family, which helped to make Cole well-known as a man interested in design. On the floor, Cole has a Brussels (looped-pile) carpet, with a dark green ground and a discrete red spot, which went well with the curtains.

It is interesting that Cole avoids the Victorian *cliché* of placing a large plate-glass mirror over the fireplace. In the first sketch that George Smith made for the picture, in April 1852, there is a large landscape in a gilt frame in this position, but a year later, when the picture was finally carried out, Cole had changed the arrangement to a grouping of two small paintings one above the other, surrounded by family miniatures, watercolours and prints, which he set in simple frames with wide mounts. The use of wide mounts was new at this date, though prints were sometimes framed complete with their own wide margins, but more often they were cut round close to the image. It was a recognition that delicate water colours needed to be separated from the busy wallpapers then so much in vogue that brought about the change. The chimney piece is a white marble one of a standard pattern that was put into many houses all over the country from about 1810 to 1840; it was prob-

ably in the house when the Cole family moved in in March 1848.

At the top left-hand side of the picture there is a cornice with a band of plaster decoration flat on the ceiling and square rosettes at the corners. It is a Regency design, and could have been put in at the same time as the chimney piece. Below it is a large print of the interior of the Crystal Palace – the Great Exhibition of 1851 was the peak of Cole's career to date. He had been one of the men who campaigned during the 1840s to hold a big exhibition of British goods, and after it was decided to open it to foreign exhibitors, he was put in charge of the arrangements inside the Crystal Palace in Hyde Park. At the close of the exhibition he was invited to re-organise and expand the Government Schools of Design. He set about enlarging the little museum that belonged to the head school in London. In 1857 it moved and became the South Kensington Museum, and was renamed the Victoria and Albert Museum, in 1901. Until he retired in 1873, Cole dominated all the design decisions that were taken not only for the new buildings for the Museum and schools, but also for other buildings going up at South Kensington, notably the Royal Albert Hall. It was due to him that the South Kensington style evolved, which was based on Italian architecture of the 15th century, using red brick, with terra cotta embellishments. Where plaster was used, Cole added sgraffitto decoration, and used mosaics both inside and outside the buildings.[5]

Towards the end of 1860, perhaps encouraged because he knew that he was to be given an official house inside the Museum, he decided to build a country house in pine woods on a ridge near the railway station at Witley, five miles south of Guildford. Some years before, he had rented a plain little cottage at Shere, between Guildford and

FIG.1 The Awakening Conscience. William Holman Hunt, 1853–4
The room is decorated in an out-of-date rococo revival style.
Tate Gallery   Photograph Tate Gallery

FIG.2 Evenings at Home. George Smith,
1852–3
Henry Cole and his family in the drawing
room of his house in Kensington. The
decoration is unusually simple for the date.
Cole family   Photograph Curtis Lane

FIG.3 No 1 The Terrace, Kensington High Street, London
Henry Cole's home 1848–1954. The house dates from *c.* 1740, with the front door and room over it added about fifty years later. The photograph was taken shortly before it was demolished in the 1890s
Royal Borough of Kensington and Chelsea Libraries and Arts Service

Dorking, to which he had added a Gothic porch and gables.[6] The new house was to be altogether grander with seven bedrooms, large reception rooms, a coach house, stables and a gardener's cottage. The neighbourhood was popular with painters, and Seymour Haden often visited a house nearby. Together they bought a large site, which they divided. The two houses were designed in the office of John Kelk, one of the largest builders in the country, who was employed at the museum and elsewhere at South Kensington. He had trained with Thomas Cubitt, and had been used by the Government in the negotiations to buy the land at Brompton that became South Kensington. Cole first mentioned him in his diary in 1856, and they were soon on friendly terms. The two houses (FIGS.5 & 6) are partly tile-hung in deference to the local vernacular style of architecture, but otherwise they are typical raw-boned Victorian houses of irregular outline, built of 'South Kensington' dark red bricks with black mortar in the joints and diaper patterns of blue headers. Linden Hall, as Seymour Haden's is now known, is hardly relieved by its barge boards, porches and bell-cote. Cole's house, which he named The Heights, is a little warmer; the massing is more compact, and Cole girdled it, at first floor level with a sequence of mottoes in Minton tiles, including his favourite text from Ecclesiastes,

164

'Whatever, thy hand findeth to do, do it with thy might'. He also set Minton roundels in the chimneys, as he had done in the picturesque new gables on the cottage at Shere.

As soon as the decision to buy had been taken, Cole began to be exasperated with Haden, which comes out from time to time in his diary. In March 1861 they were, 'On the grounds measuring and considering site of houses. Haden seemed to wish that the houses should not be seen from each others windows!'[7] Ten days later, 'Haden called & objected to ye charge for wood at Witley & wanted the land re-measured'. By the middle of June, Haden was ready to give up the project saying that the cost was 'rather beyond him'. However, he got Snell, a drawing clerk in the South Kensington Museum drawing office, to revise his plans. Cole's house was begun on 1 July, and on the same day he and Haden met on the site. Cole was firm: 'Told him that if he wished Kelk to build he must not meddle, but be content without superintending: or must go elsewhere.'

By the first week in August, Cole's house was built to first floor level, while Haden's was still at the discussion stage. The pine trees were cut down to make way for the new garden. It was designed by Cole with help from George Eyles, the garden superintendent of the Royal Horticultural Society, who had once worked in Kelk's office. The planting was done by Robertsons of Box Hill. Sadly the gardens of both houses have largely disappeared; no design can be seen, though

FIG.4 Harmony in Green and Rose: The Music Room. James McNeill Whistler, 1860–61
The scheme of decoration, though a little more elaborate than that in Figure 2, has much in common with it.
Freer Gallery, Washington.
Photograph Freer Gallery

some beeches and typically Victorian conifers survive.

In the middle of October, Cole gave a 'Feast' in Witley school-room to celebrate the topping out. About thirty-eight workmen were present. Cole was away in Italy on official business until the end of November. On Sunday 1 December, three days after his return to London, Cole wrote, 'Went to Witley. Plasterers & carpenters at inside work; planting for hedges nearly done: ... Haden had done nothing with his ground.' Nor ever did he. Though there is no documentary proof, it seems likely that Kelk took over the site and built the house as a speculation. Its style and materials are so very much 'South Kensington', that, given the previous history of the project, it is the most likely explanation. Kelk helped Cole to finance his house by building it for him and letting it to him at 4 per cent on the capital, but he declined to make the same arrangement with Haden. However, Cole was either too busy with the 1862 International Exhibition, which was held at South Kensington, or, with his children almost grown up, he was unable to afford a country house. Certainly, until midsummer he used the house only for odd nights, though he evidently enjoyed his visits, going for long walks, meeting his new neighbours and noting in his diary, 'Nightingales singing most lovely'. In July he bought a railway ticket from Witley to Waterloo for six months, which cost £19 1s 6d. At the end of the year he was discussing giving up the house with Kelk, and judging by the conversations they had about Cole paying the wages of the servants until the sale was completed, it is possible that he, too, sold his house to Kelk.

Little remains of the time of Cole's ownership of the house. There is an English fossil marble fire surround in the drawing room, though the chimney

piece has been altered. (A similar surround survives at Linden Hall.) The pretty plaster ceiling (FIG.7) is pure Italianate South Kensington, and must surely have been designed by Godfrey Sykes, the chief decorative designer at the Museum. The house was lived in by the novelist George Eliot for a few years towards the end of the 1870s, and shortly after that, someone added a large wing to the east. It is tile-hung and in a R. Norman Shaw style, with some Baroque revival plasterwork in the hall.

The house has been an old people's home for at least twenty years, and a few years ago, Linden Hall was put to the same purpose. The present owners are interested in the history of the houses and concerned to preserve them.

One of Cole's attempts to popularise good design came in 1869, when he had a piano decorated in an unusual way as an example of cheap decoration[8] (FIG.8). James Gamble designed and executed the painting in true 'South Kensington' style, and the work is very similar to the decoration of the Museum buildings and the Albert Hall. Gamble had succeeded Sykes a year or two earlier as the chief designer at the Museum. In spite of what Cole called 'his Yorkshire roughness', he carried out Cole's wishes for over fifteen years. The piano was exhibited at the 1871 International Exhibition,[9] which was held in galleries that stood south of the Albert Hall. Cole's son Alan, gave it to the Museum in 1913.[10]

It is, perhaps, worth noting here that in 1881 Cole must have been one of the first people to vandalise a four-poster bed by turning the carved posts into stands. The well-known firm of Barrett & Jordan did the work for him.

It can be seen that Cole was as original in the decoration of his houses, as he was in his career as museum director and public servant. As in his work, he

FIG.5 Linden Hall, Witley, Surrey. A 'South Kensington' house in the Surrey Hills, built in the mid-1860s.
Photograph Elizabeth Bonython

FIG.6 The Heights, Witley, Surrey. The house that Henry Cole built for himself in 1861. The verandah was altered and extended when the house was turned into an old people's home.
Photograph Elizabeth Bonython

FIG.7 The ceiling of the drawing room at The Heights. It can only have been designed by Godfrey Sykes of the South Kensington Museum.
Photograph John Bonython

FIG.8 Henry Cole's Piano. The pitch pine case is by R. Wornum & Sons, with black painted decoration by James Gamble, 1869.
V&A Museum.
Photograph V&A Museum

FIG.9 Sir Philip Cunliffe-Owen's drawing room in about 1892. A conventional interior of the period.
Lady Bragg

dominated what went on at home, and it was he who made the decisions and chose the furnishings of the houses that he and his family lived in. It even looks as though his wife was not consulted, for she often did not go with him when he visited shops or warehouses. His diary does not say whether there was any discussion, but knowing Cole and his autocratic ways, this writer suspects that there was none.

By contrast, the final illustration (FIG.9) is of the drawing room belonging to Sir Philip Cunliffe-Owen, who became Director of the Museum after Cole retired in 1873. It was photo-graphed in the 1890s, after his own retirement. There is nothing *avant garde* about this interior: it is typically late Victorian, though with some interesting features. The walls are papered, with one pattern below the picture rail and another used as a frieze above it. The carpet is an English (or Scottish) one woven in strips and sewn together. The pattern is taken from a 19th century Turkish Melas carpet. It is interesting to notice that on the left is a rug, made up of the same design, which is put down by the tea table, to protect the main carpet from wear. The chimney piece has a looking glass over it, and is heavily draped in curtains in a way that is seldom seen in illustrations. Other interesting details are the scarves knotted on the backs of chairs; the depressing vases of dead grasses (which are popular to this day); and the spindly copies of English late 18th century chairs. Lady Cunliffe-Owen was the daughter of Baron Fritz von Reitzenstare, an officer in the Royal Prussian Horse-guards, and this could account for the un-English feel of the room, and also suggests that the room was arranged by her rather than Sir Francis. Cole would never have allowed that.

1 A. Bowness, *The Pre-Raphaelites.* Exhibition Catalogue Tate Gallery. (Tate Gallery and Penguin Books, 1984.) pp 120-121.

2 For Cole's relationship with Haden see E. Bonython, *King Cole*, (Victoria and Albert Museum, 1982.)

3 A. McL. Young *et al, The Paintings of James McNeill Whistler.* (Paul Mellon Centre for Studies in British Art, 1980.) Hobbs, 'Whistler at the Freer Gallery of Art, Washington, D.C.' (*The Magazine Antiques*, November 1981, pp 1195-1202.)

4 S. Bury, 'Felix Summerly's Art-Manufactures', *Apollo*, 15 January 1967, p. 28.

5 J. Physick, *The Victoria and Albert Museum – The History of its Building* (Victoria and Albert Museum, 1982). *The Survey of London, Volume XXXVIII* (University of London, 1975).

6 E. Bonython, 'A Victorian Commuter: Sir Henry Cole's Life at Shere' (*Country Life*, 22 April 1982).

7 Henry Cole's manuscript diary forms part of the Cole Collection in the Library of the Victoria and Albert Museum.

8 M. Wilson, 'The Case of the Victorian Piano', (*Victoria and Albert Museum Yearbook*, 1972.) p. 133.

9 No. 3049 in the Official Catalogue, p 153.

10 Museum number W.11-1913.

PROVENCE ANTIQUES, INC.

Louis XVI mirror
circa 1785
carved and gilded wood
with original plate.
Height 84", width 42".

35 EAST 76th STREET
Carlyle Hotel
NEW YORK, N.Y. 10021
(212) 288-5179

A classic with intrinsic appeal.

Arzberg 1382 – Designed by Dr. Hermann Gretsch.

Feature: design quality and unpretentious form. The beauty is its simplicity.

The advantage: a classic that has outlived many design epochs, that has stayed young and intrinsically appealing. Designed back in 1931, still popular and sought after today. Quality that never fails to impress.

Benefit: timeless, functional. Designed to give pleasure daily.

Arzberg. Good design for every day.

GERMANY

Living with Art

'Art is an aspect of everyday life'
Eduardo Paolozzi, Great Britain.

The Artist
Eduardo Paolozzi, born in
Edinburgh in 1924, has succeeded
in defining the twentieth century in
relevant form and visual language.
He has constantly expressed our
modern environment in terms of art.

'Suomi' – Object no. 3
Paolozzi's design on the shape
'Suomi' by Timo Sarpaneva may
be regarded as an element in the
microcosm of technology –
coloured circuits brought to life like
currents in the stream of consciousness. This coffee pot is one of four
limited 'Suomi' objects by Eduardo
Paolozzi which can be combined

with the unlimited service pieces in
the 'Suomi' shape.

'Suomi' combines art and design.
The limited objects are at the same
time works of art and items for
practical use.

Rosenthal Studio-Linie
For almost 30 years Rosenthal has
worked with over 100 important
artists and designers in the
development of the Rosenthal
Studio-Linie. The aim is to produce
unique works which correspond to
the spirit of our time, and to make
these available to a wide public. The
result is a collection which reflects
the variety of expression in the art of
our time.

The Rosenthal Jury
Every design for the Rosenthal
Studio-Linie is judged by an
independent jury of recognised art
and design experts. Only a positive
majority decision ensures the
acceptance of a design into the
collection.

**The Rosenthal Studio
Department**
The Rosenthal Studio-Linie
collection is found exclusively in
Rosenthal Studio Departments and
in Rosenthal Studio Houses
throughout the world.

Rosenthal
studio-linie

'Suomi'-Object no. 3 Coffee pot.
Limited edition of 500 numbered and signed piece
Combined with Coffee Service 'Suomi White Go

McMillen Inc. 155 East 56th Street New York, N.Y. 10022 Plaza 3-5600

LORENZO RUBELLI
TESSUTI PER L'ARREDAMENTO

VENEZIA – Palazzo Corner Spinelli, S. Marco 3877

ROMA – Via Due Macelli 80/82

PARIS – 6, Av. de Breteuil, 7ᵉ – showroom: 6bis, Rue de l'Abbaye, 6ᵉ

LONDON – H. A. PERCHERON LTD – 97 Cleveland Street – tel. 580 5156

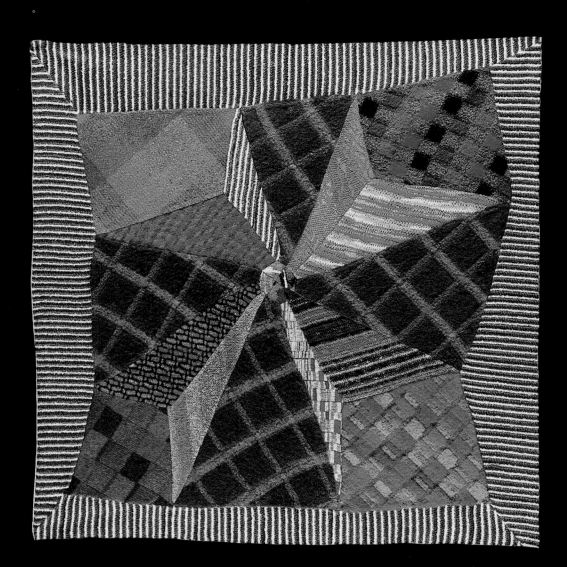

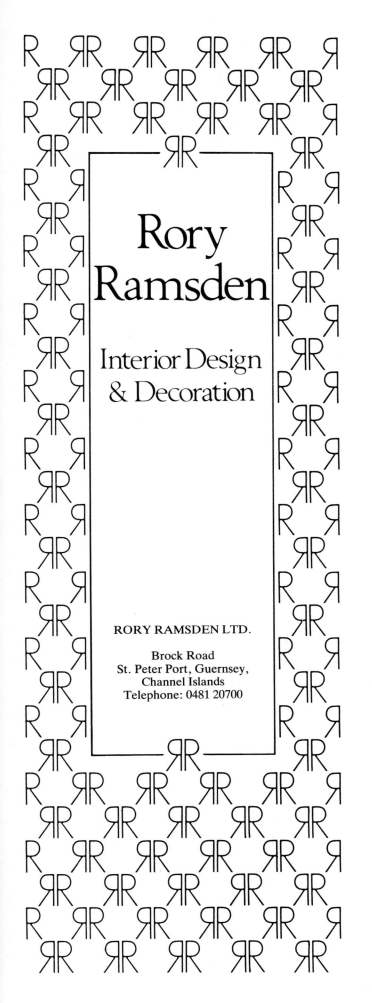

Rory Ramsden

Interior Design & Decoration

RORY RAMSDEN LTD.

Brock Road
St. Peter Port, Guernsey,
Channel Islands
Telephone: 0481 20700

GALPERIN & DAVIDSON LTD

PRINTERS & DESIGNERS
OF EXCLUSIVE
WALLCOVERINGS

**G P & J Baker
Colefax & Fowler
Interior Selection
Watts & Co.
Tissunique**

Are amongst our
most noted clients

No Commission is too small for
us.

5-11 Lavington St
London S.E.1.
Tel 01-633 0076.

★BACKGROUND DESIGN BY KIND PERMISSION OF WATTS & CO.

175

THE V&A AND ANOTHER COLE

Jean Hamilton

Over the last twenty years or so, an increasing interest in the historically accurate restoration of interiors has extended to an appreciation of the importance of wallpapers, which after all, have formed the background to the furnished room at least since the beginning of the sixteenth century.

Cole & Son (Wallpapers) Ltd is one of the oldest family-owned wallpaper firms in this country, who besides their modern range of designs, continue to print from wood blocks in their possession, some of which show patterns dating back to the eighteenth century.

Eight block-printed designs were chosen for reprinting from the Museum's large collection of historic wallpapers, and are advertised for sale in the Museum Book Shop.

The restoration of Clandon Park, Surrey, a National Trust property, formerly the home of the Earls of Onslow was carried out by the late John Fowler, and the wallpaper entitled 'Clandon' (FIG.1) was reproduced from late eighteenth century fragments (FIG.2) found in the State Bedroom. A replica was made in red flock, matching the fragments in the bedroom as closely as possible, but for general sales and considerations of cost, Coles have produced a simple block-printed version in different colourways. The red flock Greek key and flower border (also found in a green flock to match the paper in the State Dining room), has been reproduced by the screen printing process and can be obtained from Coles in different colourways.

The second paper, 'Shepherd and Sheep' (FIG.3) is based on a sample of one of the pictorial papers given to the Museum by Mr G.E. Jarvis of Doddington Hall, Lincolnshire in 1914. These wallpapers were hung in Dod-

dington Hall in the 1760s. The designs which incorporate medallions, landscapes and figures within moulded 'picture' frames, or rococo borders of leaves and flowers, seem to have been intended to imitate the fashionable Print Rooms of the period, affording, in modern jargon, an 'instant' Print Room.

The design entitled 'Temple Newsam' (FIG.4) is a block-printed version of a red flock, possibly dating to the mid-eighteenth century, but with later versions made in the nineteenth century. The flock is hung in the ballroom (as a straight match) and in the drawing room (as a half drop) at Lydiard Park, Lydiard Tregoz, Wiltshire, where it may have been the original wallhanging of c.1743. A slightly variant version of the pattern was found in a storeroom at Temple Newsam, Leeds.[1]

The paper entitled 'Regency Bamboo' (FIG.5) is a reprint of one of the many chinoiserie designs, perhaps by Robert Jones, which were produced by Crace & Sons in 1820 for the Royal Pavilion at Brighton. The pattern was among those which decorated the rooms on the upper floor of the Pavilion, which included the Duke of York's and the Duke of Clarence's bedrooms.

The blocks which belonged to the Crace firm are among the most important of the three thousand blocks stored in Cole & Son's cellars, for they include the patterns based on A.W.N. Pugin's designs, produced by John Gregory Crace in the 1840s for the decoration of the Houses of Parliament. One of these, used throughout the building, is the pattern, known as the 'Crace Diaper' (FIG.6), which was produced in both block and flock, and in several different colourways.

Another Pugin/Crace design, 'Lough Cutra' (FIG.7), was made for Lord Gough's castle of that name in

County Galway, Ireland. This paper, which incorporates the coat-of-arms, is enriched with flock.

One of the most attractive of the set is 'Nowton Court' (FIG.8). This sophisticated neo-Gothic design of window tracery, was reprinted for the owner in the 1970s from fragments found at Nowton Court, Bury St Edmunds, Suffolk. An order for the original paper in flock and block, was given to the firm of interior decorators, Cowtan & Sons on 1 December 1840. This firm, founded by J. Duppa in 1791, finally to become Cowtan & Sons in 1863, absorbed the Crace firm in 1899, and by 1930, Mr A.P. Cole of Berners Street, had acquired Cole & Son's present important and unique collection of eighteenth and nineteenth century wallpaper archives.

The last of the set, 'Large Trieste' (FIG.9), a pattern from the Cowtan collection is based on a design which is probably an early nineteenth century version of an eighteenth century flock. At any rate, variations of the pattern have re-occurred regularly; one variant appears in John Lines & Sons 'Studies in Harmony' series in the 1920s.

The hand-printing of wood blocks, virtually the only means by which wallpaper was produced in the past, is carried on at Cole's John Perry Factory in Islington. John Perry & Co, which has been owned by Cole's since 1942, was established in 1875 and originally produced simple designs of one or two colours for the use of architects, but in later years specialized in flocks of high quality, jaspe papers and 'satinettes'. Hand printing is a slow procedure compared with power-driven machinery production, which first became used commercially in the middle of the last century, but it is a method which reveals the quality which is inherent in all hand crafts. The block, usually of pearwood, is raised and lowered by a foot-controlled pulley, guided first by

FIG.1 'Clandon.' Colour print from wood block. E.594–1982.

FIG.2 Original fragments and border, mounted with reproduction paper. E.2234, 2247, 2247A–1974.

FIG.3 'Shepherd and Sheep.' Colour print from wood blocks. E.597–1982.

FIG.4 'Temple Newsam.' Colour print from
wood block. E.592–1982.

FIG.5 'Regency Bamboo.' Colour print from
wood blocks. E.596–1982.

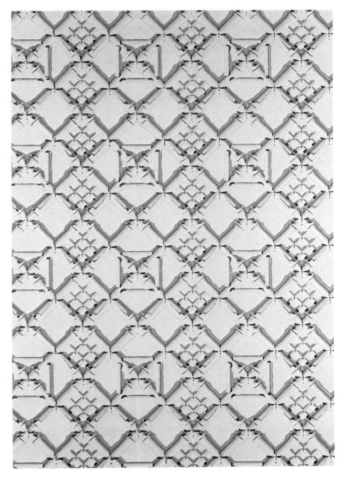

FIG.6 'Crace Diaper.' Colour print from wood block. E.593–1982.

FIG.7 'Lough Cutra.' Colour print from wood blocks and flock. E.599–1982.

FIG.8 'Nowton Court.' Colour print from
wood blocks. E.601–1982.

FIG.9 'Large Trieste.' Colour print from wood
block. E.602–1982.

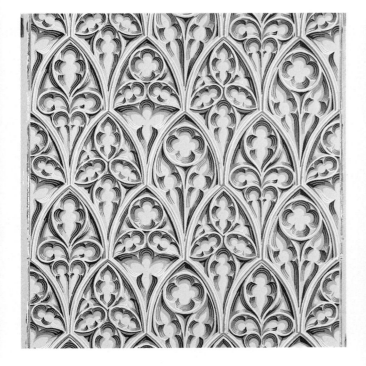

FIG. 10 A block-printer at work. Reproduced by courtesy of Cole & Son (Wallpapers) Ltd.

the printer onto a 'sieve cloth', or blanket loaded with colour pigments, then onto the sheet of paper laid out on a bench. The operation is carefully manoeuvred by the printer, and good results depend on his skill in judging placement and duration of pressure (FIG. 10).

Where blocks do not already exist, or are not repairable, Cole's have reproduced patterns by the silkscreen method, which though recognizably different in appearance, gives an approximation to the rich effect obtained by the pigments of a block-printed design. The use of screen-produced wallpapers in the restoration of an historic interior is most successful in the case of borders such as the Clandon examples mentioned earlier, where the distance from the eye renders the quality of the reproduction less discernable.

Four other wallpapers produced by Cole's from historic designs in the Museum's collection, though not in the present series, may be mentioned.

The first is based on an English wall- or lining-paper of the first half of the seventeenth century, a small embroidery-type pattern of Tudor Roses and other flowers, within a trellis formed of imitation stitchwork. This paper was produced for the Shakespeare quatercentenary exhibitions held at the Museum, as a screenprint in grey and white entitled 'The Stratford' (FIG. 11).

The second, 'Tudor Rose and Fleur-de-Lis' (FIG. 12) is a later printing (*circa* 1953) of a paper made by Samuel Scott, based on a Pugin design, for J. G. Crace for the decoration of the Houses of Parliament, between 1848 and 1850. This print was carried out in white on a bronze-gold ground, the original having been printed in flock on a gold ground.

Another later printing (1969) from original blocks is 'Scarisbrick', designed for the Red Drawing room of

FIG.11 Fragment of an early seventeenth century wall- or lining-paper. E.1974–1927.

Scarisbrick Hall, Lancashire in 1847. Scarisbrick Hall was rebuilt by A.W.N. Pugin and Edward Pugin between 1837 and 1870. Pugin's design for this paper is in the Department of Prints and Drawings (no. D.769–1908).

Lastly, a pattern of linked bamboo octagons, reproduced in silk screen, is based on a design of the 1830s, a sample of which, from Uppark, West Sussex, was given to the Museum by Mrs Jean Meade-Fetherstonhaugh. The original block print appears in the order books of Cowtan & Sons over the period between 1833 and 1861, also in the pattern-books of Jeffrey & Allen between 1837 and 1852. Its name, 'Chinese Trellis' (FIG.13) is taken from the latter volumes. It may have been produced as a paper for the smaller home, in accordance with the fashion set by the decoration of the Royal Pavilion at Brighton for large chinoiserie bamboo trellis designs in wallpaper.

In restoring historic interiors, such as Kensington Palace and Kew Palace, the Department of the Environment has searched the Museum's collections for suitable material, and in the case of wallpapers has been rewarded by searching Cole's archives and finding original blocks from which historically authentic interiors can be re-created.

1 Anthony Wells-Cole, *Historic Paper Hangings from Temple Newsam and other English Houses,* catalogue of the exhibition held at Temple Newsam in 1983.

FIG.12 'Tudor Rose and Fleur-de-Lis.' Print
from wood block. E.887–1979.

FIG.13 'Chinese Trellis.' Colour screenprint.
E.595–1982.

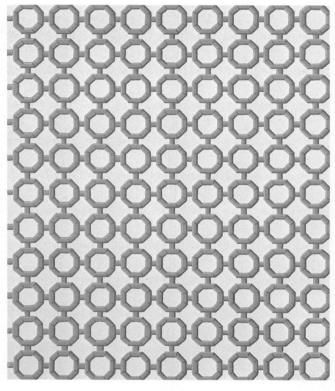

HARTOUM

CELLO

clarence house

40 EAST 57 STREET NEW YORK THROUGH DECORATORS AND FINE STORES

TURZI INTERNATIONAL

Furnishing Fabrics
Collection Le Marais

LONDON   2 Lowndes Street SW1
             Tel: (01) 235 0911/2/3

PARIS   26 Avenue Marceau 75008
             Tel: (01) 7238014 Tlx 205575 F

GENEVA   1 Rue Gautier
             Tel: (22) 314509 Tlx 28146 DAST CH

ROME   Via del Babuino, 99. 00187
             Tel: (06) 6798435

CORAUX: glazed chintz.

Brunschwig & Fils, Inc.

NEW YORK   LONDON   PARIS

Pallu and Lake Ltd., London

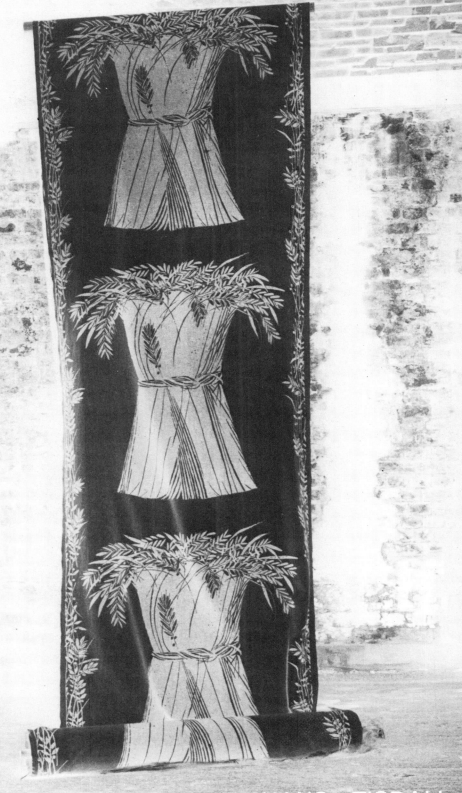

≪ WHEATSHEAF ≫
A LARGE SCALE PRINT DESIGNED BY HANS TISDALL

CHEERFUL, CHARMING, CHALLENGING, CHIC.... THAT'S

- Alan Swarbrick's new Cherry designs for 84/85 are getting rave reviews.
- They're in bright primary colours to cheer you up.
- They're in tough scrubbable vinyl, to go anywhere in the house.
- They're in the Design Council Index.
- See them in good decorating shops, DIY supermarkets and major stores.
- Have fun. Choose Cherry.

Cherry

by
ALAN SWARBRICK

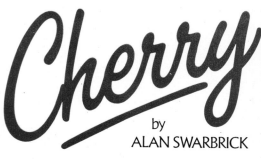

A **crown** wallcovering.

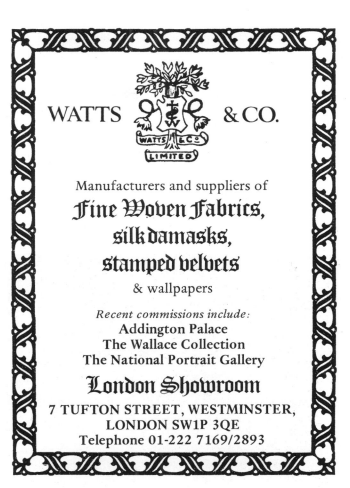

AN HERALDIC WALK ROUND THE V&A

Michael Maclagan

My interest in heraldry began when I was about eight years old, and was fostered by my father as he walked me to school every morning. While I regret to recall that at this time my brother and I actually preferred the Science Museum, I began soon to notice and to start to understand some of the lovely pieces of heraldic evidence in the V&A. Naturally I rejoiced when there was an exciting new acquisition, such as the Anstis tabard (FIG.1) in 1937.

As I learned more about blazon, I soon realised that positive evidence of its military application was not often to be found. The shield by which the warrior identified himself in battle or in joust was obviously itself perishable and prone to disfigurement through use. Very few medieval shields survive anywhere, though there are some fine examples in Germany dating back to the thirteenth century. But it is still possible to learn a lot from sepulchral effigies, which were originally as richly painted as were most medieval churches. Few things would so surprise a modern church-lover were he to be transported back to the Middle Ages as the riot of colour, often perhaps garish, in the churches which we see today so much in monochrome. The splendid tomb of an armoured knight from Lesnes Abbey (FIG.2) originally displayed a painted shield. We know this because some idle medieval hand (dare we conjecture a boy proudly fidgeting with his first dagger?) traced the outline of one of the charges on the shield. It is a pike-like fish and from its position there must have been three of them. The Lucy family were patrons of Lesnes Abbey, and bore as their arms three 'luces' – the common medieval term

for a pike. Like many families they derived their armorial bearings from a play on words. Without this idle scratching the identification of the monument would not be certain.

Shields of war from the Middle Ages are indeed rare, but shields do survive in the ritual of parade and pomp, which includes funeral displays such as the insignia of the Black Prince at Canterbury. The Museum is lucky to possess a splendid example from Florence (FIG.3) which can be ascribed to the early fifteenth century and shows the arms of the family of Villani, to which the historian belonged. The actual shape of the escutcheon is distinctly Italianate, but well accommodates the handsome figure of the griffin, in that posture which is technically called 'segreant'. The accusation is often levelled against heralds that their language is obscure and laden with jargon. The indictment loses much weight, if it is remembered that when the language developed, the speech of the English land-owning and knightly classes was still Norman-French. It has to be confessed that in the sixteenth and seventeenth centuries, the officers of arms did try to cultivate a certain mystery about their duties; but can either the lawyers or the physicians escape a similar censure?

The development of gunpowder and changes in the fashion of personal armour eliminated heraldry from its primary purpose of identification by the end of the Middle Ages. But it was already clear that this stylised and attractive form of art, with its relatively rigid definitions, could be extended into almost any available form of artistic manifestation. We can seek it therefore in every department of the V&A, for there can hardly be any medium in which a coat of arms cannot be displayed. I recall an ossuary of a great Bohemian family where their shield has been depicted entirely by the use of

human bones (FIG.4): but this is perhaps a little on the macabre side. Certainly enough, two of the great medieval techniques lent themselves with facility to the depiction of heraldry – enamel and needlework: both have magnificent examples acquired in the earliest days of the Museum's history. Few families achieved such international fame in the epoch of the Crusades as that of Lusignan. In the eastern Mediterranean their ramifications expanded over Jerusalem, lesser Armenia and Cyprus: in England, thanks to the second marriage of King John's widow, and the kindliness of Henry III to his kinsfolk, they became Earls of Pembroke. Near the end of the thirteenth century there was wrought for them a marvellous casket with lozenge-shaped depictions of their heraldic relationships (FIG.5). I do not know for what this lovely box was made, but it must, surely, have given the highest pleasure to those who first commissioned it. Although the techniques are Continental, as were the origins of the family, which came from Poitou, it is possible that the object was actually made in this country. It is one of my favourite pieces in the whole Museum.

Another early love was the Sion cope, a striking example of the triumphs of English embroidery, which made 'Opus Anglicanum' coveted all over Europe in the thirteenth century. A papal inventory of 1295 cites over one hundred examples already in the Vatican. To the herald the attraction lies in the rich armorial decoration round the edges of the vestment: in the illustration (FIG.6) are shown the 'canting' (or punning) arms of Castile and Leon – a castle and a lion – which pinpoint the marriage of Edward I and Eleanor of Castile (1254) as a date before which the cope can hardly have been designed. The Museum also possesses another signifi-

FIG.1 Tabard of embroidered velvet made for John Anstis the younger, Garter King of Arms from 1744–54. T1-1937.

FIG.2 Tomb effigy of a member of the Lucy family from Lesnes Abbey. Sandstone decorated with gesso, painted and gilt. The shield with three pike (luces). School of London, about 1320–40. A10-1912.

FIG.3 Pavoise with the arms of Villani. Wood, gessoed and painted. Florentine, early 15th century. 3-1865.

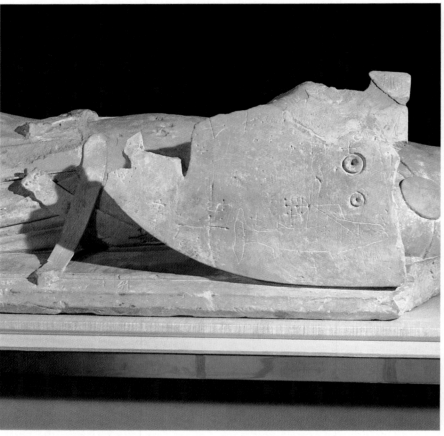

cant chasuble, emblazoned with the arms of Edmund of Cornwall and his wife, Margaret de Clare (both dead by 1312). There is evidence on sculptured tombs of similar usage of heraldic vestments, for example in Beverley Minster. It must be feared that many splendid examples of this technique may have perished at the time of the Reformation.

The same, alas, is all too true of stained glass; and in this medium, the efforts of Tudor reformers may have been surpassed by the bigotry of Cromwellian zealots. Fortunately, enough has survived to give us at least a scrapbook of the splendours which illuminated the windows of the greater medieval churches. A problem which

heraldry had to face was that of combining the arms of two inheritances which had passed to a single heir. The arms of Castile and Leon, already mentioned, are one of the earliest examples of such a combination. The lovely stained glass panel (FIG.7) shows how the Fitzalan family combined with their own lion rampant the fretty arms of the Maltravers family whose heiress they had married; the shield is divided into four, with the arms of each family repeated twice. It is probable that the blazon of Maltravers is again 'canting', and represents, with its network pattern, an 'ill traverse'. Both quarterings still represent part of the full achievement of the present Earl Marshal of England, the Duke of Norfolk. The

same shield can be seen at Windsor as one of the stall-plates of the Knights of the Garter, an invaluable set of examples of medieval enamel work, still in its original setting of St George's Chapel.

Carving in wood offers another range of opportunity to the heraldic artist. It is a less enduring medium than stone, though less perishable than glass: much must have been lost in the drastic redecoration of the interior of great country houses. In the sixteenth century the idea developed that the armorial bearings of ladies should be depicted on a lozenge rather than on a shield shape. At the same time the notion began to develop that the sovereign could reward a deserving

FIG.4 The arms of Schwarzenburg in bones.
Sedlec (Seidlitz), Czechoslovakia.

subject by an addition, or 'augmentation' to the latter's coat of arms. King Henry VIII was generous in granting such augmentations to his wives (after the first). His third queen, Katherine Seymour, actually presented him with a son, the future Edward VI, though this cost her her life. The grateful sovereign added to the arms of her family a quartering which combined the lilies of France (of which he, like his forebears, claimed to be king) and the lions of England. In due course this honorific was added to their arms by both the main surviving branches of the Seymour family and is still so used today. In this example (FIG.8) the arms are shown on a lozenge with a Tudor rose. It would be pleasant to think that this attractive piece dates from the poor Queen's lifetime.

I have suggested earlier that the uses and display of heraldry extend to almost every form of applied art, and in consequence to the earliest intentions of the V&A. In some areas, these do not lend themselves most easily to coloured reproduction. There is a rich range of heraldic manifestation on, for example, silver. The great silver-gilt Stanhope salver[1], made in 1727 for the author of the celebrated letters, is a good example. Then again there is bookbinding, such as the Villiers and Fleet example[2]; and doubtless within fine bindings, many an illustrious bookplate. On the other hand, later textiles still have much to tell us. I well recall the acquisition in my schooldays of the wonderful St John of Bletso carpet[3] – unfortunately not easy to reproduce – which illustrates profusely the elaborate matrimonial programme of the family in about the year 1559.

Another whole realm of armorial display lies in the area of fine porcelain, whether commissioned from China or from local factories in Britain, such as Worcester, or abroad. The mention of ceramics brings at once to mind

FIG.5 The Valence Casket. Copper-gilt with
champlevé enamel. French (Limoges). About
1300. With the arms of England (pre-1340),
Brittany (Dreux), Angoulême, Brabant and
Lacy. 4-1865.

FIG.6 Detail of the Sion Cope, *Opus Anglicanum*. In the centre, at the top, the arms of Castile and Leon – a castle and lion. After 1254. 83-1864.

FIG.7 Stained glass panel showing the lion
rampant of the Fitzalan family combined with
the fretty arms of the Maltravers family.
English. 15th century. 6908-1860.

FIG.8 Panel of oak carved with the Seymour arms, including the lilies of France and lions of England granted from the royal arms by Henry VIII in gratitude for the birth of a son to his queen, Katherine Seymour, in 1536. W63-1925.

another of my early favourites, and another very early acquisition by the Museum. René of Anjou was one of the significant figures of the fifteenth century, living from 1406 to 1480 and holding his court at different times in Naples, Lorraine, Anjou and finally in Provence. The splendid *stemma* (FIG.9) was made for him towards the end of his life by the celebrated Luca della Robbia. His elaborate coat of arms reveals the wide pretensions of his ancestry. He is linked with English history by the marriage of his daughter Margaret to the Lancastrian King, Henry VI. Her arms are preserved in the blazon of Queens' College, Cambridge, which she founded. The achievement here shows five 'quarterings' for René's various dynastic claims, and in the centre, a small shield for Aragon to which he also advanced a claim (based on an invitation from the insurgent Catalans). From the earlier Angevin dynasty in southern Italy René had inherited the phantom titles of King of Hungary and King of Jerusalem. These are divided in the top rank of his escutcheon by the arms of Naples (the oldest house of Anjou) which shows the lilies of France with a red label. The traditional arms of Jerusalem show five gold crosses upon a white (or silver) field: this arrangement breaks one of the basic laws of heraldry, that gold charges should not be placed on a silver field, or *vice versa*. Legend has it that this was a particular tribute to the supreme sanctity of Jerusalem. In the lower rank are the family arms of Anjou (the lilies of France within a red bordure) and René's county of Bar. Here again is a canting coat, for the fish there are barbels, a distinctive bearded freshwater species. On either side of the shield is shown René's device of a flaming brazier. Absent from the composition is René's duchy of Lorraine, possibly because by this date he had made it

FIG.9 The coat of arms of King René d'Anjou
(1406–1480) showing his various dynastic
claims. Tin-glazed earthen-ware. By Luca
della Robbia. 6740-1860.

FIG.10 Tomb front. Mosaic. Roman, late 14th or early 15th century. A81-1949.

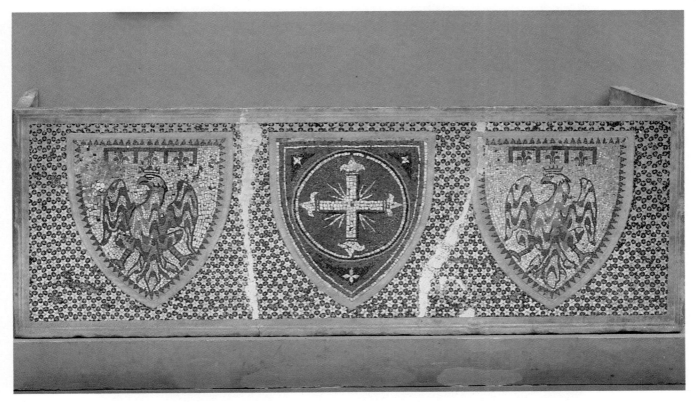

over to his son, John of Calabria. This shadowy monarch, who is remembered as 'le bon roi René', was very much a man of his age and of the new learning: he was the author of a treatise on tournaments and cultivated the fictitious heraldry associated with King Arthur and the Knights of the Round Table. A copy of the rare, first, elegant, printed list of these (1502) is in the admirable library of the V&A.

After the establishment in Naples of the ruthless Charles of Anjou in the thirteenth century, Italy was torn by strife between his party, the Guelfs, and that of the Emperor, known as Ghibellines. It was not unusual for Guelf partisans to add to their family blazon a red label and two or three fleurs-de-lys from the arms of Anjou/Naples. On a recent visit to the Museum I was delighted to notice an illustration of this practice on a tomb frontal, only acquired after the war (FIG.10). Supporters of the Empire added an eagle in the same way; there is a good example in a Florentine chimney piece of sixteenth century workmanship.

In England jurisdiction over heraldic matters has long been in the hands of the College of Arms. 1984 is for them an historic year, for their first charter of corporation was granted by King Richard III on 2 March 1484. Officers of arms were already wearing tabards by this date, though their form and the manner in which they were worn have changed down the centuries. Today, Pursuivants wear tabards of silk, Heralds of satin, and Kings of Arms of velvet. John Anstis the elder was Garter King of Arms from 1718 to 1744 and was followed by his son; the Museum has a fine tabard, made for the latter (1744–54). The observant will notice that the royal arms differ in some particulars from those in use today. The close conjunction of England and Scotland in the first quarter reflects the Act of Union of 1707; the second quarter still vaunts the claims of our Kings to France, while the fourth shows the insignia of the Electorate of Hanover. Their usage lasted till 1801 (FIG.1).

In this article I have touched only on a few objects which have taken my fancy. There is a vast and further wealth of heraldic evidence on display throughout the Museum, scattered through almost all the departments, a paradise for the heraldic enquirer.

1 Inv. No. M.72–1950   4 Inv. No. 6338–1860
2 Inv. No. L.610–1938   5 Inv. No. 6738–1860
3 Inv. No. T.152–1930

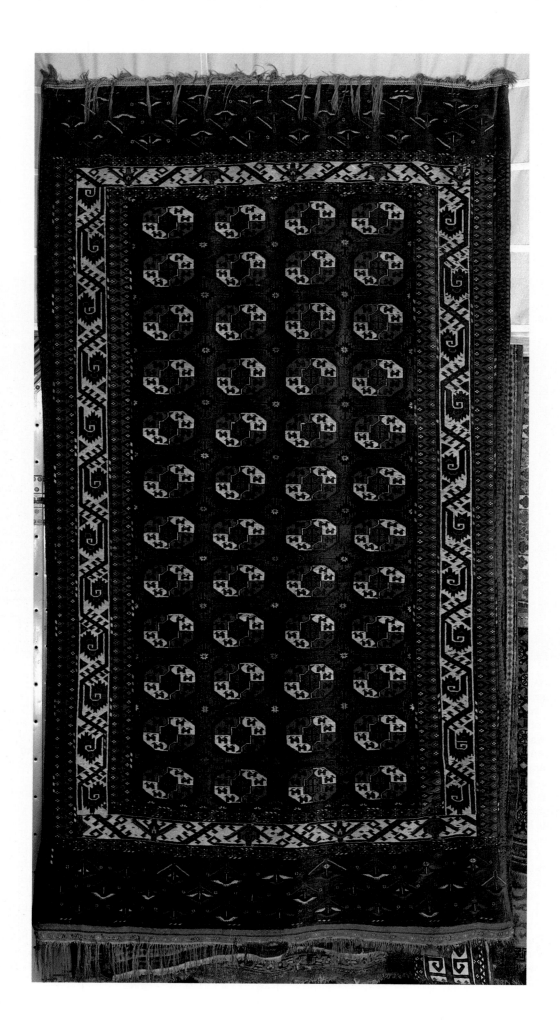

204

TÜRKMEN IN VICTORIAN KENSINGTON

Donald King

Perhaps the most popular of all Victorian narrative pictures was 'And when did you last see your father?', painted by William Frederick Yeames in 1878 and now in the Walker Art Gallery, Liverpool. The artist included in his picture much seventeenth century period detail, among which an Oriental rug, lying on the table between the youthful Cavalier and his Roundhead interrogator, seems at first sight an authentic touch. On closer inspection, however, it reveals itself as an anachronism. Certainly seventeenth century people used Oriental carpets on tables – commercially produced carpets from Turkey, Egypt, Persia and India, countries accessible to European sea-borne trade. But the carpet depicted by Yeames was produced by tent-dwelling Türkmen in the heart of Asia, the steppe country which lies eastward from the Caspian Sea towards the Amu-Darya, the ancient Oxus river. Such rugs, made by the Türkmen for their own tents, seem to have been unknown in Europe until a few years before Yeames painted his picture.[1]

The Türkmen or Turkoman tribes, except for fractions of them living within the northern frontier of Persia, were incorporated into the Russian empire from 1869 onwards and their carpets began to figure in exhibitions in Russia from about that time. But the examples acquired by the South Kensington Museum from 1875 onwards seem, as far as is known, to have been the first to enter the permanent collection of any European museum. This was largely due to Robert Murdoch Smith (1835–1900), an officer of the Royal Engineers, who had earlier played a leading role in the excavations at Halicarnassus, including the Mausoleum (1856–59), and at Cyrene

FIG.1 Floor carpet. Yomut Türkmen, 18th–19th century. 10ft. 9in. × 5ft. 7in. Acquired from Jules Richard, Teheran. 854-1876.

(1860–61); the finds from these excavations are in the British Museum. From 1865 to 1885 he was director of the Persian telegraph at Teheran, a vital link between Britain and India. There he became an excellent Persian scholar and devoted much time and attention to accumulating a large collection of Persian art-objects for the South Kensington Museum, including several examples of Turkoman carpets. From 1885 onwards he was director of the Science and Art Museum, Edinburgh.[2]

The first two Turkoman pieces collected by Murdoch Smith came from the Richard collection of Persian art, which had been formed over a period of nearly thirty years by Monsieur Jules Richard, a French Muslim long resident in Teheran. The first to arrive in London, in 1875, is a woollen carpet of moderate size (FIG.1) with a simple repeating pattern of rows of octagons containing small animal figures, with crosses between the octagons, and with borders of boldly geometrical flowers and leaves. The second piece, which reached London in 1876 (FIG.2), is smaller, but finer and richer, with some details in silk, and again with a simple repeating pattern of octagons. Both pieces are notable for the high quality of the design, dyeing and execution. Though differing in details, they show an obvious family relationship in colour and pattern, including the unusual feature of floral panels at the ends, outside the borders.

Similar carpets were also arriving in London through ordinary commercial channels. A mixed collection of carpets purchased by the Museum in 1880 from the leading London carpet dealer, Vincent Robinson and Co. of Wigmore Street, included four Turkoman pieces. One of these (FIG.3) is almost a twin of the preceding piece, though differing in small details, and is of still higher quality. Another (FIG.5) is a larger but incomplete carpet, with a

repeating pattern of rows of lobed octagons, with crosses between, and a border pattern also including octagons and crosses. The two other pieces, much smaller but complete (FIG.6), have a reduced version of the same type of repeating pattern.

Further examples collected by Murdoch Smith in Persia arrived in London in 1883–84. Two of these, both with designs unlike those already in the Museum, were acquired from the collection of Mr Sidney Churchill in Teheran. One (FIG.4) has complex geometrical patterns within a border of eccentric outline; in its colouring and texture, its use of silk as well as wool, the pattern of the border and other details, it is related to some of the pieces acquired earlier (FIGS.2, 3). The other Churchill piece (FIG.7) resembles that depicted in Yeames's painting, with the field intersected by a cross shape, like a panelled door. Another example which reached the Museum in 1884 was a further acquisition from the Richard collection in Teheran (FIG.8); it has a repeating pattern of rows of geometrical forms within boldly patterned borders.

Besides these pile carpets, a few other Turkoman textiles were acquired by the Museum about the same period. A piece made up from sections of a Turkoman tent band formed part of a collection of Persian artifacts obtained from Messrs. Pearson and Heath in 1877 (FIG.9). A similar tent band nearly twenty-five feet long and a little more than one foot wide was bought from Sidney Churchill in Teheran in 1886. Both pieces have bold patterns in coloured woollen pile on a flat-woven white ground. The silk-embroidered cloak of a Turkoman woman – romantically described by the vendor as having belonged to a Tartar princess – was bought in London in 1884.

All the pieces acquired in Teheran were catalogued in the Museum as

FIG.2 Face of storage bag, *chuval*. Salor
Türkmen, 18th–19th century. 2ft. 11in. ×
4ft. 8in. Acquired from Jules Richard,
Teheran. 2324-1876.

FIG.3 Face of storage bag, *chuval*. Salor
Türkmen, 18th–19th century. 3ft. × 4ft.
11in. Acquired from Vincent Robinson &
Co., London. 394-1880.

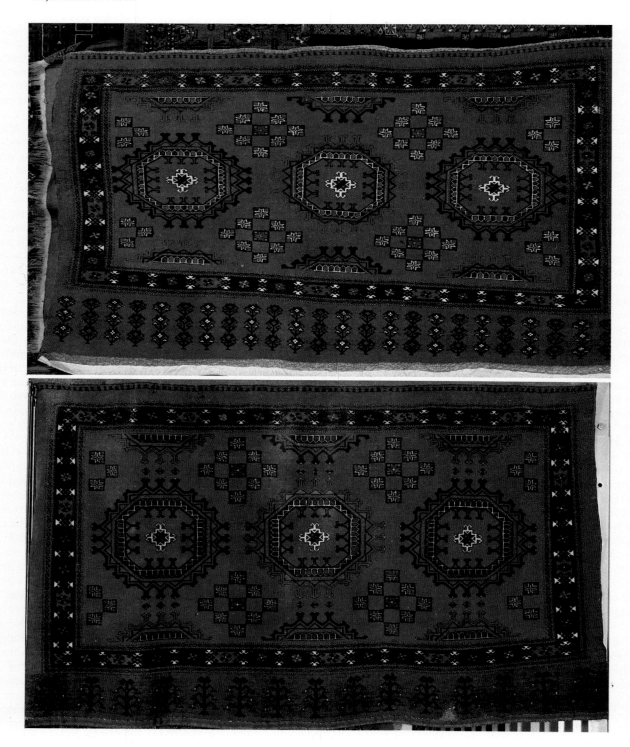

FIG.4 Animal trapping. Salor Türkmen, 18th–19th century. 2ft. 6in. × 6ft. 7in. Acquired from Sidney Churchill, Teheran. 143-1884.

Persian, of 'Turcoman make', presumably following information supplied by Murdoch Smith; a similar attribution was given to the tent hanging acquired from Pearson and Heath. A piece acquired in London was described simply as 'Turcoman' (FIG.5); some others were not specifically attributed. Several pieces were assigned to the nineteenth century (FIGS.2, 4, 6, 9), two to the eighteenth (FIGS.5, 7) and one to the seventeenth century (FIG.8); others were undated. Since nothing was known of the stylistic development of such carpets, these datings can have been little more than guesses, based on the amount of wear and damage that the pieces had suffered. Obviously the textile furnishings of Türkmen tent-dwellers, without the shelter of permanent buildings, were not likely to endure for more than a few generations, so that dating any of this material prior to 1800 can only be speculative.

In any case the Museum's purpose in collecting such material was not to acquire objects of high antiquity or of great rarity, but to obtain good examples of the art-manufactures of other parts of the world, which might serve as models or inspirations for de-signers and manufacturers in Britain. The Museum's modest expenditure on these Turkoman pieces was appropriate for such an aim. The prices paid seem to have been roughly proportional to the size of the pieces. For pieces acquired in Teheran, they ranged from £1 7s. for the smallest (FIG.8), through £1 9s., £2 10s. and £3 for medium sizes (FIGS.4, 2, 7 respectively), to £10 for the largest (FIG.1). London prices were two or three times more at £6 and £7 for medium sizes (FIGS.9, 3 respectively) and £20 for a larger piece (FIG.5). Some of these pieces are now worth several thousand pounds in today's money.

The Museum may have played a pioneering role in collecting Turkoman carpets from 1875 onwards, but before many years had passed innumerable examples were being shipped west-wards to become admired and familiar furnishings in Europe and America. The first illustrations of Turkoman carpets and tent bands were published in St. Petersburg in 1883. Two years later, an article published in the same city showed how borders and other pieces cut from Turkoman carpets could be used for curtains, cushions and seat furniture. In 1893 the catalogue of an exhibition in Vienna noted that old Turkoman carpets, very thin and fine, were considered more suitable than any others for upholstery, table covers and wall hangings. The Hallwyl Museum in Stockholm owns settees and chairs, made for the Hallwyl family 1893–95, covered with large and small Turkoman carpets like those in FIGS.5 and 6. There is abundant evidence of similar use in England and elsewhere. Obviously the smaller pieces of Turkoman carpet work came in sizes particularly suitable for seat furniture and cushions. Moreover, the deep, rich reds of the Turkoman carpets, their dense velvety pile and their stately repeating patterns were especially congenial to late 19th century taste in interior decoration. To satisfy western demand, carpet dealers descended like locusts on the tents of the Türkmen. By 1900 a traveller in Russian Turkestan, J.W. Bookwalter, reported 'It is well nigh impossible to obtain superior examples of the old work even here, so thoroughly have the Persian, Armenian and other merchants searched the country'; recent Turkoman rugs, he observed, were

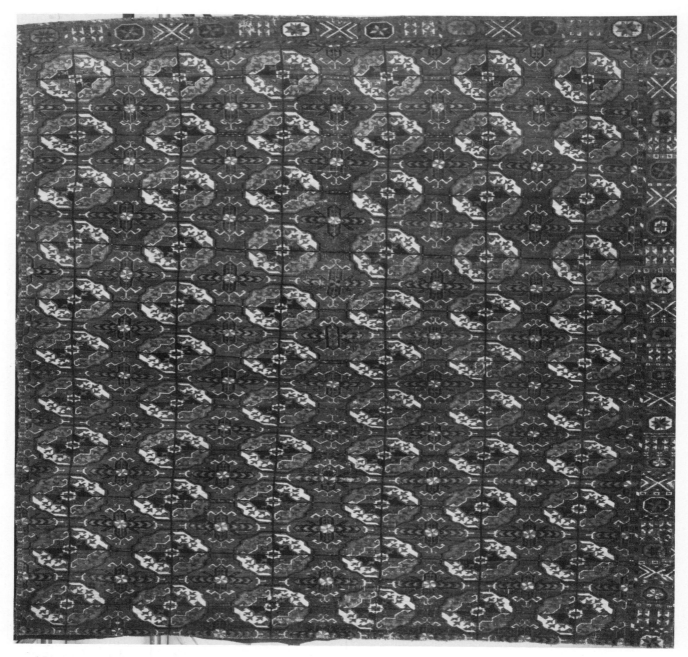

FIG.5 Floor carpet, incomplete. Tekke
Türkmen, 18th–19th century. 6ft. 4½in. ×
6ft. 4½in. Acquired from Vincent Robinson
& Co. London. 404-1880.

FIG.6 Face of storage bag, *torba*. Tekke
Türkmen, 18th–19th century. 1ft. 3in. × 4ft.
2in. One of two similar examples acquired
from Vincent Robinson & Co., London.
411PP-1880.

FIG.7 Tent-door hanging, *ensi*. Yomut
Türkmen, 18th–19th century. 5ft. 6in. × 4ft.
Acquired from Sydney Churchill, Teheran.
1050-1883.

FIG.8 Face of storage bag, *chuval*. Yomut
Türkmen, 18th–19th century. 2ft. 3in. × 3ft.
11in. Acquired from Jules Richard, Teheran.
311-1884.

FIG.9 Sections of tent girth, *ak yüp*. Türkmen,
18th–19th century. 5ft. 6in. × 4ft. 4in.
Acquired from Messrs. Pearson and Heath.
91-1877.

FIG.11 Silk textile. Central Asia, possibly
Bokhara region, 8th–9th century 11¾in. ×
10in. Acquired from Jules Helbig, Liège.
1754-1888.

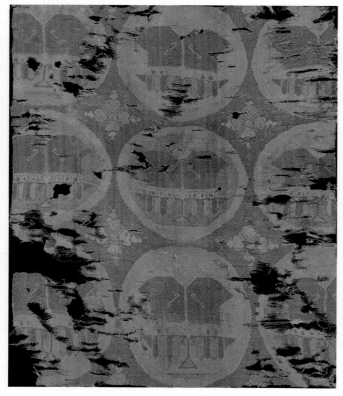

FIG.10 Sketch map showing approximate locations of tribes.

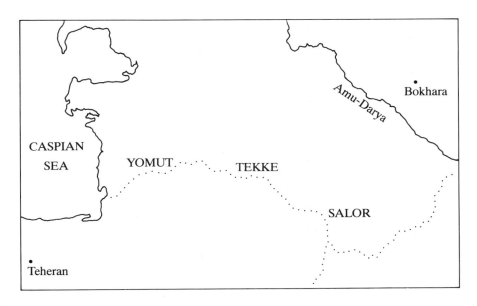

vastly inferior to the old. Soon the use of Turkoman carpets in Europe and America had passed its fashionable peak and was moving down market. J.K. Mumford in 1900 deplored 'the unvarying octagonal devices which are the feature of . . . these rugs, which are now found in almost tiresome plenty'. By 1905 a German firm was selling seat furniture and cushions covered, not with Turkoman rugs, but with factory-made reproductions of them. The old Turkoman patterns have continued to be reproduced by the Türkmen and by carpet-weavers in other parts of the world down to the present day, but these modern products cannot vie with the beautiful colouring and exquisite quality of the fine old pieces.[3]

In the meantime, the Türkmen and their rugs have become a target for academic research. The first monograph on the carpets, published in St. Petersburg in 1908, has been followed by numerous other studies by Russian and western authors. Collections have been formed by many museums in Asia, Europe and America and many private collectors are also active in this

field. Many dozens of carpets have been added to the collection at South Kensington. As a result of all this activity much additional information has come to light. We know the purposes for which the carpets were made and the Turkoman names for the various types and patterns. The large pieces (FIGS.1, 5) served as floor carpets in the circular Turkoman tents. The long narrow bands (FIG.9) were fixed around the interior walls of the tents. Many other pieces were the fronts of storage bags which were likewise hung on the walls, the larger ones called *chuval* (FIGS.2, 3, 8) and the smaller called *torba* (FIG.6). Pieces called *ensi*, with a cross intersecting the field (FIG.7), were hung in the door opening of the tents. Pieces with eccentrically shaped fields (FIG.4) were originally made as trappings for the camel which carried the bride in the wedding procession and later were also hung up in the tent. The study of the designs and technical details of the carpets has permitted their attribution to various tribal groups. Thus of the pieces illustrated here some can be attributed to

the Yomut (FIGS.1, 7, 8), others to the Tekke (FIGS.5, 6) and the finest pieces to the Salor (FIGS.2, 3, 4); approximate locations of these tribes are indicated in FIG.10. It was a strange quirk of fate that nearly all such carpets, so intimately linked with the tribal life and traditions of the Türkmen, were carried off in the late 19th century to grace the fashionable drawing rooms of Europe and America.[4]

The origin of Turkoman carpet designs has been much debated. By a coincidence, shorty after acquiring the rugs which are illustrated here, the Museum also purchased some patterned silk textiles which may throw some light on the problem. These came from reliquaries in various European churches and belong to a large group of patterned silk textiles which have been found both in Western Europe and in the East.[5] One of the silks, in a Belgian church, bears an ancient inscription which suggests that it was woven at Zandane, a village in the neighbourhood of Bokhara, and it is generally supposed that the whole group was made in that area of central Asia, very close to the present territory of the Türkmen, about the eighth–ninth century A.D. The example illustrated, which was bought at Liège in Belgium in 1888 (FIG.11), has a pattern of rows of circles, with crosses between, resembling the layout of many Turkoman carpets (FIGS.1,2,3,5,6,8). The cross motifs have some points in common with those in some of the carpets (FIGS.5, 6). The motif in the circles shows ambiguous geometrical abstraction of natural forms quite similar to that seen in the carpets; it presumably represents a flower, but the upper part looks like two birds' heads in profile. The triangular base and the stem with curling tendrils at the top resemble similar forms in the carpets, while the leaves in alternating colours, below the flower, are nearly identical with a common Turkoman ornament called *barmak* (fingers), seen for example surrounding the octagon motif associated with the Salor tribe (FIGS.2, 3). It in no way diminishes the originality and the high artistic qualities of the Turkoman weavers – who were mainly women – to suggest that they followed an age-old tradition of design in central Asia. But it is curious and remarkable that this tradition should twice have exported great quantities of its textiles to appreciative buyers in the West – first silks and, later, carpets – at two different periods, separated by a thousand years.

1   *Hali*, Vol. 1, No. 1, 1978, p.92.

2   *Dictionary of National Biography.*

3   R. Pinner and M. Franses (eds.), *Turkoman Studies I*, 1980, pp. 6ff., 63ff., 96ff.

4   Pinner and Franses, *op. cit.*, p. 14ff.; A.A. Bogolyubov, *Carpets of Central Asia*, 1973, ed. by J.M.A. Thompson from the 1908 edition; D. King, R. Pinner and M. Franses, 'Turkoman Rugs in the Victoria and Albert Museum', *Hali*, Vol. 2, No. 4, 1980, p. 30lff; L.W. Mackie and J.M.A. Thompson (eds.), *Türkmen, Tribal Carpets and Traditions*, 1980; P.A. Andrews, 'The Türkmen Tent', *Hali*, vol. 4, No. 2, 1981, p.108ff.

5   D.G. Shepherd, 'Zandanījī Revisited', *Documenta textilia, Festschrift fur Sigrid Müller-Christensen*, 1981, p. 105ff.

VIGO CARPET GALLERY

ANTIQUE SULTANABAD
12 ft. × 8 ft. 5 in. (3·66 × 2·57 m.)

"The soul of the apartment is in the carpet"

A superb late-19th century Ukrainian carpet of spectacular design and color palette . This example personifies the elegance and richness inherent in the European tradition of carpet weaving. The size is 9′5″x 7′2″making it adaptable to any room.

This gallery features an eclectic array of room size carpets and small collector pieces of outstanding merit in Oriental and European weaves.

An Appointment Is Suggested

Doris Leslie Blau

ANTIQUE AND EXEMPLARY CARPETS AND TAPESTRIES
in New York
at 15 East 57th Street
212-759-3715

Robert E. Haynes, Ltd.

1221 Union Street • San Francisco, California 94109

Telephone: (415) 928-2235

KOIKE YOSHIRO NAOMASA

MASTERPIECE TSUBA BY KOIKE YOSHIRO NAOMASA. The iron plate shows more attention to forging than the other two examples and the brass inlay is in the classic style with a carved groove in the iron plate at the edge of the inlay. The six mon are solid brass inlay. See lot ____ for an earlier example. The hitsuana are shakudo filled, with nekko yasuri surface. The face is signed: Koike Yoshiro on the left side. The back is signed: Izumi no Kami, on the right, and Naomasa on the left. This is the classical signature that is recorded in the books. (See note above.) The quality and beauty of this tsuba brings the work of Naomasa to full bloom. The later work of the Bizen Yoshiro and Saburodaiyu continued this style and in some cases equalled it. From the Alexander G. Mosle collection and listed in the text, vol. I, page 177, number 468, also illustrated in volume I of plates, number XLI-468. Ht. 8.4 cm., Th. (center) 3.75 mm., (edge) 3.25 mm. (I-290)

KAMAKURA KATCHUSHI

HIGHLY IMPORTANT AND RARE EXAMPLE OF KAMAKURA PERIOD TSUBA. Iron plate with concave hachi gata (eight sided) slightly rounded point shape. Squarish edge with iron bones visible. The plate surface is well hammered and also shows the signs of its great age. Eight mm. inside the edge is a raised ridge complimenting the outer shape. This ridge once was gold uttori covered; all that remains today are the thin lines of gold where it was buried in the iron plate at the low edge of the ridge. The reverse side of this tsuba is undecorated and shows signs of hammering and the folds of the plate in forging. The rio-hitsu were added at a later date, probably in the late Muromachi period (ca. 1500). The plate treatment and the age of the piece is evident in the appearance of the plate today. The shape is very rare at this or any time, but could very well of happened at this early inventive time. Ca. 1300. Ht., point to point, 10 cm., and at concave, 9.2 cm. Th. 2 mm. Ht. of ridge, 1.5 mm. Note: with original box with hako-gaki signed Kodo (Dr. Kazutaro Torigoye) and dated Showa 30 (1955). Provenance: illustrated in Tsuba Geijutsu-ko by Dr. Kazutaro Torigoye, published 1960, vol. II page 7 top. Also illustrated in Christie's auction catalogue (New York) of November 5, 1980, lot number 19.   Sold for $4000

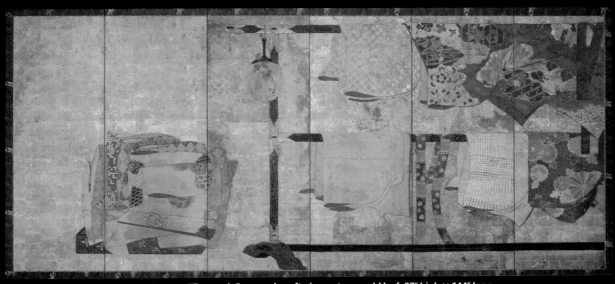

THREE JAPANESE LACQUERS

Joe Earle

Thanks to the recent enormous success of James Clavell's historical novel *Shōgun* and its film and television versions, the English-reading world thinks it knows more about the Momoyama period (1568 or 1573 to 1600, 1603 or 1615) than any other epoch in Japan's past. Clavell's manipulation and compression of events is extreme and his moralistic idealisation of Japanese culture is no more than a device to illuminate the process of self-discovery of the barbarous, prudish English hero Blackthorne and, by extension, contemporary Western readers of the novel.[1] Nevertheless, he is remarkably successful in bringing to life the atmosphere of that extraordinary age, when a series of great military leaders brought unity to Japan after centuries of civil war.

Oda Nobunaga (1534–1582) entered the capital, Kyoto, in 1568, deposed the last of the Ashikaga shoguns (military rulers) in 1573 and by the time of his murder had broken the power of the Buddhist church. Toyotomi Hideyoshi (1536–1598), by birth a common footsoldier, reunified the country and twice attempted to invade Korea. Tokugawa Ieyasu (1542–1616) defeated the majority of his rivals in 1600 in probably the greatest land battle the world had ever seen, in 1603 had the Emperor declare him shogun and in 1615 at last extinguished all opposition to his supremacy by reducing Osaka castle.

Through improved communication and the creation, from military necessity, of castle-towns, the economic expansion which had started earlier in the sixteenth century intensified dramatically and was further encouraged by the rapid development of international commerce following the arrival of Portuguese and later Dutch traders. The extravagant tastes of the *arriviste* martial elite, especially Hideyoshi, and the emergent urban merchant class, together with the stimulus of unprecedented contact with the outside world, brought to a climax the momentum of cultural transformation which had been felt in all areas of artistic endeavour during the preceding half century. Three lacquers in the Far Eastern Department, two of them acquired during 1983, exemplify some of the changes which one of the most characteristic of Japanese craft traditions underwent during the Momoyama period.

By the end of the fifteenth century, the extraction and refining of the sap of the lacquer tree, *Rhus vernicifera* D.C., and its combination with gold and silver powder and flakes to decorate wooden objects had reached a very high level of technical sophistication. The time-consuming *takamaki-e* method in particular, in which lacquer is mixed with charcoal dust and worked in relief, was especially prized and much used in the ornamentation of writing boxes and other pieces associated with the court of of the Ashikaga shogun Yoshimasa (1435–1490). Yoshimasa, a feckless politician but an enthusiastic patron of the arts, gathered about him a coterie of creative talents whose tastes combined a reverence for Chinese artefacts with a nostalgic regard for the court culture of the Heian period (897–1185). The lacquers made for this group, of which the so-called 'Five Writing-boxes of Yoshimasa' (*Jishōin-Yoshimasa-kō gomensuzuri*) recorded in a sixteenth century document are the most famous[2], epitomise this nostalgic and more purely Japanese strand in *Higashiyama* ('Eastern Hills') culture, named from the location of Yoshimasa's celebrated Silver Pavilion (Ginkakuji). Thus a writing box decorated with deer and autumn grasses calls to mind the lines:[3]

> Yamazato wa
> Aki koso koto ni
> Sabishikere
> Shika no naku ne ni
> Me o samashitsutsu[4]
>
> It is in autumn that the mountain village is at its most lonely –
> time and again I am woken by the cries of the deer

This poem from the great anthology of court poetry, the *Kokinshū*, completed around 905, would have been immediately familiar to the educated aesthetes of Yoshimasa's circle to whom verse-capping (*renga*) was a daily pastime, and the reference is underlined by the inclusion of a few of its words, hidden in the design. Wares such as this one, elaborate in technique, rich in literary content and deeply tinged with *yūgen*, the elusive melancholic sensitivity which finds its fullest expression in the *Nō* drama, represented the peak of lacquer art at the end of the fifteenth century.

In the sixteenth century there are gradual changes. The penchant for literary allusion continues, but there are also signs of a less rarified taste in the closely observed animal and plant forms that make an occasional appearance. It is not until the Momoyama period, however, that an entirely distinct lacquer style, the *Kōdaiji maki-e*, takes shape. It takes its name from the Kōdaiji temple in Kyoto, in whose precincts Hideyoshi's widow Kita no Mandokoro (1541–1624) built a mausoleum, the Reiokuin, for herself and her husband, completed in 1606 but incorporating elements from an earlier structure. *Kōdaiji maki-e*, as much a grouping of techniques as a style, constitutes a rejection of the aesthetic assumptions of earlier lacquerwares, especially those held in high esteem in Yoshimasa's time.

FIG.1 *Tebako* ('handy box') Wood decorated in black and gold lacquer. *c.* 1620.
8.5 × 17.0 × 20.5cm. FE.3-1984.

FIG.2 Another view of FIG.1.

FIG.3 The Rushbrooke Hall Coffer. Wood decorated in riveted mother-of-pearl and black and gold lacquer, with copper-gilt fittings. *c.* 1580–1610. The stand English; 17th century.
55.0 × 110.4 × 44.5cm. FE.33-1983.

FIG.4 Detail of FIG.3

While the *Higashiyama* wares are deliberately time consuming and even mannered in their technique, the *Kōdaiji* wares are deliberately rapid and expressive. *Takamaki-e* is avoided and even the finishing coat of lacquer, applied after the sprinkling of gold and silver powder, is often dispensed with. As far as we can judge from the finished products, freehand sketches, quickly painted in red lacquer directly onto the object to be decorated, are preferred to carefully worked out designs transferred from thin paper. Details such as the veins of leaves are scratched through the gold-sprinkled lacquer before it has dried, instead of, as before, being incorporated in the original application of lacquer, a far more difficult procedure.[5]

The Reiokuin mausoleum is itself decorated in these techniques and there has been handed down in the temple a group of wares which, together with pieces of the same type in other collections, is collectively called *Kōdaiji maki-e*.

On a rain-soaked visit last autumn[6] to this atmospheric spot, which includes as well as the temple buildings a celebrated teahouse with an umbrella-shaped roof, the Karakasatei, where many of the great figures of the age disported themselves, I learned of some of the doubts surrounding the history of the mausoleum's construction. It is probable that the two pairs of doors to the niches containing images of Hideyoshi and Kita no Mandokoro may be separated in date by as much as twenty-eight years and there are technical reasons for doubting the authenticity of the date corresponding to 1596 which was discovered, scratched on the back of one of the doors, in the late autumn of 1939. In any case, recent research has established that the Kōdaiji style and technique was in existence as early as 1586.[7] The more the lacquers of the late sixteenth century and early

seventeenth century Japan are studied, the more it becomes apparent that the time-saving techniques exemplified by the Kōdaiji wares were employed in the creation of most of the innovative work of the time, and are by no means to be seen as being confined to the sphere of particular places or individuals. The Museum's recently-acquired *tebako* ('handy-box', FIGS.1,2), decorated with willow trees

in gold on a black background, shares few features in common with the strictly-confined canon of *Kōdaiji maki-e*, but its free-flowing design, closely akin to contemporary screen paintings of the bridge at Uji,[8] could never have been achieved without the liberating techniques described above.

We do not know for certain when Japanese lacquerers first started making pieces to Western order, but it is

FIG.5 Detail of FIG.3

possible that Nobunaga may have owned some examples in 1569,[9] in other words before the Momoyama period had even started according to one of the accepted datings. They were definitely producing them by 1596, because there is a cabinet which was inventoried in that year as being in the possession of Archduke Ferdinand of the Tyrol.[10] Like the rest of the *Namban* ('Southern Barbarian') lacquers, it combines a number of Indo-Portuguese, Chinese and perhaps Korean, as well as Japanese, elements in its design, and these Japanese elements include several features which are found in the *Kōdaiji* group. The new acceptability of less time-consuming production processes made it pos-

sible for lacquerers to turn out wares appealing to the taste of the new military and merchant classes for immediately comprehensible and enjoyable effects and to the desire of the Portuguese traders for low-cost exotica. The Museum's most important Japanese acquisition during 1983, the Rushbrooke Hall coffer, (FIGS.3–6), is a masterpiece of this export art and has an illustrious pedigree.

The coffer is in the European shape with curved lid called by modern Japanese specialists *kamabokogata* ('fish-sausage shape'), but is highly unusual in that the exterior has no extensive areas of lacquer. Instead it is chiefly decorated with riveted plates of shell from a species of abalone or

awabi, possibly *Sulculus supertexta* or *Notohaliotis discus*,[11] separated by narrow lacquered borders, producing an overwhelmingly splendid overall effect. The inside of the lid (FIGS.5,6,7) has a more conventional, *Kōdaiji*-lacquered, design of phoenixes and vines which is in even better condition than the remarkably well-preserved exterior. The stand is English work, a very poor seventeenth century attempt to ape the achievements of the Japanese craftsman.

The coffer was until 1919 at Rushbrooke Hall, the mid-sixteenth century Suffolk residence (now sadly destroyed) of Henry Jermyn,[12] and is included in an inventory taken in 1759.[13] At that time the house still contained the bulk of Jermyn's collection, which he directed in his will should remain there 'for the well furnishing of the house'.[14] Also in the collection was a pair of English cabinets whose decoration incorporates the MHR monogram of Henrietta Maria. Henry Jermyn, Lord St. Albans (d.1684) had been a favourite of the Queen's since before the Civil War and was even rumoured by Pepys[15] to have married her upon their return to England at the Restoration. We know from the inventory compiled on the orders of Charles II at her death in 1669[16] that she owned cabinets (not coffers) 'inlaid with mother-of-pearl' and the intriguing possibility exists that the Rushbrooke Hall coffer may have come to Jermyn from her in the same way as the English cabinets. This speculation is supported, perhaps, by evidence that mother-of-pearl decorated furniture was very popular at the late sixteenth century French court.

The 1589 inventory[17] of the effects of Catherine de Medicis, widow of Henri II, contains five such pieces, four of them coffers ('coffre de bahu'). It is conceivable, then, that the present coffer, along with the cabinets which

FIG.6 Detail of FIG.3
FIG.7 Detail of FIG.3

the Queen retained until her death, may have been sent with her to England at the time of her marriage in 1625. Unfortunately the inventory of Denmark House taken after her arrival has not survived and unless it comes to light it will be impossible to establish the coffer's history.

Because the *Kōdaiji* and *Namban* wares have in recent years monopolised the attention of both Japanese and European scholars, it has tended to be assumed that the elaborate, literary style associated with Higashiyama taste disappeared during the Momoyama period. Certainly there are few if any examples which can be securely dated to the years 1568–1615 and, as a rule, pieces made around that time about which there is doubt are assigned either to the late Muromachi period (i.e. before 1568) or the early Edo period (i.e. after 1615). One example is a writing box in Kyoto National Museum[18] which has been given a late Muromachi date and is very close in design to a writing table (*bundai*) from the collection of W.C. Alexander, given by his daughters to the V&A in 1916. A comparison of these two lacquers, as well as establishing that they do not, as had been thought likely, form a set, tells us much about the popularisation of this esoteric style of decoration.

The Kyoto National Museum box in many ways typifies the traditional use of poetic material already described in connection with the lacquers of the Higashiyama court. When the front and back of the lid and the interior of the box are viewed together in reproduction, the design is superficially similar to that of the V&A table, but there are significant differences. The box, unlike the table, has characters hidden in the rocks and trees of the two islands, probably indicating a poem by Minamoto no Yorimasa (1104–1180):

FIG.8 *Bundai* (writing table). Wood decorated in gold and silver lacquer with gold and silver details. *c.* 1620.
8.9 × 59.7 × 35.0cm. W.339-1916.

Sumiyoshi no
Matsu no koma yori
Miwataseba
Tsuki ochikakaru
Awajishima yama[19]

Gazing across from between
the pines of
Sumiyoshi
I see the moon about to sink
behind the mountains of Awaji island

Sumiyoshi, in modern Osaka, is the site of an ancient Shinto shrine frequently referred to in the poetry of the Heian period (the earliest lacquer to take it as subject matter is inscribed with a date corresponding to 1228[20]) and Awaji, in the inland sea, is a real island whose name implies both *mono no aware*, the awareness of material transience, and *awa* 'foam'. However,

the Kyoto National Museum box, unlike its predecessors, cannot be tied exclusively to a single poem of thirty-one syllables or a specific geographical location, however evocative. There are many elements in its design which call for further explanation: broken blinds and shutters, holes in the roof, disused salt-makers' kilns and abandoned water-dippers are superfluous to the Sumiyoshi theme. Memories of many poems may have been present in the lacquerer's mind or that of his patron, and among these may be, in Japanese:

Kimi nakute
Keburi taenishi
Shiogama no
Ura sabishiku mo
Narinikeru kana[21]

Now that you are gone
How lonely
Has become the shore
Where smoke no longer rises
From the saltburners' huts

or

Kimi nakute
Aretaru yado no
Itama yori
Tsuki no moru ni mo
Sode wa nurekeri[22]

Now that you are gone
My sleeves are soaked
By the moonlight seeping
Between the planks
Of this ruined mansion

Or, in Chinese

Xiang xiao lian tou sheng bai lu
Zhong xiao chuang di jian qing tian[23]

FIG.9 Detail of FIG.8.

Towards dawn frosty dew grows above
the blinds
All night long I see the clear sky
through the foot of my bed

All three poems come from the *Hataku* ('Dilapidated residences') subsection of the *Kokyō* ('Ancient capital') section of the *Wakan rōeishū*, an anthology completed in 1013 which includes poems in Chinese by both Chinese and Japanese poets as well as purely Japanese *waka* lyrics. Other, Chinese, poems in this subsection refer to 'broken fences', tattered blinds' and 'precariously hanging lattices',[24] all features which are faithfully observed by the lacquerer. The Chinese poem given above is specifically alluded to in chapter 12, *Suma*,[25] of the early eleventh century *Tale of Genji* which in the late sixteenth century enjoyed a revival of interest destined to last

throughout the Edo period and down to the present day. The *Suma* chapter relates Prince Genji's self-imposed, elegant and wistful, exile at Suma, not far from the Sumiyoshi shrine, and is filled with images of deserted shores, empty salt kilns and damp sleeves entirely appropriate to the affected sensibilities of the sixteenth century aesthete. In fact, even a brief examination of the textual background reveals that the writing box was made for an educated patron who expected detailed literary justification for its design.

The V&A's writing table, reproduced here, has no hidden characters and the mansion at the left (FIG. 9) bears none of the marks of neglect, except broken railings, called for by the poems just quoted, although the sleeve draped over the lattice may intended as a reference to one of the

ladies with whom Genji corresponds during his exile. If so, it is anomalous, since none of his loves actually visits Suma. All in all, the table appears to be a much less learned lacquer than the writing box. It exemplifies the shift in patronage from aristocrat to merchant which accounts for many of the changes in the Japanese decorative arts between about 1570 and 1620. We are well on the way to the generalized, even hackneyed, atmosphere of nostalgic decay which pervades much of the more conservative lacquer of the seventeenth century and later, and was so integral a part of the craftsman's stock-in-trade that it is even found, in the form of abandoned salt kilns and fishing huts, in the later types of lacquer intended for export to ignorant Europeans.[26]

1   Henry Smith ed., *Learning from Shōgun: Japanese History and Western Fantasy*, (Santa Barbara, 1980), fills in the correct historical background of the novel and assesses its educational worth.

2   Kyoto National Museum, *Kōgei ni miru koten bungaku ishō* ('Motifs from classical literature as seen in the decorative arts'), (Kyoto, 1980), pp. 302–306.

3   This famous piece, the *Kasugayama maki-e suzuribako* in the Nezu Museum, Tokyo, is reproduced in Okada Jō ed., *Nihon no shitsugei 2 maki-e II* ('Lacquer art of Japan volume 2: maki-e part II'), (Tokyo 1978), plates 58–59.

4   *Kokinshū* IV (214), by Mibu no Tadamine.

5   There is a good discussion in English of *Kōdaiji maki-e*: M. Yoshimura, 'Some Connections between Kodai-ji Makie and Export Lacquer', *Transactions of the Japan Society of London* 69, 70 (1973), pp. 34–38.

6   Through the good offices of Professor Yoshimura Motoo and Mr. Haino Akio.

7   Tokugawa Yoshinobu, 'Tenshō jūyonen o kagen to suru Kōdaiji maki-e chōdo' (Kōdaiji

Makie datable to 1586 or earlier), *Shikkōshi* 2 (1979), pp. 46–50.

8   For two examples see William Watson ed., *The Great Japan Exhibition*, (London 1981), cat. nos. 5, 6.

9   Oliver Impey, 'Japanese Export Lacquer of the 17th Century', in William Watson ed., *Lacquerwork in Asia and Beyond*, (London 1982) p. 126.

10   Impey, p. 126.

11   Information provided by Solene Morris of the British Museum (Natural History).

12   Victoria and Albert Museum, *The Destruction of the Country House*, (London 1975), plate 25.

13   S.H.A.H. ed., *Rushbrook Parish Registers 1567 to 1850...* (Woodbridge 1903), 403–4, 413, 416.

14   S.H.A.H., p. 159.

15   Robert Latham and William Matthews *eds.*, *The Diary of Samuel Pepys*, Vol. III, (London 1970), p. 263 (Sat. 22 Nov 1662).

16   S.P.D. Fr. 78.128 (Public Record Office).

17   Edmond Bonnaffé ed., *Inventaire des Meubles de Catherine de Medicis en 1589*, (Paris 1874), cat. nos. 186, 216, 292, 304, 305.

18   Kyoto National Museum, cat. no. 63.

19   From the *Jusammi Yorimasa-kyō shū*, cited in Kyoto National Museum, cat. no. 63.

20   Komatsu Taishū, 'Shitsugeihin ni okeru bungaku ishō' ('Literary motifs in lacquerware'), *Museum* 360 (March 1981), p. 4 ff.

21   *Wakanrōeishū*, 538.

22   *Wakanrōeishū*, 537.

23   *Wakanrōeishū*, 536.

24   *Wakanrōeishū*, 534, 531, 530.

25   Edward G. Seidensticker *trans.*, *The Tale of Genji*, (London 1976), p. 241.

26   Examples of such lacquers for export, incorporated in French furniture, may be seen in the Jones collection at the V&A.

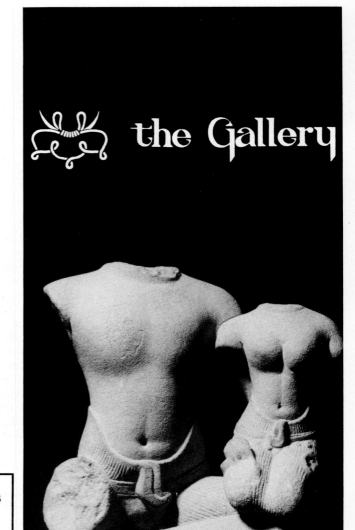
230

231

A GROUP OF CHINESE PORCELAINS OF THE DAOGUANG PERIOD (1821—1850)

Rose Kerr

Note: The Chinese dynasties referred to in this article are the Ming (1368–1644) and Qing (1644–1911) dynasties. Within the dynasties the reign periods mentioned are: Wanli (1573–1620): Kangxi (1662–1722 and previously romanized as K'ang Hsi): Yongzheng (1723–35, previously Yung Chêng): Qianlong (1736–95, previously Ch'ien Lung): Jiaqing (1796–1820, previously Chia Ch'ing): Daoguang (1821–50, previously Tao Kuang). Shende tang, the 'Hall for the cultivation of virtue', was previously romanized Shen Te T'ang.

'The reign of Tao Kuang is the last period of which collectors of Chinese ceramics take any account' stated R.L. Hobson in 1915.[1] Hobson was one of the most noted scholars of Chinese porcelain, and was to become Keeper of the Department of Ceramics and Ethnography at the British Museum. His views, published in his many works on Chinese ceramics, set the tone for the generally unfavourable view of nineteenth century products which has prevailed in recent times. European ceramic historians were unanimously of the opinion that post-eighteenth century pieces were both technically and artistically inferior to those produced during the golden reigns of Kangxi, Yongzheng and Qianlong.

'The Tao Kuang porcelain in the main is saved from utter banality by the traditions on which it was grounded and by the innate skill of the Chinese potters . . . But, speaking generally, the porcelain is a weak edition of the Yung Chêng type. The forms are correct but mechanical, the monochromes are mere understudies of the fine old colours, and the enamels are of exaggerated softness and weak in general effect.'[2] 'In the Tao Kuang period the decadence observed in the wares of the previous reign becomes more and more apparent. The porce-

lain material shows a marked degeneration in quality; the body is chalky and coarse in grain; and the glaze, which is bubbly, has that muslin-like texture which characterises the coarser Japanese wares, and an exaggerated oily sheen. Such is the common ware of the period, and its inferiority is emphasised by a few finer types which were still made, the last flicker of an art on the verge of extinction.'[3] 'By the reign of Tao Kuang there is a marked deterioration in both body and glaze. The body becomes a chalky white and thin, and the glaze of an oily sheen and muslin tone.'[4] 'For the greater part of the porcelain of the early 19th century, Ch'ien Lung themes were repeated . . . In fact, a considerable part of the Tao Kuang porcelain was made in revived Yung Cheng styles, themselves imitations of Ming shapes and patterns.'[5] 'The decline in standards, started in the reign of Ch'ien Lung, continued rapidly in the subsequent reigns of the Ch'ing dynasty . . . The decline is particularly noticeable in the quality of the porcelain itself and the white glaze. The clear smooth slightly greenish glaze of the early 18th century was replaced by a glaze of poor colour, often greyish, with a slightly uneven surface of the type described as "orange peel".'[6] 'In the absence of Imperial orders of importance, the porcelain of the period shows a marked degeneration which continued until the destruction of Chingtechen by the T'ai-p'ing rebels in 1853.'[7]

However, these uniformly harsh views of the lack of quality in Daoguang porcelain were not held by all Chinese scholars, and by those living at a closer historical remove to the period. At the very end of the Qing dynasty a civil servant called Chen Liu, who chose to write under the name of Ji Yuan Sou, 'The old man of the quiet garden', wrote a book called *Taoya* or 'Pottery Refinements'. First published

in 1906, the book is compounded of expert aesthetic judgements, practical advice on how to date one's pieces and how to distinguish original from reproduction and both from fake, and a leavening of wry comments (not meant for foreign ears) on the state of western knowledge and appreciation of Chinese ceramics! The author, a man with a deep love of porcelain and an income sufficient to allow him to indulge that passion, has rather more appreciative things to say on the subject.

'Tao Kuang reproductions do not differ by a grain or a scruple from eighteenth century wares. Until you turn them over and examine the label it is hardly possible to distinguish them. The polychrome dishes of Chia/Tao [i.e. the reigns of Jiaqing and Daoguang] depicting the "sixteen boys" on a ground of rubbed red closely follow K'ang [i.e. Kangxi] ware; for this reason the prices of the two do not differ much.' 'Dukes, ministers, chair-men and menials were not born so. People admire self-made men. Is this beyond belief? Consequently one rates the really splendid polychrome drawings on Tao Kuang pieces as no less valuable than K'ang polychromes.' 'The artists of Chia Ch'ing ware are very commonplace; far below those of Tao Kuang ware.'[8]

The first generation of Englishmen to become interested in the study of Chinese pottery were doing their own research in the same years as 'The old man of the quiet garden'. In spite of Chen's barbed comments the more learned among them were laying the foundations for a strong and ordered research tradition in this country. Stephen Wootton Bushell, physician to Her Britannic Majesty's Legation in Peking, was a scholar and connoisseur fluent in Chinese, who published two seminal works on the history of Asian ceramics in addition to translating important reference works from the

FIG.1 Bowl, porcelain decorated in enamels with hall-mark 'Made for the Hall for the cultivation of virtue' D: 17.5cm. C.293–1918.

Chinese. In his *Oriental Ceramic Art* of 1896 he comments in the chapter on the 'Modern Period, 1796–1895': 'A century has passed since the death of *Ch'ien-lung*, and there has been hardly any check to this steady progress of degeneration in any of the five reigns of his successors.' Such a gloomy view is modified with reference to particular items, and of Daoguang he says 'The finest work was lavished at this time on articles intended for ordinary use, such as soup-basins, rice-bowls, teacups with covers, and miniature wine-cups, and the seal mark of *Tao-kuang* is usually well represented in collections of such things.' William Giuseppe Gulland, a merchant and collector of fine porcelain opines in his *Chinese Porcelain* of 1902 that 'Many of the rice bowls made at this time are very beautiful, and much sought after by collectors.'

In the face of this equivocal assessment it is imperative to examine the Daoguang porcelain itself. The enormous bulk and range of ceramics produced during any one reign period necessitates the choice of top-quality wares for comparison. These 'official wares' were those produced at kilns set up and overseen by Imperially-appointed officials, and they were destined for use at court and in the homes of the wealthy and privileged. Their quality at most times exceeds that of ceramics produced at privately-owned kilns for the ordinary domestic and export trades.

There is no doubt that the Daoguang glazes do not approach the sparkling brilliance of Kangxi, nor the lambent honey tones of Yongzheng. The clear bright colours used in decoration in both reigns are unmatched, as is the calligraphic expressiveness of the painting on even the humblest vessels. On the other hand, the Daoguang porcelain compares favourably with many pieces produced during the second half of the eighteenth century. The cold white glittering glazes of late Qianlong are quite different to the lustrous glazes of Daoguang, which are warm in tone. The open 'muslin' texture of the latter only adds to their attractiveness. And the restrained and beautifully controlled painting which is a feature of Qianlong is continued on the best Daoguang ware. We should take care to view the porcelain production of the whole dynasty in its proper perspective. Nineteenth century wares do not match up to the brilliant products of the early eighteenth century; but in the parallel case of the preceding Ming dynasty, we are able to admire the late sixteenth century wares of Wanli, while according due honour to the incomparable porcelains of the fifteenth century.

The group of bowls chosen to illustrate this essay are all save one, examples of good quality ware. All except one bear the reign mark of Daoguang in sealscript on the base; the other piece has a hall mark which dates it to the period. The occurrence of reign period marks on Chinese porcelain has led to a certain amount of misunderstanding, although the mystery is easily resolved. Reign period marks are simply a way of writing the date. In the case of these Daoguang examples the mark is written in six characters *Da Qing Daoguang nian zhi* 'made during the Daoguang period of the great Qing dynasty'. (FIGS.2, 4, 6) Daoguang was not the personal name of the Emperor, but a title chosen on his accession in 1821 and meaning 'The Way (i.e. of government) Resplendent'. The fact that early reign marks are often copied onto later examples is a complication only resolved by appraisal of the porcelain itself. Happily, the Daoguang mark is very seldom seen on pieces made after the period.

The bowl illustrated in FIG.1 is decorated with cranes, one of the most common emblems of longevity. The sharp, acid enamel colours distinguish this as a late product, while the painting is rapidly executed and lively. On the base is the hall mark *Shende tang zhi* '*made for the Hall for the cultivation of virtue*'. Hall marks were first used during the sixteenth century, and continued to be inscribed on porcelains of the later Ming and Qing dynasties. They refer to the names or rooms, studies and libraries in the homes of the aristocracy and the scholarly, and were often used to designate pieces for specific halls in the Imperial Palace. Stephen Bushell claims that the Hall for the cultivation of virtue was a pavilion within the Palace founded by the Daoguang Emperor, although there is no positive confirmation for this. Chen Liu in his *Pottery Refinements* comments 'Shen Te T'ang pieces are unsurpassed Tao Kuang ware, able to rival Yung Cheng in beauty. For whiteness of the ground-work or elegance of colouring there is little to choose between them.' 'Shen Te T'ang is official ware of Tao Kuang. They fetch as much as top class pieces of Yung (Yongzheng) and Ch'ien (Qianlong). This is thanks to a passing vogue. I consider the best to be those with an upright label of three characters' (i.e. pieces like this bowl). [9]

Recent studies in China have sought to clarify the nature and dating of these hall marks. *The Palace Museum Journal* is a quarterly magazine devoted to research on the vast collection of the former Imperial Palace in Peking. In an article on porcelain inscriptions of the Ming and Qing dynasties Ye Peilan describes hall-marked pieces in the Palace Collection. [10] She quotes from a book entitled *Yinliu zhai shuo ci* 'Descriptions of porcelain from the study where drink flows', by a scholar called Xu Zhiheng who died in 1934. Xu has this to say: 'The Emperor, members of the aristocracy, ranking

Below: FIG.2 Bowl, porcelain decorated in
enamels outside and underglaze blue inside
with the reign period mark of Daoguang.
D: 14.6cm. 668–1903.

Bottom: FIG.3 Bowl, porcelain decorated in
enamels outside and underglaze blue inside
with the reign period mark of Daoguang.
D: 14.6cm. Circ. 631–1931.

Below: FIG.4 Bowl, porcelain decorated in enamels outside and underglaze blue inside with the reign period mark of Daoguang. D: 14.6cm. Circ. 494–1928.

Bottom: FIG.5 Dish, porcelain decorated in underglaze cobalt blue with the reign period mark of Daoguang. D: 17.7cm. FE.79–1983.

officials and top artisans all had pieces with hall (tang) and studio (zhai) marks. Marks like "library" and "mountain dwelling", like "treasure", "rare curio" and "elegant manufacture" were used by the aristocracy and officials, but not by the Emperor, and for this reason are referred to as "personal household marks".' 'In the Kangxi period there were (the marks) "Study where heaven is respected" and "Hall for the attainment of harmony"; in the Qianlong period there were the "Peaceful mirrored hall", the "Hall where harmony is nourished" and the "Hall where careful action is reverenced", which were all the names of halls within the palace. Hence names with a Confucian philosophical flavour quickly became fashionable among the newly-created noblemen and princes. Such names were the "Study where I lead my humble existence" and the "Hall of continuing reputation" during the reign of Kangxi; the "Hall of reverent awe" and the "Library of upright conduct" during the reigns of Yongzheng and Qianlong; the "Study of peaceful repose", the "Study of remote tranquillity" and the "Study of virtuous honesty" during the Qianlong and Jiaqing periods; and the "Hall for the cultivation of virtue", the "Hall for planting roots" and the "Hall where permanence exists" during the reigns of Jiaqing and Daoguang. On the whole all these marks are on objects owned by the newly-created noblemen and princes.' In the article Ye Peilan goes on to cite examples of more than fifty Daoguang period hallmarks that occur on porcelains in the Peking Palace collection. This is a surprisingly large range, and contrasts with the half dozen or so marks quoted in most western reference works on the subject.

The bowls in FIGS.2, 3 and 4 are painted in an interesting combination of underglaze and overglaze colours. The insides bear scenes painted in underglaze blue, while the same subjects are repeated in delicate enamelled 'medallions' outside, set in a thick enamel ground which has been engraved while still wet with feathery scroll patterns. Brightly-coloured enamelled designs which covered the whole surface of the porcelain came into vogue during the second half of the eighteenth century. The first inspiration for this rich, dense style of decoration came from Ming dynasty 'three-coloured' enamelled wares, and it is a style which has remained popular in China down to the present day. These pieces interpret the theme in a manner typical of Daoguang, combining a number of disparate colours, textures and motifs in an integrated scheme. The blue-ground bowl contains scenes from the Chinese story about the Herdsman and the Weaver-girl, mythical figures corresponding to the star constellations Aquila and Vega. These two lovers, cruelly separated by the Sun-king, are only able to meet once a year. On the seventh night of the seventh moon myriads of magpies fly up to the firmament, to construct a living bridge across the flood of stars of the Silver Stream of Heaven (The Milky Way). The second bowl is decorated with three rams, because the Chinese word for ram is a pun on yang, the positive principle in nature; thus 'triple yang' signifies great good fortune. The bowl with an engraved dark pink background is painted with auspiciously-combined flowers and fruit, both inside and outside.

Bowls with this style of decoration have always been numerous and popular with collectors, and the V&A's collection contains examples with a variety of coloured grounds. They used to be known as 'medallion bowls' or 'Peking bowls', two rather silly names that Stephen Bushell condemns with scorn. 'The "medallion bowls" of this period are perhaps the most general favourites, and in London, at Christie's auction-rooms, where they are wont to figure under the name of "Peking basins", they are seldom sold for less than ten guineas a pair. The name is as misleading as that of "Nanking blue and white", as porcelain was never made at either Peking or Nanking. The bowls are found at Peking today, because they were sent there from Ching-te-chen at the time they were made for the service of the emperor.' [11]

The designs on the insides of these three bowls make it clear that underglaze blue was still being used with some skill as a decorative medium in the nineteenth century. Following the introduction of a fresh range of enamel colours during the third decade of the eighteenth century, blue and white became less popular, and by the 1820s formed only a very small percentage of the total ceramic output. The dish in FIG.5 is an example of high-quality Daoguang 'official ware', and is painted in a clear, strong cobalt blue. The garden scene depicted contains an ornamental rock with growing plants which all represent longevity. The plum puts forth blossom on leafless and apparently lifeless branches, the pine is evergreen and does not wither in winter, while the bamboo flourishes all year round and bends before the fiercest storm without breaking. Together these plants are known by the Chinese as the 'Three Friends of Winter'. The sprigs of fungus are also emblematic of longevity, because of their durability when dried. Symbolic decorations of this kind reached their peak of popularity during the Qing dynasty, and this particular design was so suitable as to be used on official wares of other eighteenth and nineteenth century reigns.

The most important addition to the ceramic painter's palette in the eighteenth century had been a rose

Below: FIG.6 Bowl, porcelain decorated in enamels with the reign period mark of Daoguang. D: 11.8cm. C. 763–1909.

Bottom: FIG.7 Octagonal bowl, porcelain decorated in enamels with the reign period mark of Daoguang. D: 14.6cm. 669–1853.

pink derived from gold. This pink enamel was discovered in Europe and used in France and Germany in the seventeenth century, and it reached China in the 1720s. At the same time it became possible to add white enamel to the whole range of overglaze colours, thus doubling the range of tones available by producing an extended range of opaque pastel tints. This new and expanded range of colours, with the pink enamel predominating, gives rise to the Chinese porcelain wares which Europeans have called 'famille rose'. It is an attractive form of decoration, and one which has remained favourite with the Chinese till now. The bowl in FIG.6 reflects the Daoguang treatment of this style. Minutely detailed painting sets a range of lucky animals and plants in an improbable landscape; huge flowers grow to half the height of a tree, while a large red carp pops up behind water weeds. This whimsical quality is often found in late Qing painting on porcelain.

Having illustrated a range of the better quality Daoguang wares, we shall glance briefly at those which have caused the connoisseurs to shudder with such exaggerated disdain. The octagonal bowl in FIG.7 bears a six-character mark in red on the base, and was acquired by the museum in 1853. We may surmise that it was made not long before 1850, for it resembles a class of ordinary-quality porcelains which were produced in large numbers during the second half of the century. The thickly-potted body is covered with glutinous enamel glazes, producing a marked 'orange peel' effect. While the decoration outside is related to that seen on the 'medallion' bowls, the crudity of execution precludes comparison. Nonetheless, there is a vigour in both potting and painting which made these wares popular both at home and among the overseas Chinese communities in Malaysia and Singapore. Bowls like these are the ancestors of the brash, attractive tablewares which you may use in your local Chinese restaurant today.

Photography by Ian Thomas.

1   R. L. Hobson, *Chinese Pottery and Porcelain, An Account of the Potter's Art in China from Primitive Times to the Present Day*, volume II, (London 1915), p. 263.

2   *Ibidem*

3   R. L. Hobson, *The Later Ceramic Wares of China* (London 1925), p. 89.

4   Soame Jenyns, *Later Chinese Porcelain* (London 1951) p. 72.

5   W. B. Honey, *Guide to the Later Porcelain* (London 1927), p. 58.

6   Sir Harry Garner, *Oriental Blue and White* (London 1954) p. 51.

7   H. A. van Oort, *Chinese Porcelain of the 19th and 20th Centuries* (The Netherlands, Lochem 1977), p. 23.

8   Transl. Geoffrey R. Sayer, *T'ao Ya or Pottery Refinements* (London 1959), sections 284, 482, 207.

9   *op. cit.* sections 213, 102.

10   *Gugong Bowuyuan Yuankan*, 1983 no. 2, pp. 62–69.

11   S. W. Bushell, M.D. *Oriental Ceramic Art*, (London 1896), p. 240.

240

AN ATTIC BLACK-FIGURE NECK AMPHORA: 530–500 BC

Side A: depicting the god Hermes seated to the right, holding a caduceus and kantharos. The god Dionysus reclining and leaning against a cushion, a kantharos in his right hand, quiver and sword in the field above him.

Side B: depicting two pairs of Satyrs and Maeneads dancing.

This amphora belongs to the Antimenes painter.

Height 12 inches (30·5 cm.)

BARAKAT

Klaber and Klaber

Antique Porcelain & Enamels

A rare pair of Bow goat and sheep groups with putti representing Spring and Autumn.
Brillant colours. Circa 1770. Height approx. 8 inches.

2a Bedford Gardens, Kensington Church Street, London W8 7EH
Telephone: 01-727 4573

salviati&c.

glassmakers in Murano since 1859

Venice, San Gregorio 195
Murano, Fondamenta Radi 16
Milan, Via Montenapoleone 29

Victoria and Albert Museum, Room 112 Bethnal Green Museum, Room 18 Other pieces may be seen on request.

Röbbig, Munich

Rare pieces from the Swan Service made for Count Brühl. Modelled by J.J. Känder and F.R. Eberlein. Meissen, circa 1738.

EARLY GERMAN PORCELAIN

Prannerstraße 3-5
8000 Munich 2, WEST Germany
Tel: 089/227509

ARCHIMEDE
SEGUSO

CHINESE PORCELAIN AND ENGLISH GOLDSMITHS c.1560 TO c.1660

Philippa Glanville

'The principal wares after the jewels... consisted of spices, drugges, silks, calicots, quilts, carpets and colours... the rest of the wares were many in number but less in value; as elephants' teeth, porcelain vessels of China, coconuts, hides, eben wood as black as jet.' (Cargo of the carrack *Madre de Dios* captured by an English privateer off the Azores, 1592.)

Chinese porcelain was so rare and highly prized in Tudor England that it could not be valued as other Eastern commodities were; bowls, dishes and flasks which arrived here in the sixteenth century were treated as treasures equal to other exotic materials such as lignum vitae, serpentine, coconut, ostrich eggs and crystal, and they acquired handsome silver-gilt mounts, and romantic associations. It is these mounts with their hall-marks and date letters that enable us to trace the rapidly evolving late Elizabethan taste for porcelain.

The V&A has been fortunate recently to acquire by private treaty purchase the Trenchard bowl, of Jia Jing [Chia Ching] porcelain, which has been in a Dorset family since the sixteenth century (FIG.1). It is painted in underglaze blue with peony flowers outside and fish inside, and has been well known to students of Chinese porcelain for over a century. According to family tradition, it was a gift, together with another bowl, from Philip, Archduke of Austria and Joanna, his wife. The royal couple, whose ship was driven ashore at Weymouth in 1506, were entertained at Wolfeton House, near Dorchester, by Sir Thomas Trenchard, High Sheriff of Dorset. These two bowls, portraits of their royal guests, a cedar coffer and an ironbound chest, were

FIG.3 Bottle: Wanli with silver-gilt mounts, London, maker's mark three trefoils slipped. Metropolitan Museum of Art 44.14.3.

supposedly passed down in the Trenchard family as souvenirs of the visit. However, in the Trenchard wills and probate inventories of the seventeenth century examined so far, these treasures are not mentioned and the earliest printed reference to them occurs in Hutchins's *History and Antiquities of Dorset* (1868)[1]. Unfortunately, this charming account of how the two bowls came to the Trenchard family is also at odds with the evidence of both the mounts and the porcelain vessel they enclose, for the bowl was made in China in the second half of the sixteenth century, (the reign name Jia Jing covering the period 1522–1566), and the mounts are struck with the London hall-mark and date letter for 1599.

The English were slow to develop a taste for porcelain, partly because the country was poorly placed, on the fringe of Europe, to acquire it by the long-established overland route through Turkey. Judging by the Jewel House inventories, neither Henry VII nor Henry VIII owned any mounted porcelain, despite the latter's anxiety to acquire rarities in competition with other European princes, and the celadon bowl at New College, Oxford, said to have been presented by Archbishop Warham before 1530, is the sole example with an English provenance before the 1560s (FIG.2).

Gradually, from the 1560s, porcelain appeared in England, thanks initially to the trading activities of the Portuguese. Once their trading station in Macao was established in 1557, they broke into the long-established export trade in porcelain from the Jingdezhen kilns to South East Asia. Tributaries from this trade had carried porcelain up the Red Sea to Persia and Turkey for a century or more. A pair of small Jia Jing bowls, one of which is in the museum, were brought from Turkey by Count Eberhardt von Man-

derscheidt in 1583 and given European mounts; these are typical of export porcelain intended for the Turkish market. Englishmen active in the Levant trade were also clearly well-placed to dip into the stream of porcelain reaching Istanbul. But the greater bulk of Wanli export porcelain was carried by the Portuguese carracks directly to Lisbon and most remained in the Iberian peninsula – the 1602 inventory of Philip II's possessions shows that he owned hundreds of pieces of blue and white porcelain.

As Portuguese carracks increased in capacity, (by 1600 they had reached 1,000 tons), so the English privateers seized the opportunity to acquire oriental trade goods without the trouble of travelling so far. Sherds of export porcelain found in Drake's Bay near San Francisco, are apparently souvenirs of Sir Francis Drake's visit in the *Golden Hind* in 1579.[2]

Captain Burroughs' capture of the heavily-laden carrack *Madre de Dios* off the Azores in 1592 is only the best-documented of the means whereby wealthy English noblemen came by porcelain; but it remained rare at least until the second decade of the seventeenth century. Even lavishly-equipped Hardwick Hall in Derbyshire could boast in 1601 of only one piece of porcelain, 'a pursland cup with a cover trimmed with silver and gilt weighing 14 ounces',[3] and cabinets of curiosities, such as the one in London visited by Thomas Platter in 1599, now contained a few pieces among the 'Arteficialia', or man-made wonders.

All the larger wares known to have reached England before 1600 are standard Wanli or Jia Jing export porcelain – bowls, small and large, dishes, wine ewers and *kendi* (bottles for the Malayan market, later adopted by the smokers of the Near East as nargilehs or water-pipes). Production in quantity specifically for the European mar-

FIG.1 The Trenchard bowl: Jia Jing porcelain with English mounts. London, 1599, maker's mark IH in a shaped shield. Ht. 16.6cm. VAM M.945-1983.

FIG.2 Archbishop Warham's cup: Yuan celadon ware with English silver-gilt mounts, unmarked *c*. 1516. New College, Oxford.

FIG.4 Bowl: Wanli, with silver-gilt mounts, English, unmarked, *c.* 1580–1600, engraved with a band of scrolling flowers. Ht. 21.5cm. Burghley House, Stamford.

ket began only in the early seventeenth century for the Dutch East India Company, although the Portuguese had apparently placed orders for bottles specially painted with the sign IHS as early as the 1540s. Wine ewers and bowls made handsome sideboard display plate when mounted up and it is likely that the group of porcelain in late Elizabethan mounts sold in 1888 from Burghley House, in Lincolnshire (now in the Metropolitan Museum, New York) were originally paired up for this purpose, like their equivalents in silver-gilt (FIG.3).[4]

The English royal collection in the 1580s still contained only a few porcelain vessels: two mounted bowls were gifts from members of the Cecil family (which, given the group of porcelain formerly at Burghley, is suggestive) and a third was given by a Mr Lichfield. Although there may have been unmounted porcelain elsewhere in the palace (the Queen is said to have

eaten dessert from porcelain dishes) it is likely that, given its rarity and value, it would have been stored in, and listed by, the Jewel House, along with other valuable materials such as jasper and crystal.[5]

The Trenchard bowl is not unusual in being linked to a royal personage. Mounted porcelain, with its quality of rarity and exoticism, frequently attracted royal associations, whether genuine or spurious. A cup in the Museum of London, mounted on a silver-gilt stem in about 1580, is said to have belonged to Mary Queen of Scots. This association cannot be authenticated and the link with that unfortunate queen may well have been the product of an enthusiastic later owner's fancy. A Wanli bowl at Burghley House, with simple strap mounts and a lipband engraved with scrolling flowers, is said to been a christening gift from Elizabeth I (FIG.4).[6]

An earlier bowl, now in the

Metropolitan Museum, has a rather stronger claim to royal ownership. This bowl, of Jia Jing porcelain with *kinrandi* red enamel outside and underglaze painting inside, was fitted with silver-gilt mounts in about 1570. Only a maker's mark, a bird in a shaped shield, is struck on the mounts. This anonymous goldsmith is noted for the very high quality of his work, from a nautilus cup of 1557 recently acquired by the Victoria and Albert Museum to a handsome standing salt of 1572 at the Vintners' Company. The dates of his hallmarked plate, coupled with the years of activity of the Jewel House supplier Affabel Partridge, suggest that the bird punch may have been adopted by this royal goldsmith.[7] The cup was a gift from James II to his Groom of the Stairs, H. Green of Rolleston Hall and descended in the latter's family until purchased for the collection of Sir Samuel Montague. How this cup came to England and into the hands of a royal goldsmith is unknown, and the same is true of one more small drinking vessel, the earliest of this handful of Elizabethan mounted porcelains. The Lennard cup, a white porcelain bowl, painted inside in underglaze blue with animals, in mounts of 1569, descended from its first English owner, the Devon gentleman Samuel Lennard (1553–1618), until it was sold in the 1930s to that eminent collector of Chinese porcelain Percival David (FIG.5). The maker's mark, RF conjoined, has been assigned recently to the goldsmith Roger Flynt. These small bowls and rectangular boxes, like one in the University of Toronto Museum, with mounts of about 1570 (formerly in the Lee of Fareham Collection) are the smallest and most portable of the typical export wares reaching Turkey in the mid-sixteenth century and may have come to England via the Levant.[8]

Although the Trenchard bowl is of

Below: FIG.5 The Lennard cup: Jia Jing painted in underglaze blue, with silver-gilt mounts and cover, London 1569, maker's mark RF conjoined. Ht. 11.9cm. Percival David Foundation, University of London.

Opposite: FIG.6 Wine ewer: Wanli porcelain with silver-gilt mounts. London, *c.* 1600, maker's mark three trefoils slipped. Ht. 25.5cm. VAM 7915-1862

Bottom: FIG.7 Bowl: Wanli porcelain with silver-gilt mounts. London, *c.* 1580, maker's marks three trefoils slipped. Diam. 19.6cm. Franks Collection, 22.

Jia Jing porcelain and so was made earlier than the rather greater number of Wanli bowls, flasks and dishes with late Elizabethan mounts, there is a homogeneity about the mounts of these larger porcelain vessels which suggests that they may have arrived in London and been dispersed among members of the court at one and the same time, presumably the fruits of a raid on a carrack. Because the same figure handles appear on the two bowls from Burghley and one of the Burghley ewers, it has been argued that a single London workshop was responsible.[9]

Another version of this double-tailed handle is known on an agate ewer of 1579, belonging to the Duke of Rutland; on this the grotesque figure is reversed and faces inwards towards the lip. The goldsmith's mark on the marked pieces in this group, three trefoils slipped, is associated with other high-quality mounted wares, such as the V&A's porcelain wine ewer, of a type popular in Persia, with London mounts of 1585 (FIG.6). But the Trenchard bowl bears another London goldsmith's mark altogether, despite the close similarity of its handles. In addition to the Burghley bowls, three more Wanli bowls with English mounts are known, one in the Franks collection by the three trefoils maker (FIG.7), another very similar, but unmarked, in the Schroder collection, and a third in Ireland; the last has the faun and mermaid-tailed handles of the Trenchard bowl.[10] Versions of these cast caryatid straps are found on English-mounted wares from the 1550s and with the marks of several different goldsmiths. Thus it is probable that these common elements were supplied by a goldsmith specialising in cast components such as handles and straps. Once assembled, the components were then marked with the retailing goldsmith's punch. For this reason it is unwise to attribute unmarked

FIG.8 Ewer: Wanli porcelain with English mounts, unmarked *c.* 1600. Ht. 28.5cm. Schroder collection.

pieces, such as the mounted ewer in the Schroder collection (FIG.8) to a particular goldsmith on the basis of stylistic parallels with a fully-marked object. In the second half of the sixteenth century there were too many goldsmiths at work in London for us to be able to pick out and name individuals without supporting evidence; the proportion of Elizabeth plate surviving is so small that we simply do not have enough examples from which to generalise.

To take the mounts of the Trenchard bowl as an example: the goldsmith's mark, IH in a shaped shield, is found on three mounts for Chinese porcelain between 1585 and 1599, two in the V&A and one at Hardwick. However, at least three other versions of the IH mark are found on late Elizabethan plate, one with an arrow bisecting the H, another with pellets above and below the letters, and a third with IH above a bear. The arrow IH maker has been convincingly identified as John Harrison, who practised his trade at the sign of the Broad Arrow, in Cheapside. The goldsmith using the IH mark with pellets certainly made mounts occasionally: there is at Burghley a coconut cup of 1591 with mounts by him of exceptional quality (although the coconut presumably cracked and so has been replaced later in silver).[11] It is impossible to associate these IH marks with a named individual. Forty-four goldsmiths with these initials were potentially active in London in the 1590s. Their names were noted in the Wardens' Minute Books and first Apprenticeship Register at Goldsmiths' Hall, some for trade offences, other when they became free or took apprentices or were appointed to some Company office. Some of these men were no doubt jewellers and a few may never have registered a mark, but there remains a substantial body of candidates.[12]

FIG.9 Ewer: Wanli porcelain with English mounts, London 1589, maker's mark IH in a shaped shield. Ht. 32cm. National Trust (Hardwick Hall).

The history of the Hardwick Hall, Wanli ewer, with mounts of 1589 (FIG.9) by the goldsmith who mounted the Trenchard bowl, is not known. It was restored in the nineteenth century, when a fresh porcelain disc was inserted in the lid. At that time, the thumb piece and flange were replaced in mock-Tudor style, although, since the full hall-marks are struck on the lid's lining and agree with those on the handle mount, the Elizabethan goldsmith clearly did provide a lid originally. It may have been bought by the sixth Duke of Devonshire (1790–1858) whose passion for refurnishing the house in antiquarian style is well-documented; certainly a flourishing collectors' market in Elizabethan mounted wares can be detected by the 1850s. Thanks to this buoyant demand, a set of mounts and caryatid straps have survived from a large decagonal porcelain dish and were acquired by the V&A from the J.C. Robinson collection. These bear the hall-mark and date letter for 1595 and again, same IH mark (FIG.10). The bowl, of a shape unusual in Wanli export porcelain, had been broken and was replaced some time before 1879 by the antique dealer, Durlacher, with an elegantly carved walnut bowl.

The Portuguese had never considered porcelain an important article for the northern European market, but after 1602 when the Dutch East India Company was founded, the bulk trade in export porcelain was dominated by the Dutch and far more porcelain percolated through to England. The cargo of the *Witte Leeuw*, or White Lion, a Dutch trading vessel sunk in James Bay at St. Helena in 1613, contained large quantities of standard Wanli export porcelains – some three hundred plates, dishes and bowls in standard sizes with a few kendi, flasks and boxes.[13]

All these types of *kraakporselein* are

FIG.11 Transitional porcelain vase, with English silver-gilt mounts, *c.* 1665, maker's mark of Wolfgang Howzer. Ht. 30.5cm. VAM M.308-1962.

FIG.12 Detail of chasing on cover of vase: the hound finial and probably the greyhound handles are heraldic, referring to the crest of the purchaser.

FIG.10 Mounted wooden bowl: detail of caryatid strap. Mounts London 1596, maker's mark IH in a shaped shield. VAM 163-1879.

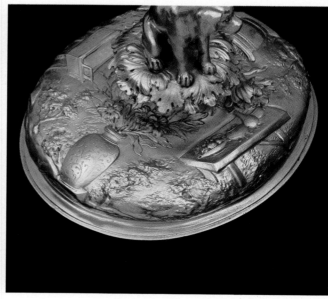

familiar from Dutch paintings from about 1605–1640; the general custom was to set out fruit at the dessert stage of the meal in a porcelain dish, to honour guests with objects of beauty. A similar attitude inspired early Italian artists, the first of whom to depict a porcelain fruit bowl was Francesco Banaglio in about 1470.

In England, as porcelain rapidly became less of a rarity and more of a commodity, values reflected this shift. When the plate and household goods of Henry Howard, Earl of Northampton, were appraised in 1614, a cupboard containing 'Seeven parcels of Purslane cuppes trimmed with silver and gilt' was valued at twelve pounds whereas a single ivory cup garnished with pearls and precious stones was valued at more than thirty-eight pounds.[14] Sets of porcelain cups and plates begin to appear in English inventories and a clear distinction emerges between these tablewares, and 'cabinet' or curious pieces, such as the martaban (container jar) and Wanli jar in the Tradescant collection, both presumably acquired before 1637. The inventory of the possessions of Lettice, Countess of Leicester, taken on 7 January 1634, lists in her sweetmeat closet 'six pursland fruit dishes, unmounted', but these, even when thrown in with 'bone lace of diverse sorts, glass bottles, many glasses and diverse other trifles', were still only valued at forty shillings. By contrast, among her plate and jewels was a 'pursland bottle with a gilt foot and a gilt cover' valued at forty-five shillings, but rather more, three pounds and four shillings, was set on a relatively common object, a stone jug, 'covered and bounden with silver-gilt'.[15]

When the goods of Charles I at the Wardrobe in Denmark House were appraised for sale in August 1649, one piece, 'a great Porcelain Basson sett in a Foote and Frame' of silver-gilt with two handles had survived all the vicissitudes of the previous decade and was valued at the high figure of forty pounds. Also at Denmark House were seven parcels of porcelain, mostly sets and some valued as low as ten shillings. Some were display pieces, like the waterpots and beakers noted, significantly, straight after a set of hanging shelves, but thirty-six porringers and saucers indicate that tableware was present. By 1614 the Dutch East India Company was specifying European forms such as mustard pots, beer mugs and butter dishes and sending wooden models to be copied from the 1630s; this reference to porringers and saucers demonstrates that the English market was benefiting too. It has been estimated that by 1638 over three million pieces of Chinese porcelain had been shipped to Europe by the Dutch.[16]

Among the mounted wares in the Upper Jewel House, which contained exotic and precious materials – agate, amber, rhinoceros horn, lapis lazuli, heliotrope, jasper, and mother-of-pearl – there was in 1649 only one piece of porcelain: 'a cheynye large pott with an eagle beake and serpent handle with a cover richly garnished', valued at £50. This was clearly exceptional, both in weight and in quality, and presumably therefore highly saleable.[17]

By the 1620s London potters were producing imitations in tin-glazed earthenware of such Wanli designs as the bird on a rock; these painted earthenware versions were so popular that they have been found not only on widely-scattered English sites of the period, but also on colonial sites in Virginia, an indication of how familiar porcelain had become within less than a generation and how rapidly the taste for it had spread to Londoners.[18]

Porcelain reaching England after the Restoration, like the splendid collection at Burghley House, was either unmounted or given trumpery mounts, an indication that it was no longer seen as an immense curiosity, to be given mounts worthy in value and complexity of its own rarity and beauty, but that it was either display ware or practical tableware, suitable for teapots, small jugs and the like.[19]

Certainly there were exceptions; the museum is fortunate to possess a high-quality Transitional export jar, which has been fitted in London in about 1665 with silver-gilt mounts of a commensurate quality (FIG. 10). These are marked by the Zurich-born goldsmith Wolfgang Howzer, who was noted for his skill in embossing and was employed on several Jewel House orders in the 1660s. The cover is chased with a table, incense burner and a vase, all motifs which are inspired by the painting on the porcelain. The goldsmith's work is very different from the sketchy flat-chased chinoiseries of the 1680s; here Howzer has consciously created an objet d'art to grace a king's or nobleman's cabinet.[20] However, porcelain was now normally regarded far more casually in England, as an incident recounted by a French visitor in 1671 illustrates:

'Walking in the beautiful orchard at Epping the Countess of Castlemaine ordered a syllabub to be prepared, and people hurried to the house to bring the necessary things. These consisted of a great basin of Chinese porcelain with silver handles, into which before our eyes, was put a good quantity of white sugar already pounded, and then two flagons of Canary wine over the said sugar, mixing until the wine looked clear, the sure sign that the sugar was sufficiently melted. Then, and I could scarcely believe my eyes, while Mon. de Grammont and de Saint-Evremont were unable to prevent themselves laughing, the basin was placed between the hind legs of a great cow which happened to be grazing in the orchard just where we were walking; and behold, a dairy maid set herself to milking the cow over the basin, and the milk flowed gurgling and foaming into the wine. Some goblets were quickly filled with a large silver gilt spoon, and I can affirm that it is an excellent beverage'.[21]

1 O. Pickard-Cambridge 'On the relics left by Philip and Joan of Castile in 1506 at Wolfeton House, Dorset and preserved in the writer's family'. *Dorset Natural History and Antiquarian Field Club*, XXXV (1914), pp. 1–7; John Hutchins *The History and Antiquities of the County of Dorset* III, (1868), pp. 328–30.

2 Rijksmuseum, Amsterdam *The Ceramic Load of the Witte Leeuw 1613* (1982). O. Impey *Chinoiserie* (1977), pp. 92–3.

3 L. Boynton 'The Hardwick Hall Inventory of 1601' *Furniture History* VII (1971).

4 Burlington Fine Art Club *Early Chinese Pottery and Porcelain* (1910), pl. XXXIII; L. Avery 'Chinese Porcelain in English Mounts' *Bulletin of Metropolitan Museum of Art*, New York, May 1944, discusses the Burghley pieces.

5 A.J. Collins *Jewels and Plate of Queen Elizabeth: the 1574 Inventory* 1955, nos. 1577, 1580, 1582. By 1550 there were in the Jewel House two 'faire Laires (ewers) of Purslaine' among the Banqueting House plate, nos. 1080 and 1099. Another 1550 cup, no. 347, was almost certainly made of shell, not porcelain.

6 I.G. Lang *The Wrestling Boys: Chinese and Japanese ceramics from the 16th to the 18th century* (Stamford 1983), p.126.

7 However, his shop sign was the Bull so the bull's head device is also a strong candidate. T.F. Reddaway 'Goldsmiths Row in Cheapside 1558–1645' *Guildhall Miscellany* III (1963), pp. 181–206. This cup is illustrated in *Highlights of the Untermyer Collection* (1977) no. 3

8 M. Medley *Porcelains decorated in underglaze blue and copper red in the Percival David Foundation* (1963); W. Watts *Works of Art in Silver and other Metals* (of Fareham collection) (1936), p.15. The stem has been damaged and foreshortened.

9 T. Schroder *Virtuoso Goldsmiths Work* (exhibition catalogue 1979), no. 69.

10 H. Read and A. Tonnochy *Catalogue of Silver Plate: the Franks Bequest* 1928, 22; Schroder, 68. The Irish bowl is pl. 17 in Y. Hackenbroch 'Chinese Porcelain in European Silver Mounts' *Connoisseur* CXXVIII, (1956).

11 T. Webster, *Catalogue of Silver at Burghley House* (1984)

12 The Wardens' Minute Books run from 1334 to the present; the only gap is the volume 1578–1592, destroyed in the Assay Office fire of 1681. Fortunately this coincides with the first Apprenticeship Register, the Book called the Dormant, started in 1578.

13 *Witte Leeuw* (1982) pp. 44–5.

14 'The inventory of Henry Howard, K.G. Earl of Northampton, 16 June 1614' *Archaeologia* XLII, (1869), pp. 347–74.

15 J.O. Halliwell *Ancient Inventories* (1854).

16 O. Millar 'Inventories and Valuations of the King's Goods 1649–1651' *Walpole Society* XLIII, (1972), pp. 121–2; T. Volker *Porcelain and the Dutch East India Company* (Lieden 1954), pp. 121–6.

17 Millar, p. 30. It weighed forty-one pounds.

18 I. Noel-Hume *Early English Delftware from London and Virginia* Colonial Williamsburg Papers in Archaeology (1977).

19 E.J. Lang (1983), pp. 171–3.

20 C. Oman *Caroline Silver* (1970), pp. 33–4.

21 Sieur de Noyer, quoted in 'Syllabub: A French View', Elizabeth David, *Petit Propos Culinaires*, 6, Oct. 1980.

BOSSI
JOAILLIER
GENÈVE

ANCIENNE MAISON LOMBARD

Who has not heard of the prestigious HOUSE of LOMBARD in Geneva, which under the magic touch of its creator, Mr. Jean LOMBARD, has supplied for several decades his faithful 'clientèle' from all over the world with a great and unique variety of 'objets d'art'.

During his marvellous career, Mr. Jean Lombard had the quite unique opportunity of co-operating with Fabergé's grandson, Carl-Théodore Fabergé, for more than 15 years.

How many fascinating objects can be admired in the House of Lombard: historical pieces, Russian objets d'art by the most famous Imperial silversmiths as Fabergé, Morozov, Ovchinikov, Sazikov, Fabergé's grandson, ancient jewels belonging to various European Royal Families and a great number of Mr. Lombard's original creations.

Today, Mr. Jean Lombard has retired and he has passed on the torch to Mr. André BOSSI, who took over the House in September 1983. But don't worry, nothing will change at 19 Rue de la Cité, in the old town of Geneva... Everything will be carried out in the same spirit, in the same atmosphere of tradition as before and at the same time, Mr. Bossi, who is admirably backed up by his artistical wife, will introduce a younger touch, in order to always maintain this famous House as: *'Le Dernier Rempart de la Joie de Vivre!'*.

Mr. André Bossi will be exhibiting at the PALACE of ST. MORITZ from February 7th to February 12th 1985 and will be very happy and honoured to welcome you.

19, rue de la Cité, Vieille Ville   1204 GENÈVE   Tél. 022 213244/213245

PAUL STORR

A fine pair of George III Entree Dishes and Heater Stands. Maker Paul Storr. London 1819
Weight 155 oz.

TESSIERS LTD

SPECIALISTS IN ANTIQUE JEWELLERY, SILVER & OBJECTS D'ART

ARMS

The arms are those of Codrington for Sir Edward Codrington (1770–1851), GCB, KLS, KSG, admiral of the Red. He commanded HMS *Orion* at the battle of Trafalgar in 1805, the allied fleets at Navarin in 1827 and was MP for Devonport from 1832 to 1839.

26 NEW BOND STREET, LONDON W1Y 0JY

01-629 0458

Members of The British Antique Dealers Association

Set of four George III Silver Wine Coolers
Two by Paul Storr London 1815
Two by Philip Rundell London 1819
Weight: 363 oz.

260

J. KUGEL

ANTIQUAIRE

279, RUE St HONORÉ, PARIS. 8ᵉ

TÉL. 260.86.23
——— 260.19.45

A pair of ormoulu wine-coolers by Matthew BOULTON ca 1780
Height: 8½″

262

264

HARRY WINSTON
of New York

NEW YORK	GENEVE	PARIS	MONTE CARLO
718 Fifth Avenue	24 Quai du Général Guisan	29 Avenue Montaigne	Hôtel de Paris

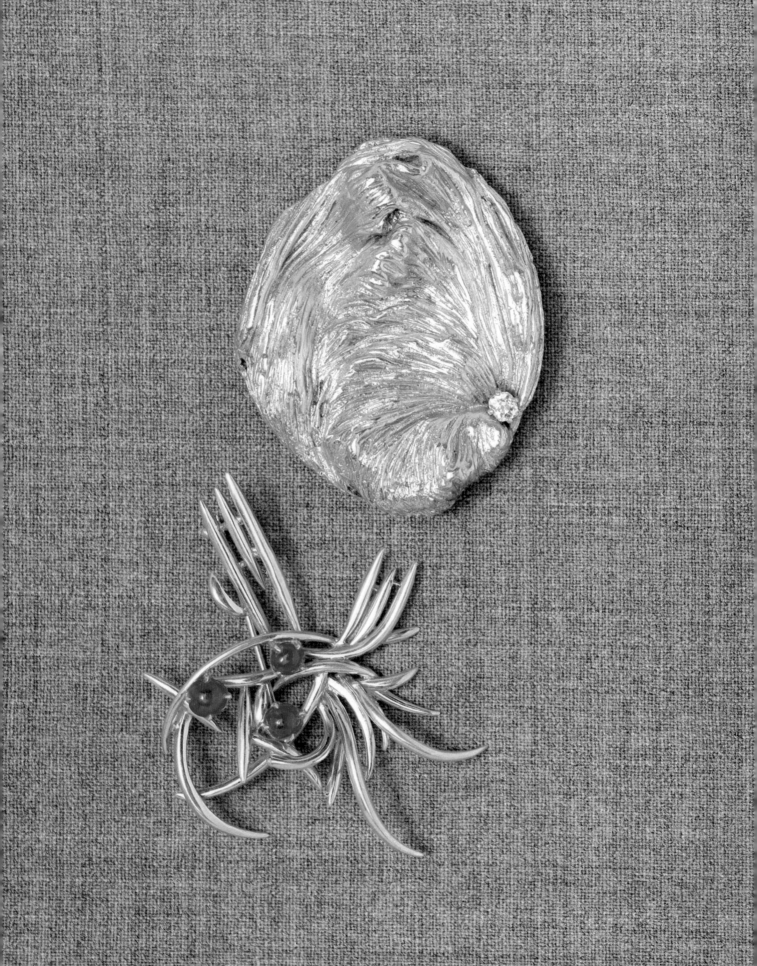

THE COLLECTION OF POST-1920 JEWELLERY IN THE V&A

A. Somers Cocks

Any account of the modern jewellery scene in England has to start with the vast 1961 exhibition of jewellery from 1890 to 1961 in Goldsmiths' Hall in the City of London. This assembled nine hundred items, valued even then at three million pounds, and showed Jean Schlumberger's fashionable gem-studded creations with Jean Fouquet's abstract Modern designs, next to a wire necklace by Alexander Calder, next to artist-craftsman's work by Gerda Flockinger. It was an extraordinary, unprecedented, and most catholic event, free from the quasi-political prejudice of those who think that if one admires the Arts and Crafts movement and its modern successors, one is morally obliged to despise the expensive commercial end of the market. It also avoided parochialism, and showed work from nearly every European country, and as far afield as Brazil and India. The sucess which the exhibition enjoyed lasted far beyond it because it gave great stimulus to the art colleges and schools of design to see jewellery-making as more than a merely repetitive manual skill verging on the industrial, but as an art form with great opportunities for design; writing nine years later Graham Hughes, one of the organisers, said, 'Jewellery design used to be the harmonious use of stones, but it then became a conscious wish to be different, to express individuality'.[1]

In 1961, Graham Hughes was the Art Secretary at Goldsmiths' Hall, and in conjunction with Carol Hogben and Shirley Bury, both then of the Circulation department of the V&A, he made the selections for the show. Apart from the pre-1920s pieces, for which Mrs Bury was responsible, there were three categories: the expensive gem jewellery such as Cartier's; fine art jewellery, designed as a side-line by sculptors or painters, usually as a present for the woman in their life; and designer jewellery, then still quite a rarity.

For the second category, Carol Hogben had the idea of sending a match-box full of wax to a number of English artists, and asking them to model a piece of jewellery with it. These designs were then executed by centrifugal casting in the workshops of the H.J. Company Ltd. for which Andrew Grima worked. De Beers Consolidated Mines paid for this (as indeed they financed the British Jewellery Competition just before the Exhibition), and so the public had the opportunity of seeing what sculptors like Elizabeth Frink, Robert Adams and Bernard Meadows (FIG.1) envisaged as jewellery.[2] Many of these pieces ended up in the V&A and Goldsmiths' Hall to form the basis of their permanent collections, neither having owned more than a few items before, the V&A because of its firmly antiquarian collecting policy, and Goldsmiths' Hall because it had only been buying silverware.

But more exhibits were also bought from the 1961 show by Carol Hogben: among others a necklace of brass spirals with rather an African look to it, made by Alexander Calder in 1938 (FIG.2); a pebble and silver brooch designed about 1960 by Jean Arp as a gift and executed by Johanan Peter in Israel,[3] and a gold ring cast from a rosewood model carved by Yves Tanguy in 1937.[4]

Thereafter, however, collecting languished for a while because of lack of funds, since the acquisition of modern art was still thought peripheral to the Museum's real purpose. In 1971 Circulation department held a two-man show of the work of Gerda Flockinger and Sam Herman. Gerda Flockinger is now the doyenne of the British craft-jewellery world and many of her pieces have subsequently come into the Museum, two of them through her endearing habit of giving the V&A Christmas presents of her own work; but in those days it was difficult to persuade the Director to make money available for even one purchase from these craftsmen who had, after all, made considerable efforts to get this strictly non-commercial exhibition together – it was felt to be rather improper to enter into financial transactions with a living artist whose work was being displayed in the Museum. However, one item was acquired, but Shirley Bury and our colleague David Coachworth were unlucky in their attempts to buy a necklace of enamelled gold by Wendy Ramshaw. This had been on show at the Design Centre as she had become the first jeweller to win the Council of Industrial Design Award, one of the many signs that jewellery was being taken seriously by the British art establishment for the first time since the Arts and Crafts movement. This necklace did not come to the Museum until 1976.[5] It has since been joined by one of her prize-winning ring sets of 1972.

Soon after his arrival in 1973, the new Director, Roy Strong, made available to each department a discrete fund for post-1920 purchases, and from then onwards Metalwork could really begin to exercise its judgement in buying modern jewellery. As at Goldsmiths' Hall, where, throughout the '60s and part of the '70s, Graham Hughes had completely free rein in his purchasing, so here the collection was formed by one person, Shirley Bury, who transferred to Metalwork in 1967, with her background in Circulation department, which had traditionally tried to go on buying contemporary art

Bottom: FIG.1 Brooch. Silver-gilt set with cabochon rubies. Designed and modelled by Robert Adams.
Top: Brooch. Silver-gilt, set with a diamond. Designed and modelled by Bernard Meadows. Both executed by H.J. Company, 1961.

FIG.2 Necklace. Brass. Designed by
Alexander Calder, Paris, about 1938.

Bottom left: FIG.3 Brooch-pendant. Turquoise,
black-stained chalcedony, diamonds and
white gold. Paris. By Georges Fouquet, about
1920.

Bottom right: FIG.4 Brooch-clips ('Reflection').
White gold set with sapphires, diamonds and
moonstones. Paris. By Mauboussin, late
1930s; also signed TRABERT and
HOEFFER.

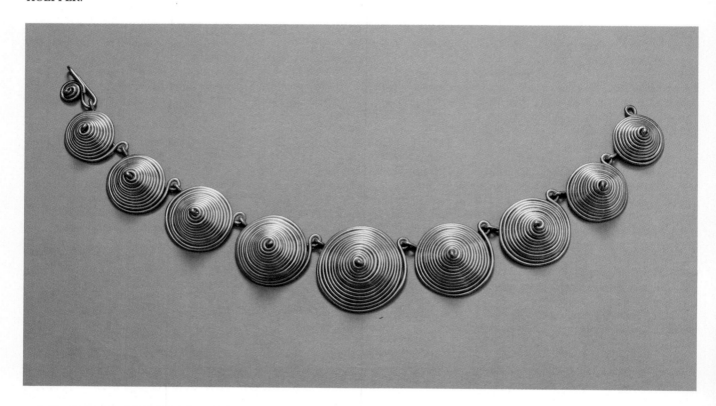

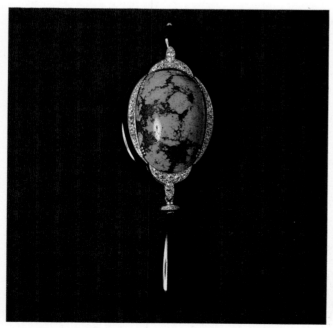

FIG.5 Watch-bracelet. Gold set with diamonds and sapphires. The watch by Vacheron-Constantin, 1950s. One of a pair of dress clips. Gold and platinum set with diamonds. By Van Cleef and Arpels, about 1955.

FIG.6 (Top) Brooch ('Mobile'). Silver, ivory and lapis-lazuli. Designed and made by Gunilla Treen, 1975.
(R) Brooch ('Flyingbird'). Silver inlaid with resin. Designed and made by Susanna Heron, 1975.
(L) Pair of earrings. Silver set with mother-of-pearl. Designed and made by Beverley Phillips, 1976.

FIG.7 Hairpin. Horn and crystal. Designed and made by Martin Baker, 1980. Given by the Hon. Alistair MacAlpine.

whenever its limited funds permitted it to do so.

There were, (and indeed, still are) three areas to be covered – the Art Deco, post-war commercial jewellery, and artist-craftsmens' work.

The major problem with collecting in the first two categories is that the stones with which so much of the jewellery is set are intrinsically expensive, and their cost has to be covered before even the artistic value can be priced. We were therefore most grateful to receive the Gollan bequest in 1976 of two fine pieces by the famous Paris manufacturers, Lacloche, who led the fashion in the 1920s for carved hardstone in the oriental manner: an inlaid hardstone vanity case,[6] and a stylised cypress tree brooch[7] set with diamonds, emeralds and black onyx. The same year an appeal was launched for the public to donate their spare Art Deco pieces, but while this yielded a great deal of useful costume jewellery, the finest piece of real jewellery – a lozenge-shaped diamond and black onyx Cartier brooch[8] – was given by the person behind the appeal, Lady Reigate herself.

Gradually, however, the gaps are being filled; in 1978 a superb brooch-pendant made about 1920 by Georges Fouquet was bought (FIG.3); this still has the curving lines and fundamentally classical shape of the earlier period, but with its bold colour contrast and outsize central cabochon of turquoise matrix it belongs to the Art Deco.

In 1980 a ring[9] of platinum and gold set with amber, black onyx and jadeite, and also with the mark of Georges Fouquet, but almost certainly by his avant-garde son, Jean, was added to the collection. In 1978 the department also bought a brooch-clip (FIG.4) of the kind so popular between the wars, by the Place Vendôme firm, Mauboussin, which still produces very stylish work.

The 1950s are represented by a very few pieces, which include a heavy watch-bracelet in the dark-coloured gold favoured then, set with diamonds and sapphires (FIG.5); the watch is by Vacheron-Constantin, who, like Patek-Philippe, have given increasing emphasis to their jewellery side and may have been responsible for the design of the bracelet as well. The two dress-clips of gold and platinum set with diamonds (FIG.5) by Van Cleef and Arpels have a slightly space-age look to them appropriate to the sputnik era.

But much more is needed; there is 'no river of diamonds' bracelet of the kind so popular between the wars, no pair of Art Deco clips; nothing by the extraordinarily successful Jean Schlumberger, whose sumptuously naturalistic jewellery of the '50s and '60s, made mostly for Americans, is still echoed, in a debased way, by costume jewellers. Nor is there anything by the Firbankian sounding Fulco, Duca di Verdura, who was born in Palermo, but worked with great success in America from 1934 onwards, designing large, lavish, romantic pieces using multi-coloured stones, and not disdaining the semi-precious hardstones like malachite, lapis-lazuli, and porphyry.[10] In most collecting areas the Museum would not need to worry unduly, as it buys, if not in the light of eternity, at least in the context of centuries; but with jewellery there is always urgency because now, as in the past, outmoded pieces tend to get broken up very fast for the sake of their stones.

In the category of artist/craftsmen's work, the department now has a collection of almost 100 pieces, and is constantly adding to it. Mrs Bury has been an enthusiastic talent-spotter at the Royal College of Art and Central School, among other colleges. She also goes to all the (alas too few) shops

FIG.8 'Stretched Square Neckpiece' with six
pendent corners. Gold and blue steel.
Designed and made by David Watkins, 1978.

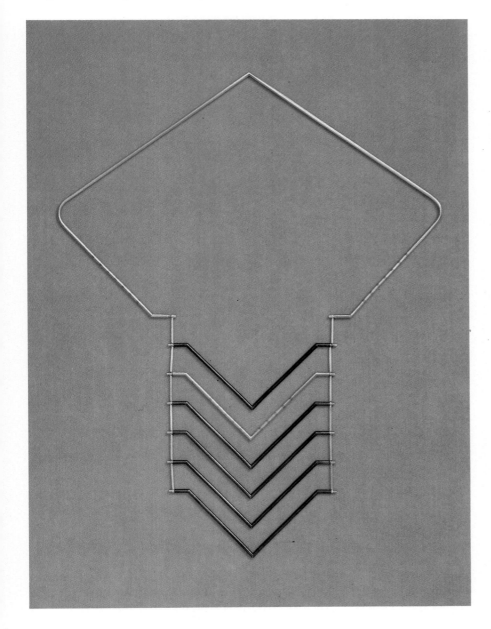

which handle artist/craftsmen's pieces;
she watches what the Crafts Council is
doing, keeps her ear to the ground, and
above all has made herself available to
craftsmen wanting to show their work
to her. In addition, there have been
some external influences: one was
Ralph Turner's Scottish Crafts Council Exhibition of Jewellery shown at the
V&A in 1976. This was cosmopolitan
and daring (it included the vast
necklace by David Poston of boulders
strung on a hawser, for elephants).
Three pieces were bought from that:
one by Rudiger Lorenzen,[11] and the
Susannah Heron[12] and Gunilla Treen
[13] brooches in FIG.6. (The ele-
phant necklace unfortunately had to be
eschewed for lack of space, but David
Poston is represented by a later, finely
curved, forged-iron necklace made for
humans)[14]. Another source, and to
some extent also an influence, were the
very successful *Loot* exhibitions
devised by Graham Hughes at
Goldsmiths' Hall. These aimed to
show exciting modern craftsmen's
work, for sale to the public, and
subject to the discipline of a price limit
(at the first show in 1975 this was £50).
A considerable number of pieces were
bought, such as a silver ring by
Michael Burton with a towering house
on it, reminiscent both of Jewish
marriage rings and of Mervyn Peake
drawings.[15]

Then the department benefited from
the generosity of Alastair (now Lord)
MacAlpine, who was the external
examiner at the Royal College of Art.
He bought from two successive Degree
Shows there, in 1976 and 1977, and
gave the pieces to the Museum. Among
them are the two silver and blued steel
rings inlaid with small gold faces by
Mary Lloyd.[16] In 1981 he added a hairpin of horn and crystal evocative of
Lalique, by Martin Baker from his
one-man show at Wartski's (FIG.7).[17]

In 1977 Lady Casson, then on the

FIG.9 Brooch. Gold set with moonstones. Designed by Malcolm Appleby, made by Roger Doyle, 1975.

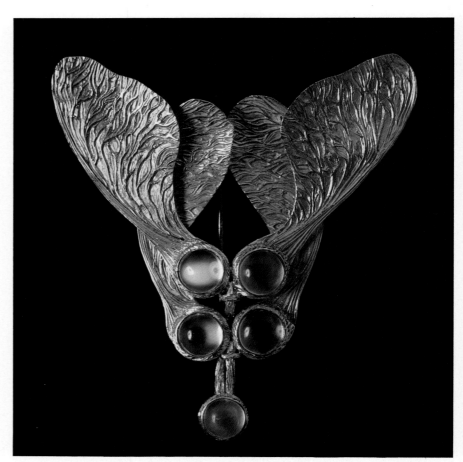

Advisory Council of the Museum, organised an exhibition of modern English jewellery in the Jewellery Gallery to celebrate the Queen's Silver Jubilee, and two items shown there were subsequently bought – a bracelet of silver and resin by Brian Glassar[18] and one of Edward de Large's *2001*-style pictures of a floating oblong over a vast horizon in coloured titanium.[19]

The idea of exhibitions of modern jeweller's work in the Jewellery Gallery was the Director's, and the first one took place before it closed in 1975 for structural improvements. The exhibitors then were Wendy Ramshaw, David Watkins, Roger Morris, Malcolm Appleby, and Gerda Flockinger. Not surprisingly all these names also appear more than once in the permanent collection. FIG.8 shows one of the David Watkins pieces;[20] he is a sculptor in geometric forms whose jewellery is austere and finely engineered. FIG.9 is a sycamore brooch designed by Malcolm Appleby, and made by Roger Doyle,[21] who must have honed his skills under the hard commercial discipline of his Cartier apprenticeship.

When, after many building tribulations, the Jewellery Gallery reopened in 1982, the first exhibition was a large retrospective of Wendy Ramshaw's work including the fruits of her experimental collaboration with Wedgwood, her necklaces and pins with hand-turned elements of jasper and basalt-ware. Since then there has been a succession of small exhibitions arranged by the writer, who has taken on responsibility for the Gallery, and the programme is full now for some years to come. This policy has contributed to a new departure, namely, the commissioning of works. It has become clear that this is often necessary if one wants to acquire the best of which one knows a craftsman to be capable. The Museum has often

bought a piece at the end of the shows, and from there it has been an easy step actually to commissioning a piece. The economics of craft jewellery are so under-financed that, as with all goldsmiths' work before the 19th century, only relatively mundane pieces can be made 'on spec'. Thus we await an enamelled necklace by Ros Conway, whose work is displayed in the gallery at the time of writing; the remarkable craftsman, Charlotte de Syllas, who painstakingly carves semi-precious stones, and whose jewellery boxes even are works of art in their own right, is also contracted to make a necklace for the Museum. The brooch/miniature sculpture, 'Athene Noctua',[22] FIG.10,

by Dr. Kevin Coates, harpsichord-maker and goldsmith, was completed in 1983. A possible criticism of this policy is that the Museum will end up with a series of freak objects which would never have emerged in the outside world. The answer to that is, that if the craftsman has already proven himself in the market, it does not matter if the piece is somewhat more lavish than the ordinary commission: the Museum has merely played the role of an outstanding patron like, say, François I and the great salt made for him by Cellini (risking the accusation of *hubris*). The danger would only be if the Museum intervened in the market to the extent of distracting and divert-

FIG.10 Brooch 'Athene Noctua'. Gold,
platinum, oxidised silver and titanium.
Designed and made by Kevin Coates, 1983.

ing craftsmen from what would have been the normal direction of their development: we would have to start worrying if *all* an artist's oeuvre were in our collection, and none outside. Of course, buying and commissioning work from the contemporary scene is fraught with dangers and invites impassioned criticism – one need only read the 'right-wing' versus 'left-wing' ding-dong arguments in the letter pages of *Crafts,* after Peter Fuller's critical review of the avant garde exhibition, *The Jewellery Project,* held by the Crafts Council in 1982. It is not enough for us to invoke Cicero and say that there is no disputing about taste, even if it is predominantly one person's taste which has formed a collection, so I have taken upon myself to attempt a rationale, however brief, and however many questions it may still beg, for what has been bought up until now.

The age-old idea of jewellery as decorative of the person has been retained: experiments in the wider definition of jewellery do of course

interest us, but apart from the Lorenzen piece, we have not acquired any such for the Museum. We admire quality and originality of design before anything else, but also expect these to be carried through into execution. This does not mean that everything has to be in finely-tooled precious metals. Far from it: we have bracelets and earrings by Alison Baxter of printed nylon,[23] necklaces and bangles by Lesley Miller of perspex,[24] and a wooden painted beechwood bead necklace decorated with gold leaf, by Valerie Robertson,[25] to name just a very few pieces in unconventional materials bought from the 1983 exhibition of costume jewellery. But where a craftsman chooses to work in the traditional materials, using traditional techniques, such as enamelling and inlay, it is impossible for us to put aside our experience of old works – the perfection and precision of chasing and hingeing on an 18th century French snuff box, for example, cannot be forgotten by anyone who has handled it – so skilled execution is definitely

admired. Similarly, aspects of our old collection may lead us to recognise with delight a craftsman's innovation: the presence, until recently, in our collection, of the Japanese sword mounts, with their extraordinary coloured and inlaid metals, has predisposed us to understand and admire work such as Malcolm Appleby's; the 15th century Mérode cup, and the Feuillâtre dish of 1900, both decorated with plique-à-jour enamel, inclined us to be interested in Georgina Follett's work using the same demanding technique. And herein, I believe, lies the difference between Goldsmiths' Hall's huge pioneer collection of modern jewellery and our own: theirs is probably the most comprehensive, purely modern collection in the world, beginning with the 1960s; but our is the continuation of a collection covering all the centuries back to the Pharaohs and we cannot fail to be conscious of what has been produced in the intervening years.

1 G. Hughes, 'The Renaissance of the Artist – Jeweller' *Optima* XX i–ix (1970).

2 Mary Kessell, Wiliam Scott and Terry Frost also submitted designs.

3 Circ. 395–1962.

4 Circ. 10–1962.

5 M.169–1976.

6 M.24–1976.

7 M.25–1976.

8 M212–1976.

9 M.4–1980.

10 G. Hughes, *op.cit.* part iii, p. 122.

11 M.183–1976.

12 M.181–1976.

13 M.174–1976.

14 M.49–1980.

15 M.296–1975.

16 M.402– and M.403–1977.

17 M.3–1981.

18 M.26–1979.

19 M.353–1977.

20 M.24–1979.

21 M.314–1972.

22 M.19–1983.

23 M.10+A– to M.13+A–1984.

24 M.30– to 32–1984.

25 M.926–1983.

A carat or more.
A little extra weight she won't mind putting on.

This necklace features a 1.25 carat diamond.

A quality diamond of a carat or more.

Quality. It's as important in diamonds as in anything else you own. And it's especially important in a diamond of a carat or more.

It's one of nature's most perfect gifts. Spectacular. Impressive. Crafted by a master cutter, it has exceptional clarity and colour.

Your jeweller is the expert where diamonds are concerned. He'll be happy to discuss the 4Cs: the four criteria (Cut, Colour, Clarity and Carat-weight) that determine the quality and value of a diamond.

He can show you outstanding diamonds of a carat or more that will please the most discriminating taste.

And since this isn't the type of purchase you make every day, we've prepared a free booklet to further help you understand the 4Cs and to make the right decision.

For your booklet, write to: Dept. LA, The Diamond Information Centre, Saffron House, 11 Saffron Hill, London EC1N 8RA.

4C

A diamond is forever.

*Antique Natural Pearls, Rubies and Diamonds Brooch
formerly in the collection of Empress Eugenie,
later owned by Mrs. Ernest Sassoon Raphael*

J. & S. S. DeYOUNG, Inc.
Since 1835
**Source of Fine Antique, Estate and
Modern Jewelry to the Trade
Boston — New York**

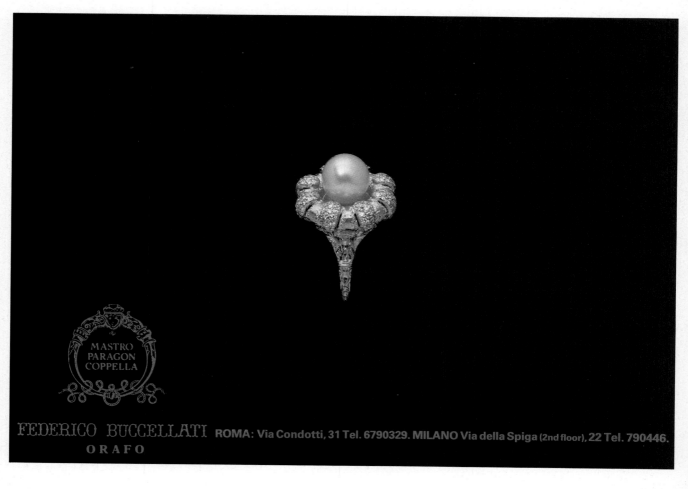

BVLGARI

10 VIA DEI CONDOTTI · ROMA
TÉL. 679.38.76

NEW YORK · GENÈVE · MONTE CARLO · PARIS

ELIZABETH GAGE

20 ALBEMARLE STREET, LONDON W1X 3HA

01-499 2879

ANTIQUE AND
ESTATE JEWELLERY

Harry Hofmann

BAHNHOFSTRASSE 87 & 79
8001 ZURICH
SWITZERLAND

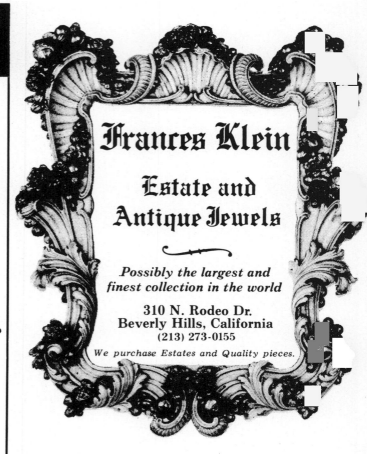
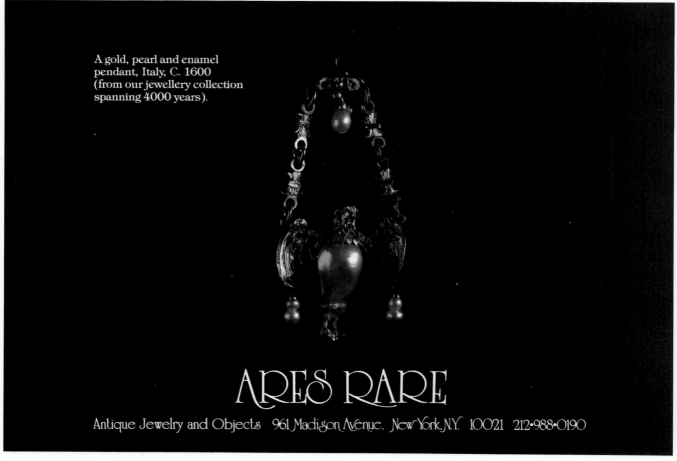

COLLINGWOOD
OF CONDUIT STREET
46 Conduit Street, London W1R 0HE.
also at

of Knightsbridge

N·BLOOM & SON

N. BLOOM & SON (ANTIQUES) LTD. Established 1912
DEALERS IN FINE OLD JEWELLERY AND SILVER
40 CONDUIT STREET LONDON W1 Tel. 01-629 5060

Victorian silver gilt and red glass decanter, 1874	£2,200
Striking and repeating carriage clock with ivory face by MARGAINE	£1,200
Diamond and sapphire clip by Cartier	£8,950
Victorian multigem set butterfly brooch	£3,600
Diamond and platinum bracelet by CHAUMET, PARIS 45cts (est)	£90,000
Queen Anne 1711 mug by Joseph Ward 5½ ozs	£2,250
'Mr Pickwick' Victorian pepper pot by Robert Harper 1879	£485
Russian enamel coin purse by Nicolai Sverev, Moscow c 1880	£785
Russian enamel knife and fork by Paula Mishurova, Moscow c 1880	£350

Please ask for our new brochure if you did not receive one in last months edition.
We would like to buy good old jewellery and silver
VALUATIONS·REPAIRS·PEARL-STRINGING

SOME FINE WATCHES IN THE V&A

A. R. E. North

The Museum's collection of watches has been assembled over the years to demonstrate the art of the European watchmaker from the sixteenth to the twentieth centuries. The emphasis has always been on the decorative qualities of the watch rather than its technical importance. The ones shown here represent various techniques and styles of ornament from the intricate engraving of the seventeenth century to the fine painted enamelling of the late eighteenth century. The collection is displayed in the Jewellery Gallery, Room 90.

The case of gilt brass mounted in silver, the dial engraved with a scene depicting Venus and Cupid in a landscape.
English, about 1625.
Signed on the backplate 'EDM BULL IN FLEET STREET FECIT'.

Fitted with a contemporary verge movement with a fusee operated by a gut cord, steel balance wheel and ratchet wheel regulator.

Edmund Bull is recorded as working in Fleet St. from about 1610 to 1630.

As with many watches of the first half of the seventeenth century the case is constructed from brass with silver covers and sides. The oval shape is characteristic of cases of the first half of the seventeenth century.

The Bull family were among the earliest recorded English watchmakers. The earliest English watch so far known, dated 1590, is signed by Randolph Bull (1582–1617). Edm. Bull may be the 'Emmanuel Bull' recorded as Clockmaker to James I.
Diam. 2¾in.   418–1893.

The case of gold, pierced with floral scrolls and decorated with translucent enamel; the dial-plate decorated with champlevé enamel. English, about 1640.

With the watch is a plain silver case engraved with the Stuart royal arms and the initials CR. An inscription engraved on the back of the outer case reads, 'This watch was a Present From Ye King to the Earl of Monteith'. It was presented by Charles I to William Graham, 7th Earl of Monteith (1591–1661). The Earl was considered by Charles I to be an authority on Scottish affairs and was made President of the Council and Justice-General of Scotland.

The verge movement fitted to the watch is a replacement made in about 1770. It is signed on the backplate 'Arlr Dobson London 1376'. Arlander Dobson is recorded as working in Convent Garden from about 1744 until his death in 1772.

An interesting manuscript note written between 1789 and 1808 by Lady Elizabeth Hastings refers to this watch. 'Charles the 2nd during his illness gave to the last Earl of Menteith the watch which belonged to his father Charles the 1st, which watch is now in possession of the present Lord Moira. I was grieved beholding it in my time modernised the dial plate was of silver coarsely engraved with the hours and minutes; the inward workmanship coarse and instead of a chain a piece of catgut was the material by which it was wound up, there was a clumsy repeater in it distinct from the main work and the ribbon which was the same the King wore it with was brocade with silver. It ought I thought to have remained in its first state as a sample of the progress of mechanism in that article.' (*The Ancestor* IV, January 1903, p. 85).
Diam. 1⁷/₈in. 446–1884.

Clock-watch, the silver case pierced and engraved with floral designs.
English about 1645.

The back-plate is signed 'Eduardus East Londini'. The watch has a verge movement and is fitted with an alarm. The alarm disc is set in the centre with the alarm being indicated by the small hand set at the outer edge of the disc. The fusee with chain-drive is a replacement for the earlier system using a gut cord. Other later replacements include the brass balance wheel with hair spring, and the over-winding wheel to the striking train.

According to an account written in 1841, this watch belonged to Charles I (1625–1649), then becoming the property of Elizabeth, Queen of Bohemia, his sister. The Queen presented the watch to Gilbert Spencer of Redleaf near Penshurst, who was responsible for supervising the stay of the Queen and her retinue at Penhurst in 1661. Edward East (1602–97) was one of the ablest watch makers working in England during the seventeenth century. He had an exceptionally long career, was a founder member and Junior Assistant of the Clockmakers' Company in 1631, becoming Master of the Company in 1645 and 1652. He made clocks and watches both for Charles I and II, so there may well be truth in this legend.

Diam. 3½in.   M64–1952.

Enamelled gold decorated with delicate white flowers. The inside of the case is painted with landscapes in which are ruins and figures. English, about 1650.

The back-plate is signed 'Eduardus East Londini'. The watch has a verge movement with gut-driven fusee and steel balance wheel. The movement has a tangent screw regulator with silver index dial. The hour-ring is of gold with white enamel.

The case-maker supplied cases of similar design and decoration to other watchmakers of the period; one with a movement by Jacob Cornelius is recorded. The style of painting employed on these watch-cases was also used on contemporary miniature cases.
Diam. 2in.   14–1888.

The case of gold decorated in enamel with designs of flowers and foliage. The dial-plate is also decorated in a similar manner. English or French, about 1660.

As with many finely decorated seventeenth century watches, the case was retained and another more modern movement substituted for the original. It is now fitted with a verge movement dating from the latter part of the eighteenth century. This is signed 'JAS Rousseau London', who is recorded as working in London from 1743 to 1761.

The watch is decorated in the enamelling technique known as 'champlevé' whereby the design is cut into the surface of the case and areas where metal has been removed are then filled with powdered enamel and fired. The combination of opaque enamel for the petals and foliage, and translucent enamel for the ground and some of the flowers is especially skillful and subtle.

As the case is not signed and the movement is later it is not possible to attribute the case to any particular craftsman. At one time it was considered to be French but miniature cases of gold decorated in a similar manner are now known to have been produced in England during the seventeenth century.
Diam. 1⁵/₈in.   M.81–1913.

A silver double-case, the outer case with scrolling foliage trophies and figures framing a medallion depicting William III (1689–1702), on horseback directing a siege.
Swiss (Zurich, about 1700).

The silver dial is signed 'Mehlin a Zurich'; the case is stamped with an unidentified maker's mark, AH beneath a crown.

The design for the pair case is almost certainly taken from a model by the Swiss medallist Jean Dassier (1676–1763). In Metalwork's collections there is an oval bronze plaque (M.45–1914) cast in relief with an identical design. This plaque was originally thought to have been intended as a design for the lid of a snuff-box, but is clearly a model for a watch-case.
Diam. 2⅛in.   464–1880.

A gold double-case, the inner case pierced, chased and engraved. On a roundel are engraved the royal arms of England under a crown. The outer case is embossed and chased with a scene of huntsmen about to give the *coup de grace* to a boar.
Polish (Cylkowa), about 1720.

The movement is signed on the backplate 'Zillichaw George Albrecht'.

This watch is a quarter repeater with a verge movement of English type. By tradition this watch once belonged to George I (1714–27). Cylkowa is a town south-east of Warsaw formerly in the province of Brandenburg. Attached to the watch is a gold chatelaine chased and embossed with designs *en suite* with the case.
Diam. 2¾in. 2398–1855.

The case of embossed and chased gold showing figures in classical costume having a meal.

English, about 1725.

The movement is signed 'Gerret Bramer Amsterdam'; the outer case is signed 'H. Manley fecit'.

This watch is a 1/4/1/2 repeater with a double case. The enamel dial has an arched minute band with diamonds set at regular intervals between each figure indicating the hour. The

hands of pierced silver are also set with diamonds. The case is stamped underneath the bell with a maker's mark SG below a fish, and it is also numbered 131. In addition the bell is scratched with the name Danckert IEI Drury.

The signature appears only on the outer case which probably indicates that the watch was made in England for export to Holland. The embossed and chased scene on the case is almost certainly taken from Virgil's Aenead,

probably showing Aeneas being entertained by King Latinus. The case-maker, H. Manley (1695–1730), was particularly good at embossed and chased work. A number of watch cases decorated in a similar manner by this maker are known, including one in the Museum's collection, also depicting scenes from the Aenead. He was a member of the Clockmakers' Company.

Diam. 2 1/8 in.   654–1872.

The outer case of gold enamelled with classical figures in a design representing the Discovery of Painting.
English, with London hall-marks for 1778–9.

The watch signed on the back-plate 'Jas Upjohn and Co. London'. The verge movement is fitted with a steel balance-wheel, hair spring and regulator; the gold inner-case is stamped with a maker's mark IW.

The enamelled decoration is in the style of the Swiss-born chaser and enameller, George Michael Moser (1707–83). Moser's work is characterised by the use of classical motifs, usually against a grey ground, and translucent

The gold case enamelled and set with pearls. The scene depicts Venus in her chariot with attendant cupids and Adonis.
Swiss (Geneva) about 1790.

The dial bears the name Orazio Somerara; the back-plate is similarly inscribed together with the number 13781. The movement is signed 'Jacques Coulin, + Amy Bry A Géneve. No. 13781'. The movement is fitted with a fusee and cylinder escapement.

The watch was commissioned by an Italian merchant whose name appears on the dial and on the dust cover. This watch is a fine example of late 18th century Swiss work, the

enamel on an engine-turned surface. He was trained as a coppersmith, later becoming a chaser and engraver. His work as an enameller seems to date from the period towards the end of his working life. He was a founder member of the Royal Academy and was appointed Keeper in 1768. In the Museum collections there are some of his designs for watch-cases in pen and wash, as well as examples of his work as a chaser and engraver, including a signed watch-case.

James Upjohn and Company are recorded as working at Red Lion St. Holborn from 1773–95.
Diam. 2½in.   1924–1898.

high quality enamelled decoration being typical of a Geneva workshop.

Amy Bry of Geneva was born in 1750, and is recorded as being in partnership with Jacques Coulin and Jean Flourney from 1784 to 1800.
Diam. 2¼in.   M.187–1919.

Select Bibliography

C. Clutton, and G. Daniels, *Watches* London, 1965
G. Brusa, *L'Arte del Orologeria in Europa,*

Bramante Editrice, 1978
J. F. Hayward, *English Watches,* V&A, H.M.S.O., 1965
Britten's Old Clocks and Watches and their Makers 8th Edition London, 1973

G. H. Baillie, *Watchmakers and Clockmakers of the World,* London, 1975
G. H. Baillie, *Watches,* London, 1929

CHRISTIE'S

Mid-17th Century Augsburg ivory clock with silver-gilt mounts,
the ivory attributed to Bernhard Straus,
the mounts by David I. Schwestermüller and Daniel Zech, 66cm. high.

Sold at Christie's St. James's in July for £842,400
A world record auction price for any clock.

8 King Street, St. James's, London SW1Y 6QT   Tel: (01) 839 9060
85 Old Brompton Road, South Kensington, London SW7 3JS   Tel: (01) 581 7611
164/166 Bath Street, Glasgow   Tel: (041) 332 8134

A LA VIEILLE RUSSIE

781 FIFTH AVENUE, NEW YORK, N.Y. 10022 (212) 752-1727   ESTABLISHED 1851

Gold and vari-colored enamel temple-form clock with carillon musical movement and singing bird.
Signed ''Melchior Monnin à Genève.''
Geneva 1794-1804.

296

Mystery Clock of Cartier
Cristal en rocher, diamond and
enamel – Paris 1930 Art Deco

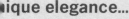
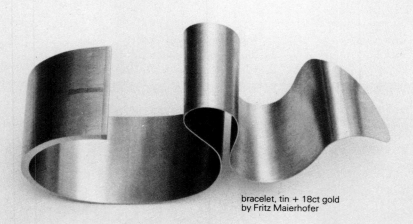

WHITE GOLD RINGS 750/1000

DESIGN RINALDO GAVELLO

ANTIQUORUM
AUCTIONEERS

genève new york hong kong

Osvaldo PATRIZZi
15, ch. de la Grande-Gorge
CH-1255 VEYRIER
Tél. 022/84 09 64

SUMPTUOUS AND EXTREMELY RARE
18-carat GOLD, PAINTED ENAMEL AND
PEARLS SNUFF-BOX. WITH WATCH,
MUSIC WITH TWO TUNES AND
AUTOMATIONS, made for CHINA,
HALL-MARKED ON THE MOVEMENT
P.M. (PIGUET MEYLAN), GENEVA,
No. 4189, cira 1818.

VERY IMPORTANT ASTRONOMIC 18-
carat GOLD HUNTING WATCH WITH
MOON PHASES, PERPETUAL CALEN-
DER, MINUTE REPEATER CHRONO-
GRAPHER, SPLIT-SECONDS AND 60
MINUTES PROGRESSIVE REGISTER,
signed DENT, 33, COCKSPUR STR.
LONDON, WATCHMAKER TO THE KIN
AND QUEEN, No. 32384, circa 1885.

VERY IMPORTANT AND RARE 18-carat
GOLD, ONE MINUTE TOURBILLON
POCKET CHRONOMETER, WITH 24
HOURS POWER RESERVE INDICATION,
signed S. SMITH & SON, 9 STRAND,
LONDON, MAKERS TO THE ADMIRALTY
AND THE INDIAN GOVERNMENT, No.
302-14, year 1901.

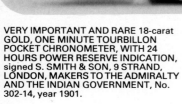

Auctions – Buying – Selling – Appraisals
Antique precious and complicated pocket watches, clocks, collector's wrist watches

THE GLC HISTORIC HOUSES

KENWOOD
The Iveagh Bequest, Hampstead Lane, NW3

An outstanding neo-classical house re-modelled by Robert Adam, 1764-73, for the 1st Earl of Mansfield, the famous Lord Chief Justice. The Library is one of the finest of Adam's creations, and has been restored in the original colours.

The house contains the Iveagh Collection (bequeathed 1927) of Old Master and English paintings, including works by Rembrandt, Vermeer, Hals, Gainsborough, Reynolds and Turner. Exhibitions are held on the first floor, usually devoted to some aspect of eighteenth century painting or the decorative arts. Chamber music concerts are held in the Orangery and symphony concerts by the Lake in summer.

MARBLE HILL HOUSE, Richmond Road, Twickenham

A complete example, both inside and out, of an English Palladian villa, built between 1724 and 1729, for Henrietta Howard, the mistress of George II, and later Countess of Suffolk. The design is based on a drawing by Colen Campbell, while the Great Room was inspired by Inigo Jones' Cube Room at Wilton. The grounds, going down to the Thames, were laid out with the advice of Alexander Pope. The house contains an important collection of early Georgian paintings and furniture.

RANGER'S HOUSE, Chesterfield Walk, Blackheath SE10

The house of the 4th Earl of Chesterfield, statesman and author of the famous 'Letters' to his natural son.

The bow-fronted Gallery he added to the house in 1749, with "the finest prospects in the world" now houses the remarkable series of Jacobean portraits by William Larkin from the collection of the Earls of Suffolk. Concerts are held in the house and there is a collection of musical instruments.

Open daily all the year, including Sundays, from 10-5 (10-4, November to January). Marble Hill is closed on Fridays, but Kenwood is open until 7 in the summer.
For further details see entries.

keep
GLC
Working for the Arts in London

THE TASTE FOR REGENCY AND EMPIRE FURNITURE IN THE LATER NINETEENTH CENTURY

Frances Collard

It has been traditional to recognise the years immediately after the First World War as a period of fashionable interest in the furnishings and furniture of the Regency and Empire styles but recent research has shown that there were indications of demand for such styles in the nineteenth century. Designs for furniture produced during the Regency period remained popular long after they were originally published as can be seen in the various books of prices produced to enable the furniture making trades to regulate prices. Designs for chair backs copied from originals by Hepplewhite and Sheraton appeared in the *London Chair-Makers' and Carvers' Book of Prices* in 1823, and the Carlton House table, one of the most familiar of Regency designs, first appeared in the *Cabinet-Makers' London Book of Prices* in 1793, and in all subsequent editions up to 1866. Even designs published right at the end of the Regency period by Thomas King in his 1829 pattern book, *The Modern Style of Cabinet Work Exemplified*, were popular enough in their debased classical style to be reprinted several times up to 1862 and were incorporated into a trade catalogue produced by William Smee & Son, one of the largest furniture manufacturers of the later nineteenth century.

Combined with a continuing interest in late eighteenth and early nineteenth century styles was a revival of earlier eighteenth century styles, epitomised by the fine pieces of French Royal furniture collected by the Prince Regent, one of a group including the Duke of Wellington and the Duchess of Rutland who encouraged such

craftsmen as the various members of the Wyatt family to create interiors inspired by the rococo styles of the eighteenth century. By the 1830s such interest had become popular enough for John Weale, an enterprising publisher, to publish a series of reprints of designs by Chippendale, Thomas Johnson and Matthias Lock. At the International Exhibition of 1862 Wright and Mansfield, a prominent cabinet making firm, illustrated the popularity of eighteenth century styles by exhibiting furniture, the details of which were, 'Gleaned from the works of the Messrs (Adelphi) Adam, and may be considered as indicating the style of English decorative furniture of the eighteenth century', according to the *Art Journal Illustrated Catalogue*. The firm also showed at the Paris Exhibition of 1867 where their cabinet (FIGS. 1 and 2) attracted a great deal of comment, particularly for its English nature, and for the satinwood ground, very unusual at a time when ebony was extremely popular and dark woods generally more common. The cabinet, for which the firm was awarded a gold medal, was immediately acquired by the South Kensington Museum, later the Victoria and Albert Museum.[1]

The 'Adams' style, the contemporary term for designs influenced by the work of the Adam brothers, has remained popular since the mid-nineteenth century and was one of the elements present in interior decoration of the 'Queen Anne' Movement. This developed from the 1860s as, 'The natural reaction among cultivated persons against the vulgarity of all the forms of furniture to which they have been for too long accustomed; these forms being in their turn a reaction against the excess of quietness and artistic asceticism of seventy years ago', as Mrs Haweis wrote in *The Art of Beauty* in 1878. An essential feature of 'Queen Anne' furnishings was their

eclecticism and whilst the 'Adams' style was just one of the suggestions for decorating drawing rooms, the contents of such rooms could include Japanese screens, fans or prints, Persian rugs and furniture of vaguely eighteenth century shape.

There was some confusion evidently about exactly what was meant by the term 'Queen Anne', confusion illustrated by Mrs Haweis's remark in *The Art of Decoration* in 1881: 'Only the other day I was shown a French mirror (Louis XIV) by some really cultivated folks as, "Queen Anne-Empire", you know – genuine Chippendale!' She pointed out that some of the difficulty arose because what, 'People now call "Queen Anne" fashions with a charming indifference to the trammels of dates, are the fashions of three Georges, Marie Antoinette . . . and especially everything which came in during the Empire (Napoleon I).'

In spite of the possibilities offered by this range of styles most furniture designs for the popular market were inspired by either Adam, Hepplewhite or Sheraton well into the 1880s. Firms like Gillows, Seddons, Edwards and Roberts, Wright and Mansfield, Jackson and Graham, Johnstone and Jeanes, and Cooper and Holt were all known to have produced furniture of this type, but it was Wright and Mansfield (FIG.3)[2] who were credited by the *Cabinet-Maker* in 1886 as, 'The leaders of that pleasing fashion which has happily brought back into our houses many of the charming shapes of the renowned eighteenth century cabinet makers'. At the sale of their stock caused by the dissolution of the partnership in 1886 the South Kensington Museum bought a pair of chairs, a card table and a pembroke table, all obviously influenced by Sheraton.

Reproductions of antique pieces and pieces which show Regency inspira-

FIG.2 Detail of the cabinet showing the
quality of the mouldings and plaques.

FIG.3 Chair, painted satinwood, in the
Sheraton style by Wright and Mansfield *c.*
1880, and very similar to a pair of chairs in the
Museum by Seddon and Sons, *c.* 1790.

tion, like those of Wright and Mansfield, were made as closely as possible to the original, although without deliberate intention to deceive, and could therefore with age and the acquisition of patina be mistaken for the real thing. Sources for reproductions included original examples, of which many survived, particularly the smaller pieces, and the various books of patterns. A special branch of the furniture trade, usually the antique dealers, since through their stock passed most of the genuine old pieces worth copying, were responsible for the reproduction furniture.

Antique shops were also a good source for collectors of Regency objects like Dante Gabriel Rossetti and his brother William Michael and Dante Gabriel Rossetti apparently enjoyed visiting antique and junk shops in the vicinity of Leicester Square, and in the Hammersmith area, a district where late eighteenth and early nineteenth century furniture could be acquired very reasonably in the 1860s. In 1862 Rossetti moved into an eighteenth century house in Cheyne Walk which he then furnished with a typically varied selection of pieces, incuding blue and white porcelain and Regency style furniture, both antique and reproduction. Rossetti's sitting room in 1863 (FIG.4) was described by H. Treffy Dunn in *Recollections of Dante Gabriel Rossetti and His Circle* as, 'One of the most curiously-furnished and old-fashioned sitting-rooms that it had ever been my lot to see'. Among the furniture was a 'Cosy little sofa, with landscapes and figures of the Cipriani period painted on the panels', while the studio was furnished with 'Chippendale chairs and lounges' and the bedroom with 'An old-fashioned sofa, with three little panels let into the back, whereon Rossetti had painted the figures of Amor, Amans, and Amata'. Whilst the sofa in the sitting

FIG.4 D.G. Rossetti in his sitting-room at 16
Cheyne Walk. Watercolour by H. Treffy
Dunn, 1882, showing an eclectic mixture of
objects including a Sheraton style settee and
two Regency convex mirrors. (National
Portrait Gallery, London.)

FIG.5 Bergere chair, mahogany with cane
back, sides and seat, with cushions covered in
the 'Tulip' chintz, made by Morris & Co.
c. 1893 and probably designed by George Jack
after a Regency example.

FIG.6 Empire Chair, described as either
Empire or Grecian in style and sanitary since
the seat was removable for cleaning, *The
Cabinet-Maker,* August 1st 1884.

FIG.7 The Pompeiian Bedroom, the Waldorf Hotel, New York, *The Cabinet-Maker*, February 1895.

room was probably one of Rossetti's antique shop bargains, the example in the bedroom, now in the Fitzwilliam Museum, is probably an early example of a Regency inspired design by Rossetti himself.

This sofa is similar to the 'Sussex' chair, manufactured by Morris and Co. in various forms from about 1865 onwards and based on a typical Regency armchair with round cane seat. Several individuals, including Rossetti, Ford Madox Brown and E.W. Godwin, have been mentioned as involved with the development of this design but it is difficult to distinguish the work of one designer in some of the products of Morris & Co. The firm also made more straightforward reproductions of Hepplewhite and Sheraton furniture and also some pieces after typical Regency designs, including the armchairs and settees with cane backs and seats, from the 1890s (FIG.5).[3]

Another artist who used late eighteenth century styles for inspiration in designing furniture was E.W. Godwin, who described his difficulties in furnishing his London house in 1867. After designing pieces for his dining room in his Anglo-Japanese style, first in deal and then in mahogany, he realised that the effect was not, 'Calculated, to say the least, to make a room look cheerful or even comfortable', and decided, after considering various alternatives, 'To hunt up secondhand shops for eighteenth century mahogany work inlaid with strips of satinwood'. His search was successful and his dining room was refurbished with, 'A bow-fronted sideboard, Chippendale chairs, flap tables, cabinets, bookcases, and a little escritoire, all of admirable colour, design, and workmanship'.

The attraction of Hepplewhite and Sheraton styles for artists can also be seen in descriptions of J.M. Whistler's rooms, since in his Fulham Road studio in 1885–7 he had an old painted Sheraton settee while his Paris studio in the 1890s was furnished with Sheraton and Empire pieces, some of which are now in the collections of the Hunterian Museum, Glasgow. Others who collected such pieces included John Sargent, whose painting of the Sitwell family depicts furniture, objects and a painting from Renishaw, the family home, including a silver bowl which was placed on an Empire table, belonging to Sargent himself. Aubrey Beardsley required candles to be lit in two tall ormolu Empire candlesticks before he could start work.

The interest in Empire as well as Regency styles was an essential part of the 'Queen Anne' Movement and, as Mrs Haweis pointed out in *Beautiful Houses* in 1882, 'The slang term "Queen Anne" means almost anything just now, but it is oftenest applied to the pseudo-classic fashions of the first Empire'. By the 1880s, interest in Empire styles was spreading among more conventional circles although Sheraton designs were still very popular, many fashionable periodicals like *The Magazine of Art* or trade papers like *The Cabinet-Maker* included references to Empire styles in interiors and furniture (FIG.6). *The Cabinet-Maker* in 1884 referred to the availability of many 'Old pieces of Spanish mahogany brass mounted furniture, betraying an unmistakable "Empire" origin', in private homes and in the trade, while designs for Empire furniture taken from the publications of Thomas Hope and Percier and Fontaine, although only the latter were acknowledged, were included in Robert Brook's *Elements of Style in Furniture and Woodwork* in 1889. He also mentioned the availability of Napoleonic relics for inspiration in Madame Tussaud's Exhibition in

FIG.8 Chair, mahogany with brass inlaid decoration, 1892 or later. The design is adapted from one in Thomas Hope's *Household Furniture* of 1807, and the chair bears the label of Edwards and Roberts.

FIG.9 Detail of table, mahogany with inlay of brass and ebonised wood, made between 1892 and 1896 by Edwards and Roberts, whose label the table bears, as a sophisticated exercise in the neo-Regency style. The design is similar to examples produced by Percier and Fontaine, the French Empire designers.

Baker Street.

By the 1890s the growing enthusiasm for Empire styles had become firmly established and fashions, wallpapers, furnishings fabrics, settings for plays, and even the interior decoration of large hotels like the Hotel Cecil and the Carlton Hotel, all showed the influence of the style, while relics of Nelson and Napoleon were fetching high prices in the salerooms. *The Cabinet-Maker* echoed popular taste by illustrating several Empire designs, including a number of illustrations copied from Continental sources in 1894 and several pages of designs copied from Hope's *Household Furniture* in 1895 (FIG.7). The reproduction of Empire designs apparently caused some difficulties to cabinet-makers because of the skill required in applying mounts and using metal inlay, although it was possible to obtain exact facsimilies of Napoleonic ormolu mounts.

Several firms are known to have produced very good copies of Empire furniture, one of the best known being Edwards and Roberts of Wardour Street who traded in antique and reproduction furniture, as well as modern pieces (FIG.8).[4] The reproductions included pieces after designs by Sheraton, Percier and Fontaine (FIG.9)[5], and Hope, as well as examples of the brass-mounted furniture of the later Regency, and since they labelled or stamped many of their pieces, it is often difficult to distinguish between a genuine antique or a very good reproduction. In 1892 Frederick Litchfield commented that in order to supply the demand in England and America for the best Empire furniture, 'The French dealers have bought up some of the old undecorated pieces and by ornamenting them with gilt bronze mounts cast from good old patterns have sold them as original examples'.

There is no doubt that the vogue for Regency and Empire styles in the later nineteenth century, and their continuing popularity in the twentieth, is due to their elegance and flexibility as the last great classic style, which has been appreciated by many including connoisseurs, collectors, artists and designers.

1 Inv. no. 548-1868.

2 Inv. no. 239-1897.

3 Inv. no. Circ. 249-1961.

4 Inv. no. W.29-1976.

5 Inv. no. W.29-1964.

WILLIAM BEDFORD ANTIQUES

PERIOD FURNITURE AND WORKS OF ART

William Bedford Antiques Limited
The Merchants Hall 46 Essex Road London N1 8LN
Telephone 01-226 9648

A fine George III Period Mahogany Breakfront Bookcase with secretaire drawer and oval panel doors. circa 1780, *100" high, 66" wide, 22" deep.*

Huntington Antiques Ltd.

Period Oak & Country Furniture, Eastern Carpets and Rugs
The Old Forge, Church Steet, Stow-on-the-Wold, Gloustershire.
Telephone: Stow-on-the- Wold (0451)30842

In our considerably extended showrooms we offer a substantial stock of fine early oak, walnut and country furniture. Always a selection of refectory, gateleg and other tables; dressers and court cupboards; wainscots and sets of chairs; and usually some rare examples of gothic and renaissance furniture.

We would always welcome the opportunity to purchace such items.

open Mon–Sat 9–6 and by appointment.

314

THE CONSERVATION OF SIX OF THE DOLPHIN CHAIRS, HAM HOUSE

Nicola Gentle

In the North Drawing Room of Ham House stand twelve chairs, known as the Dolphin chairs, which appear in the 1677 inventory of Ham as 'six arme chairs with carved and guilded frames covered with Brocade . . . , six back stooles of ye same'. Their gilded frames are ornately carved in the forms of dolphins and their overall style suggests that they may be of French origin of the 1670s. What is most remarkable about them is that they still have their original covers of brocaded silk. Each chair has a cover which slips on down over the chair-back, and a separate one which fits over the seat, fastening around the back uprights with hooks and eyes. They also have permanent undercovers of linen fixed over the upholstery.

The silk brocade covers of the six side-chairs (FIG.1), the so-called 'back stooles' of the inventory, are at present undergoing conservation at the Victoria and Albert Museum's textile workshop at Osterley Park House.

The initial stage of any conservation project is investigation. A survey was made first of the general condition of the covers. We found that the seat-covers were very dusty and that the surface of the brocade on all was sadly worn (FIG.2). Three of them were in very much worse condition: where the covers curved over the front of the seat (this being the area most rubbed against in use), the brocade had weakened and eventually broken; the fine silk warp of the fabric had almost disappeared leaving only the deep layer of weft threads hanging in a loose swag across the front of the seat. One of the other seat-covers had been repaired previously: stitches in a coarse thread had been laid across and caught down over this vulnerable front area and

FIG.9 The covers, cleaned and repaired replaced on the chair.

although this rather unsightly repair would have to be removed and replaced with a more acceptable one, it had served its purpose well and had saved the brocade from further deterioration. We decided now to give priority to the seat-covers which had not been so fortunate.

The brocade of the back-covers, although less dusty, was equally worn and, in some areas, was beginning to break up. Linings of a red wool fabric covered the reverse side of the chair-backs and these had worn thin along the top and sides against the wood of the chair-frames, while the central area, being stretched between the framework, had acted as an air filter and collected much dirt. On three of the chairs, a few fragments of what seemed to be pink silk taffeta remained stitched around the edges of the wool linings, suggesting the existence, at one time, of another lining.

Each cover had silk fringes around the outer edges. This had a gimp of parchment strip wrapped with unspun cream silk and was decorated with cords and hanging threads of different colours. Much of the parchment had become bare and discoloured, and the hanging threads were in a very delicate state. It was interesting to note that the cream and white threads, in particular, had worn away most badly, perhaps because these colours would have undergone a more drastic processing during manufacture.

Although they had generally the same construction, the covers varied in their individual measurement, shapings and positioning of the fringing. As, in turn, they were removed from the chairs for conservation work, a more detailed examination was made to discover and record how each was put together. Types of threads and stitches were noted. From these observations we established that the covers had not been altered from their original

form, as newer threads only appeared in mends, such as restitching of the fringe.

It was important that the original stitching should be preserved as far as possible, but the fabrics could not be repaired adequately while stitched together in the form of covers. Some stitches would have to be sacrificed for the sake of the fabrics but only when really necessary would a seam be opened, and stitches would only be cut if there were others similar to them that could remain intact. Before cutting any stitching, details were noted so that the fabrics, when repaired, could be put together again in exactly the same manner; the stitches were then cut but the threads were left in place as a future indication of what had been there originally.

It was necessary to open a seam when the first set of covers was removed from its chair. The back-cover was too delicate to be pulled up over the upholstery it neatly fitted, and so one of the side seams, joining brocade to wool, had first to be unpicked. We now saw that the brocade had a backing of unbleached linen fabric and that these two layers together had been seamed to the wool from the inside, therefore the cover had been made up inside-out. The linen extended a little beyond the lower edge of the brocade where it was covered by the fringe. The seat-cover had a similar layer of linen fabric which extended beyond the brocade around all the edges. This was perhaps a device for using a minimum of silk fabric: the extra linen was hidden under the fringe which lay against it and needed to overlap only a little of the brocade.

A closer examination could now be made of the brocade itself. The seat-cover was made from a full width (twenty-five inches) of the fabric with side flaps, cut from separate pieces, seamed to the selvedges. The back-

317

FIG.1 Two of the Dolphin side chairs. The covers of the one on the right have been cleaned and repaired.

FIG.2 One of the seat-covers, before conservation work.

FIG.3 Under the fringe, the surface of brocade has been preserved.

FIG.4 The reverse of the brocade of the back-cover shows some of the original colours and their asymmetrical arrangement.

FIG.5 On the underside, the fringe contains the ends of brightly coloured silk threads. The lighter coloured threads have deteriorated more than the darker ones.

FIG.6 The front of the seat-cover after cleaning. The end of the brocade has been preserved by the fringe.

cover was also made from a full width, the selvedges being seamed to the wool lining. Twenty-five and a half inches of the pattern repeat had been used for the seat and a further twenty and a half inches for the back.

Before the start of conservation work the worn silk was predominantly a dark red colour through which detail of the pattern showed as a dull golden brown. Across the front of the seat-cover, where it had begun to break up, strands of the underlayers of the weft showed through as lighter brighter colours: a pale green, a peach pink, white. But the area beneath the fringing revealed a truer picture of the original splendour of the brocade (FIG.3), for where the edges and ends of the fabric had been covered and protected, its rather startling richness was undimmed. Along part of the side-flaps, most of the surface silk remained: soft weft-faced area in two tones of pink, pale and salmon, detailing in pale green and pinkish brown, rich red satin warp-faced shapes, ground areas and small details in white. These bright colours gave a hint of the fabric's bold design of luxuriant leaves and buds. On closer study, it could be seen that the side flaps had been cut from a section of the fabric with the same pattern as the very centre of the seat where only a ghost of this flamboyant design could now be traced.

The edges of the brocade on the back-cover showed a pattern of red, white and green. At the ends, other colours were found and it seemed that the arrangement of colours was not symmetrical. This asymmetry was more obvious on the reverse side of the fabric (FIG.4). It was possible, at one corner, carefully to separate the brocade from its linen backing, thereby revealing that throughout the pattern the flowers or cluster of leaves to each side of the central motif, al-

though similar in design, were not of the same colours. Light brown and pink were balanced by red-brown and white; red-brown by yellow; pink and yellow by pale-blue and cream. During the investigation, drawings were made from the areas on which the surface silk had been preserved, and gradually, throughout work on the set of chairs, a picture could be built up of the original design and colours. The underside of the fringe itself was equally revealing. What from the faded and dusty front seemed to be pale red, yellow, green and cream threads, in fact contained many bright colours: red, peach pink, pale pink, yellow, green, cream, white and deep grey in irregular mixtures of all colour combinations (FIG.5).

It is difficult to look at the chairs in their present restored state and imagine the full effect that the rich colours of the brocade and fringes with the brightness of the gilded frames of all twelve chairs together must have had when new. No amount of work now could or can revive their original splendour: the aim of our conservation work could only be to preserve what remained of the materials and, by cleaning and repair, to slow down inevitable further deterioration.

Our first task was to clean the covers. For the most part the dust remained on the surface of the fabrics but had collected also among the threads of the fringe, and had passed through the wool lining so that its inside surface was greyer than the outside. A soft squirrel-hair brush was used over the fragile silk to remove the dust onto pads of cotton wool or paper-towel; great care was taken not to disturb the delicate fibres. A small electric absorber with a gentle vacuum pull was used to lift dust from the stronger areas of silk, the linen and the wool, through a protective layer of nylon tulle held taut across the fabrics. While the brocade of the seat-cover was surface-

cleaned, the loose weft threads were rearranged to lie in their original position. A piece of nylon tulle was then placed over this area and large stitches were taken through to the backing linen so that the silk was held in place. All the fringing was similarly stitched into a fold of tulle for safer handling during further cleaning.

To remove loosened dust and other dirt particles, a solvent (white spirit) was used. Water was impossible for several reasons: the dyes of the brocade and fringe were not water-fast; the fabrics might have changed dimensionally on drying, and the parchment would have been spoilt. So the covers, supported and interleaved with Melinex (a clear polyester film), were immersed in the solvent, and turned so that all the surface could be worked over very lightly with a soft brush. After a second bath the covers were drained of excess solvent, blotted gently with paper-towel, and the remaining solvent was allowed to evaporate away naturally.

We decided that the brocade should be repaired onto a total support of fabric using a combination of adhesive and stitching techniques. A fine polyester fabric (Stabiltex), treated on both sides with a thermoplastic adhesive (polyvinyl acetate), was chosen to fix a layer of cotton lawn to the underside of the brocade. The support fabrics were first heat-sealed together, then cut to shape and inserted between the brocade and linen backing. The weave of the brocade was gradually arranged, from the centre outwards, to lie correctly on the support fabrics, and heat from a small iron was applied to set it down, section by section. The adhesive acted as a supplementary support for the complex layered weave of the brocade. The principal repair was then made by couching stitches: threads laid across the weft of the brocade and held down, by small stitches along their length, through to

FIG.7 The front of the seat-cover: the brocade stitched to the support fabrics.

FIG.8 The brocade was stitched to the support fabrics with fine polyester thread worked with a curved needle.

FIG. 10 The seats of two chairs: the one at the back has been cleaned and repaired.

the cotton lawn. This was worked in fine polyester thread using a curved needle, with a sheet of cellulose acetate inserted under the cotton lawn to prevent catching the linen backing (FIGS. 7 and 8). The couching was taken over all the brocade, closely spaced for broken and weak areas, more widely spaced where the fabric was still in sound condition. The type of thread and stitching thus gave strength to the fabric as a whole without putting strain on the delicate fibres, and the fineness and sympathetic translucent colour of the thread made the repair unobtrusive.

The wool lining was strengthened by couching the top and sides onto strips of cotton lawn which would protect the wool from further rubbing against the chair-frame. Weak parts along the heading of the fringe were backed with a fine cotton tape and stitched over with the very fine thread. In addition, thicker thread was used to replace the broken cording across the parchment strip. To help stop further fragmenting of the hanging threads of the fringe, they were lightly sprayed with a consolidant (hydroxy propyl cellulose). Then the opened seams of the covers were re-made and the fringing re-attached, replacing the original stitches of silk or linen thread with stronger polyester thread, but using the same types of stitch and, where possible, the original stitch-holes. After all this painstaking work the covers could then be put back on their chair, and displayed once more at Ham House.

For textiles especially, deterioration with time is inevitable; conservation cannot prevent this, but can help greatly to slow the process down. It is of course also true that furniture on open display in a house is affected by changes in the environment to a greater extent than if it were in the more controlled conditions of a showcase. Because the repaired chair-covers were going back to be shown in the rooms, the conservation materials and methods had to be chosen with a view to durability and stability. But as FIGS. 9 and 10 show, the cleaning and repair have also made the textiles much more pleasing to the eye. Their revived brilliance has lent much of the original grandeur back to the chairs which were, and are an integral part of the North Drawing Room.

GOTHIC RAMPANT: DESIGNS BY L.N. COTTINGHAM FOR SNELSTON HALL

Simon Jervis

'SNELSTON HALL, a spectacular piece of romantic Gothicism by *Cottingham*, 1827. With two show-fronts, both completely asymmetrical, very pinnacled: a miniature Alton Towers. Like Alton Towers the house is to be demolished. There is never much hope for the preservation of C19 fantasy in the C20'. The combination of authority, lapidary yet brisk sentiment, and – most noticeably in the brutal abbreviations – brevity, is unmistakable: Pevsner in top form. Snelston Hall was in fact demolished in 1951 before this thumbnail portrait was published in his *Derbyshire* (1953). A more conventional valediction was that expressed by the editors of the *Journal of the Derbyshire Archaeological and Natural History Society* in 1952: 'Regrets that another mansion has been added to the list of the several classic and ancient homes which have disappeared in this century can be tempered by the fact of its comparative modernity and indifferent structure'. Burke's *Visitation* (1854) makes a nice contrast: 'This is a splendid mansion, modern as to the date of its construction, but so closely imitating the character of the olden times, that it wants nothing but the mantling ivy about its walls, and the mellowing tints of age, to make it pass for the works of other days.'

Such serried encomia are all too reminiscent of Osbert Lancaster's Pelvis Towers and Ffidget Priory or Betjeman's Tomcat Park, as briefly evoked in *Antiquarian Prejudice*. But fortunately, in the case of Snelston Hall, literary evocations are not the sole evidence. In the Derbyshire Record Office at Matlock are the Snelston papers and a number of drawings, in the National Monuments Record are

further drawings and an extensive series of photographs, and in the Print Room of the V&A there is an important group of designs for furniture. The purpose of this account is to draw attention to the latter, but in order to place them in context some account of Snelston Hall and its architect is necessary.

The manor of Snelston, in Derbyshire but close to the border with Staffordshire, was held by the Okeover family from the late twelfth century to the Civil War. Various owners then followed until in the mid-eighteenth century William Bowyer bought the manor. After the death of his great-grandson, Thomas Langley, in 1821 John Harrison, who was married to Elizabeth Evans, Thomas's second cousin and William Bowyer's senior surviving descendant, enforced her claim to the manor and estate after a protracted and contentious legal battle. The Stanton family, who now possess the Snelston estate, are direct descendants of John and Elizabeth Harrison. Why John Harrison, a successful Derby lawyer, chose Lewis Nockalls Cottingham as his architect is not known. Cottingham, born in 1787 the son of a Suffolk farmer, was apprenticed to an Ipswich builder and then worked as an architect's clerk in London, until setting up as an independent architect in 1814. He was an accomplished designer in the neo-classical style but his real love and forte was Gothic.

The earliest dated drawing for Snelston Hall by Cottingham shows neo-classical additions to a neo-classical house. It is inscribed 'June 18th 1822': apparently John Harrison was then confident of rapid success in his suit. Cottingham was still producing neo-classical schemes in March 1826. But already at the beginning of that year he was also proposing alternative Gothic designs and when, on June 11th

1827, the foundation stone of the new Snelston Hall was laid by John Harrison Junior, then aged eight, Gothic was the chosen style. Gothic was by this date highly fashionable, but it is nonetheless tempting to attribute Harrison's conversion to Cottingham's *Working Drawings of Gothic Ornaments, etc., with a Design for a Gothic Mansion* (1824), which comprises an imposing series of Gothic lithographs. The 'Gothic Mansion' in question is planned as a massive hollow rectangle symmetrically disposed around a fountain court. Its main front, well over two hundred feet long, has as its central feature a pinnacled octagonal hall surrounded by a cloister (FIG.2), and the principal apartments included a library ninety feet long by twenty feet wide. The style is an elaborate Tudor Gothic and the only major departure from symmetry a low service wing terminating in a collegiate gate house.

Although this grandiose scheme may have led to a Gothic Snelston, its three-dimensional successor was at once more disciplined and more picturesque. Discipline is apparent in the more compact plan and smaller scale, the influence of the picturesque in the varied skyline, the complete asymmetry of plan, and in the exploitation of a hilltop site. A view of the house by the antiquarian topographer, Frederick Nash (1782–1856) was shown at the Water Colour Society in 1829 but the V&A's only view is a pedestrian lithograph in Burke's *Visitation* of 1854 (FIG.1).

The eastern entrance front, about one hundred feet long, was relatively dull, eight regular buttressed bays with an off-centre projecting and gabled two-storeyed porch. But round from the south-east corner, where the east wing ended in a polygonal bay window lighting the drawing room, all was variety and drama. First a massy great hall with a great south window and

FIG.1 Snelston Hall, Derbyshire, The Seat of John Harrison Esq., lithograph printed by W. Walton, from Burke's *Visitation*, London, 1854.

FIG.2 Elevation of the Principal Front of a
Gothic Mansion, designed by
L.N. Cottingham, lithograph, printed by
C. Hullmandel, London, 1824.

FIG.3 The Drawing-room, Snelston Hall,
pencil and pen and ink, by L.N. Cottingham,
about 1843. Given by Lt.-Col. J.P. Stanton, J.P.

FIG.4 'Drawing-room Cabinet', pen and ink and watercolour, by L.N. Cottingham, about 1843. Given by Lt.-Col. J.P. Stanton, J.P.

FIG.6 'Drawing-room Sofa', pen and ink and watercolour, by L.N. Cottingham, dated 1843. Given by Lt.-Col. J.P. Stanton, J.P.

FIG.5 'Designs for Furniture. Temp. Henry VII', pen and ink and wash, by L.N. Cottingham, dated 1842. Given by Lt.-Col. J.P. Stanton, J.P.

FIG.7 'Divan Couch for Angle of Room', pen and ink and watercolour by L.N. Cottingham, about 1843. Given by Lt.-Col. J.P. Stanton, J.P.

flanking pepperpot turrets, next, after an interval, another large faceted bay window, and then, on the south-west corner there was a lofty and battlemented octagonal tower enlivened with a turret. To the south of the house a series of stepped terraces led up to a mighty retaining wall behind which, surrounding the house, Cottingham planned a 'Terrace Flower Garden' with serpentine paths, cedars, agaves, roses and irregular flower beds.

In 1854 Burke stated that, 'The interior fully answers to the expectations raised by the first view of this stately edifice . . . The principal rooms are fitted up with oaken furniture, carved and massive, according to the ancient fashion, which is so rigidly adhered to, even in the minutest details, as to completely exclude any idea of a modern mansion'. Drawings in the V&A Print Room, given by Colonel Stanton in 1951, allow a partial reconstruction of the drawing room, which is depicted in an incomplete interior (FIG.3). Cottingham designed a monument to Miss Harrison in Snelston Church in 1837, and in 1839 a Gothic garden seat, so his Snelston involvement seems to have been more or less continuous. Fortunately two of the drawing room designs are inscribed 1842 and one 1843, which gives a clear date for this scheme.

The drawing room, twenty-six feet wide by thirty-six feet long, was entered from the north, had a Gothic fireplace and overmantel on its long west wall, and was lit by a tripartite bow window to the south. The principal piece of furniture was a massive cabinet opposite the fireplace, presumably for the display of objects from John Harrison's collection. At Matlock is a large and detailed drawing of an earlier design, inscribed 'Design for a Gothic Armoire for the Great Drawing Room at Snelston Hall'. It depicts a Gothic piece of conventional recti-

FIG.8 'Design for a Table. Temp. Henry VII', pen and ink and wash, by L.N. Cottingham, about 1843. Given by Lt.-Col. J.P. Stanton, J.P.

FIG.9 'Reliquary in Box Wood, Formerly in the possession of Mr Bullock, Egyptian Hall, Piccadilly, bought from Spain', drawn by George Cattermole, engraved by Henry Shaw, 1834, and published in *Specimens of Ancient Furniture*, London, 1836.

FIG.10 'Conversational Sofa', pencil, pen and ink and wash, by L.N. Cottingham, dated 1842. Given by Lt.-Col. J.P. Stanton, J.P.

FIG.11 'Sofa Table', pen and ink and watercolour, by L.N. Cottingham, about 1843. Given by Lt.-Col. J.P. Stanton, J.P.

FIG.12 Hanging shelves and pole screen, pen and ink and watercolour, by L.N. Cottingham, about 1843. Given by Lt.-Col. J.P. Stanton, J.P.

FIG.13 'Sideboard and Chairs for Dining Room, Snelston Hall, The Seat of John Harrison Esqr.', pen and ink, by L.N. Cottingham, about 1840(?). Given by Lt.-Col. J.P. Stanton, J.P.

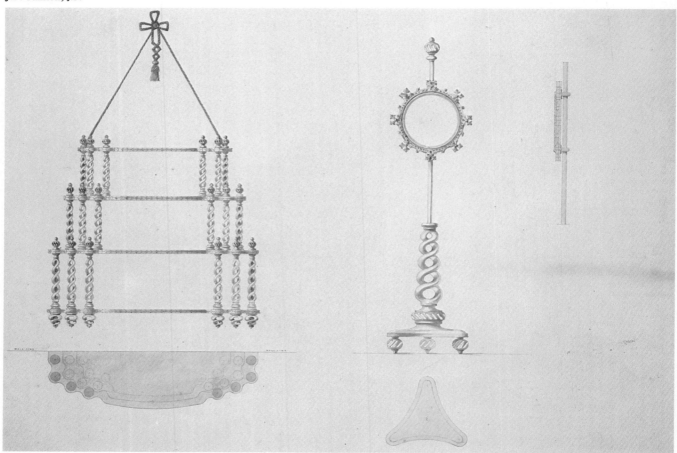

FIG.14 Stalls placed in the Music Gallery, Snelston Hall, pen and ink and wash, by L.N. Cottingham, about 1840(?). Given by Lt.-Col. J.P. Stanton, J.P.

linearity but is interesting for the inclusion of numerous objects – ewers, cups, candlesticks, caskets, books and sculpture – presumably from Harrison's collection. When Cottingham's own collection was sold in 1851 lot 894 was 'A PAIR OF VERY FINELY MODELLED DRAGONS, after an original pair in bronze, in the possession of J. Harrison, Esq. of Snelston Hall, Derbyshire; said to be by Cellini'. Judging from the objects on the Matlock 'Armoire' these 'Cellini' dragons would appear to be representative of Harrison's taste. The later armoire design shown in the V&A interior and in another large drawing at Matlock, is more interesting in form, although regrettably no objects are depicted. Its top section is tripartite, and both the taller central bay and the outer bays are embellished at the top with rich late Gothic canopy work. The general form is reminiscent of late Gothic carved wooden triptychs and it is possible that Cottingham may have been influenced in particular by a splendid Flemish triptych of about 1490 installed, prob-

ably by Cottingham himself, in St. Wilfred's Chapel, Brougham, in about 1840. This was on loan to the V&A, which restored it, from 1970 to 1976, and is now shown in Carlisle Cathedral.

The large armoire was flanked by two 'Drawing-room Cabinets' of typical late Gothic form (FIG.4), at least one of which was in turn flanked by X-framed chairs of plausibly Gothic character (FIG.5). Opposite, at the window end of the fireplace wall, was a large and exuberant 'Drawing-room Sofa', wholly unarchaeological, its back surmounted by a Gothic finial (FIG.6). This piece recalls a sofa designed for Eaton Hall by William Porden, which is depicted in an 1824 watercolour by John Buckler, reproduced in *Views of Eaton Hall* (1826), and which is now at Acton Round, Shropshire. On the other side of the fireplace was a Gothic side chair (FIG.5) and a 'Divan Couch for Angle of Room' (FIG.7). In front of this was an 'Octagon Table' for which the finished design is in Matlock.

In front of the fireplace was another

octagonal table, whose base is formed much like that of a Gothic chalice, a type recorded in illuminated manuscripts (FIG.8). However it is interesting to find that Cottingham's direct inspiration was a Flemish carved wood reliquary of about 1500 illustrated in *Specimens of Ancient Furniture* (1836), the first English book on old furniture, by Cottingham's friend, Henry Shaw (FIG.9). The Snelston drawing room also contained a round stool whose form echoes that of the table on a smaller scale (FIG.5). In the centre of the room was a hopelessly implausible 'Conversational Sofa', its feet formed as roundels of Gothic tracery (FIG.10). Curiously a parallel occurs in a stool design in Pugin's usually archaeological *Gothic Furniture in the Style of the 15th Century* (1835). Also in the drawing room, but not included in the incomplete interior, were a throne-like X-framed chair (FIG.5), a 'Sofa Table', perhaps influenced by Pugin (FIG.11), a pole screen and hanging shelves (FIG.12). The shelves are, unexpectedly, close to a two-shelf version

FIG.15 Brass candle branch 'of the time of Henry V', engraving published in the *Catalogue of the Museum of Medieval Art, collected by the late L.N. Cottingham, F.S.A., Architect,* London, 1851, and also in *The Builder,* 1851.

FIG.16 Gilt bronze candle branch, designed by L.N. Cottingham for the chapel of Magdalen College, Oxford, about 1832. Impressed 'SUMMERS', probably for W. Summers, listed as a coppersmith and brazier at Herbert's Place, Waterloo Road, in 1835.

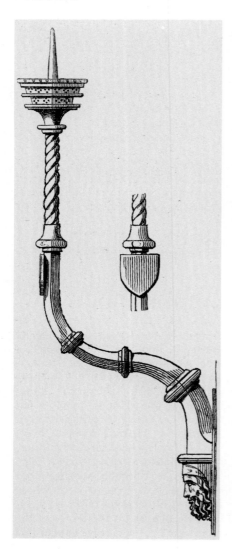

shown in a gouache interior of a summer house at Lainz in about 1840, which was included in the V&A's *Biedermeier Interior* exhibition in 1979. But the direct inspiration for the elaborately turned supports of both shelves and pole screen may have come from another plate in Shaw's *Ancient Furniture* (1836), depicting a 'Wassail Table and Candelabra', acquired by the V&A in 1976.

Since the middle of the 18th century English designers had become increasingly expert at applying the pointed tracery, clustered columns and foliate carving of Gothic to modern furniture forms, although alongside such fluent and congruous designs ran a lesser strain of quirkier inventions. In the 1830s increasing antiquarian expertise led towards a more archaeological approach, while Pugin, whose original if uneven *Gothic Furniture* (1835) is the key pattern-book of the decade, moved beyond simple copyism to the design of new forms convincingly Gothic not only in ornament but also in structure. From the evidence of the Snelston

drawing-room designs of 1842 and 1843 it is clear that Cottingham never made this creative leap.

Cottingham was however an important collector of architectural fragments and his own house in Waterloo Bridge Road was one of the great antiquarian ensembles. It did not long survive his death in 1847 being sold in 1851, despite an eloquent plea from Henry Shaw in his preface to the *Catalogue* that it be purchased by the Government as an adjunct to the Schools of Design. This suggestion was not however wholly ignored: certain items were purchased to form part of the newly founded Architectural Museum, whose collections were eventually incorporated in the V&A. A design by Cottingham for a 'Sideboard and Chairs for Dining Room' at Snelston exemplifies one aspect of the antiquarian interior: the sideboard, although modern in form, incorporates fragments of what appears to be genuine Flemish sixteenth and seventeenth century woodwork (FIG.13). Such interiors also included unaltered

objects. A watercolour by Cottingham shows a run of seventeenth century Flemish stalls, one of three such which stood in the Music Gallery at Snelston (FIG.14).

The sideboard design includes four candlesticks which are probably Flemish late seventeenth century. Cottingham was a celebrated collector and designer of metalwork. Among the objects sold in 1851 were 'A PAIR OF REMARKABLY FINE BRANCHES of brass, with prickets for candles, of the time of Henry V' (FIG.15). In 1981 the V&A purchased two gilt bronze 'branches' designed by Cottingham for the chapel of Magdalen College, Oxford, in about 1832. Their form is clearly influenced by his Gothic pair, albeit reduced, but their rich foliate decoration is a new ingredient (FIG.16). This acquisition not only gives the V&A's representation of Cottingham three dimensions, it also demonstrates that in the late C20, to use Pevsner's convention, some hope is left for the preservation of C19 fantasy.

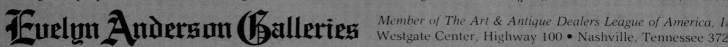

7, quai Voltaire, 75007 Paris - Tél. : 260.73.13 et 261.75.99

R.C. Paris 316 316 207 - Siret 316 316 207 00018 - A P E 6425

Once again we have re-purchased and offer stock from our past. In 1935 we acquired (through Messrs Sellick of Exeter) the suite of eight elbow chairs bearing the crest of the Connock family of Treworgey Manor, Cornwall.

We have a pair of these outstanding chairs; four of which are at Temple Newsam Museum and the other pair in a private collection. These chairs are amongst the great achievements of the chair-makers of the mid-18th century and their condition confirms the strength of a real craftsman's work.

(Fine Arts) Ltd.

1-9 BRUTON PLACE,
LONDON, W.1
Tel: 01-629 5600 & 01-499 6266

Gander & White

PACKERS AND SHIPPERS OF ANTIQUES AND WORKS OF ART SPECIALISED HOUSEHOLD REMOVALS

1 *A George III ormolu mounted commode*

2 *The commode is wrapped, padded, wrapped again and then padded again.*

3 *The inner case is lined with shock-resistant material.*

4 *A strong outer case completes the protection. The commode is now ready for shipment to French & Co. Inc. New York.*

GANDER & WHITE SHIPPING LTD
21 LILLIE ROAD, LONDON SW6 1UE. TEL: 01-381 0571 TELEX: 917434 GANITE

337

340

SPAIN AND SOUTH KENSINGTON.
JOHN CHARLES ROBINSON AND THE COLLECTING OF SPANISH SCULPTURE IN THE 1860s

Malcolm Baker

In April 1871 the architect Sir Matthew Digby Wyatt, Art Referee to the South Kensington Museum, wrote to Sir Henry Cole, the Museum's first Director, about a polychromed bust of the Virgin, today displayed in the Continental Baroque primary gallery: 'This capital head & bust of the "Virgen de los dolores", the favourite Spanish type, should certainly be bought. It is full of character, and is cheap – since I have seen many of much less merit for which higher prices have been asked in Spain. It looks very much like the work of Montanes and is both interesting and rare, of such esthetic merit. Strongly recommended'.[1] Now attributed to Pedro de Mena, rather than Montanes, this sculpture (FIG.1) forms part of a substantial but relatively little-known, collection of Spanish sculpture.[2] The foundations of the collection had, however, already been laid, and many of its most distinguished individual pieces acquired, some years before through the efforts of John Charles Robinson (FIG.2), a far more scholarly and discerning judge than Wyatt. As Art Referee, responsible for advising on potential acquisitions, during the 1860s Robinson played a crucial role in shaping the V&A's European collections, complementing the interests of Henry Cole in the applied arts and ornament with a remarkably well-informed appreciation of figure sculpture.

It is evident from the records of this period, as well as from the sale of Spanish silver from his own collection to the Museum some thirty years later, that Robinson was collecting on his own account and not merely for the South Kensington Museum. His activities as a dealer, together with per-

FIG.1 Virgin of Sorrows. Polychromed wood. Ascribed to Pedro de Mena (1628–88). 284-1871.

sonal antipathy between him and Cole, eventually led to his resignation in 1869. As a connoisseur and scholar, however, Robinson's range of taste and depth of knowledge were exceptional. His achievement in gathering together before 1870 one of the foremost collections of Italian Renaissance sculpture has already been recognised, his 1862 catalogue being described in the introduction of its 1964 successor as, 'a remarkable achievement, detached, admirably formulated, and filled with qualitative judgements that are no less valid now than at the time when they were made... Of [Robinson's] vision, persuasiveness and energy the sculptures he acquired speak for themselves'.[3] Robinson's concern with Spanish sculpture is less well-known, but both his acquisitions and the letters

FIG.2 John Charles Robinson. Bronze by Charles Marochetti (1805–67). A202-1929.

and reports concerning potential purchases seen in Spain and Portugal on two visits in 1863-4 and 1865-6 reveal an equally impressive knowledge and a comparable breadth of interests.

Robinson's first extended tour of Spain was made between September 1863 and January 1864. Entering the country from France, where he had already begun to acquire Spanish works of art, his itinerary covered a dauntingly wide geographical area, with stays in most of the major centres including Burgos, Madrid, Segovia, Avila, Valladolid, Astorga, Leon, the Escorial, Toledo, Cordova, Seville, Malaga, Granada, Alicante, Valencia, Barcelona and Saragoza. On his return he produced a lengthy and characteristically crisply written report that, even if allowances are made for the author's need to justify his tour to Cole, reveals much about both collecting in Spain at this period and the thinking that lay behind the Museum's early acquisitions.[4] The visit, he says, allowed him 'to form an estimate of the relative abundance or scarcity of works of Art both of an available, or if I may term it, floating kind, and also fixed or monumental nature, in the several districts of the country, information calculated to be of primary utility should any further operations be undertaken in Spain'. He concluded that the country 'might yet be made to yield a productive and interesting harvest', though there were some formidable difficulties. On 17 December he writes to Cole from Valencia: 'This part of Spain has evidently been completely cleared of works of art in past years, whilst the towns in the mountain districts, where I went provided with excellent introductions, although scarcely even traversed, were equally devoid of interest'. On his return he summarises the problems, commenting interestingly on the differences between col-

FIG.3 Virgin of the Immaculate Conception. Polychromed terracotta. Ascribed to a follower of Luisa Roldan. Seville, about 1700. 320-1864.

FIG.4 Shepherd Boy. Polychromed terracotta. Ascribed to Jose de Leon. Early nineteenth century. 325-1866.

lecting in Spain and Italy: 'Whatever may be the relative artistic wealth of Spain at the present time in specimens available for purchase, it is certainly more difficult there than elsewhere to find out and acquire such objects, whereas for instance in Italy, Germany and France, everything is known and noted, where every town and village has been searched to exhaustion, and the machinery of acquisition if I may so term it, organised in the most complete and practical manner, in Spain comparatively little of the kind has been done. There are as a rule no dealers, no local guides, no middle men, and possessors of works of art are either completely ignorant of their importance, and so never think of calling attention to them, or else on the other hand, delude themselves with exaggerated ideas about their value, this last being a natural result of the hasty and isolated excursions of continental dealers, and the inconsiderate offers of wealthy travellers. Certain national characteristics moreover should be taken into account as opposed to the acquisition of works of Art. The innate pride and reserve of the Spanish people indispose them to invite the attention of strangers to their possessions; and it is as difficult to obtain information as respect to objects of Art in private hands as it is easy in Italy where as a rule all classes are willing to barter away their artistic possessions'.

Reflecting both the Museum's aims and Robinson's own diverse interests, the many acquisitions made – a total of 112 items by 31 December 1863 – cover all aspects of the decorative arts and sculpture. Among these are some surprising objects, including a 'gold mounted etui of Old Chelsea porcelain' purchased in Murcia, 'a large old Wedgwood ware bowl and cover', bought in Toledo, and two 'carved boxwood statuettes of Roman emperors', now regarded as German.[5]

However, the majority of the items listed were divided between two main categories. One was metalwork, Robinson's acquisitions, along with the pieces given or bequeathed this century by Dr Hildburgh, making the Museum's collection of Spanish silver quite exceptional.[6] The other was sculpture.

Although Spanish paintings had been attracting the attention of English visitors to Spain from a much earlier date, the sculpture of the peninsula seems to have been largely unknown to English collectors before Robinson's pioneering efforts. An analysis of his sculpture acquisitions provides an interesting contrast to the pattern of Spanish picture collecting by the English during the nineteenth century. Some pieces are indeed quite compatible with the long-established taste among the English for artists such as Murillo. For example, the terracotta Immaculate Conception (FIG.3), purchased in Granada, might seem to be paralleled well by the 'Assumption of the Virgin, a beautiful figure supported by Boy-Angels, in a bright manner, by Morellio' that was recorded at Houghton by 1766.[7] Similarly, Leon's Shepherd Boy (FIG.4) is perhaps not too far in spirit from the genre subjects of peasant children by the same painter that were so popular with early 19th century English artists. But far less conventional was Robinson's enthusiasm for polychromed wood sculpture which represents such an important aspect of Spanish baroque. He was well aware of its significance, drawing attention to specific examples he had acquired: 'In the thoroughly national category of wood sculpture moreover, I would particularly specify two, if not three, original works from the hand of the greatest Spanish master in that speciality, Alonso Cano (FIG.5), and a really beautiful and truthful work by an artist of great local cel-

ebrity, Alexandro Carnicero of Salamanca' (FIG.6). Although an enthusiasm for this type of sculpture may have seemed rather unusual to his contemporaries, it should perhaps be set against the collecting earlier in the century, particularly by Catholic families, of late Gothic German and Netherlandish wood sculpture, some of which at least retained its polychromed surfaces. Indeed, any examples of Spanish sculpture that came to this country before Robinson's expedition, including the splendid crucifix figure at Arundel, were probably acquired by such families for devotional use.

The name of Alonso Cano occurs frequently in Robinson's reports. Although he is perhaps better known today as a painter, Robinson evidently thought of him primarily as a sculptor. Possibly this awareness in South Kensington of his sculptural achievements explains why, when shown on the Albert Memorial, he is given the attributes of a sculptor rather than those of a painter. Another sculptor who engaged Robinson's attention was Risueño, who like Cano and Mena worked in Granada, and to whom the terracotta Immaculate Conception was originally attributed. Outstanding among the various works now ascribed to him is the terracotta of St Joseph with the Christ Child (FIG.1), which is one of several examples of the same subject by this sculptor[8]. Another notable purchase was the terracotta of St Diego with the Virgin and Child (FIG.8), now attributed to Luisa Roldan. Subjects such as these occur frequently in the paintings acquired by the English from a much earlier date and from this point of view these sculpture acquisitions may seem unexceptional[9]. However, the representation of such subjects in a vividly painted, three-dimensional form emphasises both their baroque quality and their devotional function. These

FIG.5 The Infant St John the Baptist. Polychromed wood. Ascribed by Robinson to Alonso Cano. Probably Granada, early eighteenth century. 171-1864.

characteristics probably seemed less pronounced in the paintings, which could relatively easily become assimilated into English collections dominated by the works of Guido Reni or the Carracci. In this way, therefore, Robinson's appreciation of Spanish baroque sculpture was unusually advanced. Indeed, perhaps the relative lack of interest in this field among the English even today reflects an underlying resistance to those qualities that Robinson evidently prized.

Renaissance and Mannerist sculpture figures less prominently among Robinson's Spanish acquisitions than the Baroque, but this lack of earlier works was largely a problem of availability. Most sculpture of this date was architectural or formed part of large complexes such as altarpieces and was not therefore, in Robinson's words, 'of the floating kind'. In October 1863 he draws attention the to the main problem in a letter to Cole: 'From the little I have yet seen of Spain I am not without hopes of securing some interesting specimens in the class of decorative sculpture, though there is at present (as in Italy) a great archaeological and conservative movement in the country for the conservation of ancient monuments, the establishing of local museums etc. having been recently instituted in every province'. Nevertheless, despite these difficulties one work by a major sixteenth century sculptor was obtained; a prophet from the altar-piece of the conventual church of San Benito, Valladolid, executed by Alonso Berruguete (FIG.9) Commissioned in 1526 and completed in 1532, this *retablo major* was dismantled in the mid nineteenth century but had yet to be properly re-assembled in the museum at Valladolid when Robinson arrived there, thus giving him the opportunity to acquire a single figure. On 10 March 1864 he reports its purchase to Cole in

the following terms: 'Statuette of a saint or apostle in carved and gilded wood, the drapery is picked out in colours ("Estifado")... This statuette carved in walnut is one of the very numerous figures, which formerly adorned the now dismantled altarpiece or "Retablo" of San Benito el real Valladolid, one of the most celebrated works of the Master (see Cean Bermudez – life of Berruguette – where the

original contract is quoted). A considerable number of the most important of the statues and groups from the retablo are now preserved in the public museum at Valladolid. The present specimen, unfortunately mutilated, is also one of the most hastily executed and mannered of the series, having been doubtless one of those originally placed high up at a great distance from the eye. Purchased of Perez Minguez

FIG.6 Christ carrying the Cross. Polychromed wood. Ascribed to Alexandro Carnicero (1693–1756). Salamanca, early eighteenth century. 102-1864.

in Valladolid, price 550 reals'. Although it is likely that the figure came from the lowest register, rather than from above, and was among those carved by one of Berruguete's two Netherlandish assistants, probably Juan de Cambray, its twisting pose and elongated proportions illustrate well that Spanish variety of the mannerist style best exemplified in sculpture by Berruguete.[10]

Although, with occasional exceptions such as this, medieval and Renaissance works were largely unavailable, Robinson still considered that they should be represented, at least in the forms of photographs or plaster casts, as in the case of the Portico de la Gloria at Santiago. Indeed, in his report to Cole he states: 'My instructions were first to find out and effect the purchase of objects of

Art, more especially of Spanish national origin, suitable for the Kensington Museum; and secondly to inspect the permanent monuments of Art with a view to the procuring such illustrations or reproductions of them as might seem desirable to that collection'. He was equally energetic in acquiring publications, both current and earlier, on Spanish art: 'I took every opportunity of procuring

FIG.8 St Diego with the Virgin and Child.
Polychromed terracotta. Ascribed to Luisa
Roldan (1656–1704). 250-1864.

FIG.7 St Joseph and the Christ Child.
Polychromed terracotta. Purchased by
Robinson as from the School of Alonso Cano.
Ascribed to José Risueño (1667–1721). 313-
1864.

FIG.9 Prophet. Polychromed walnut. By
Alonso Berruguete (1485/9–1561) About
1530. 249-1864.

Spanish books on the Fine Arts, Catalogues of galleries and collections and also local guide books – in the latter class Spanish literature is comparatively rich, and such works contain much information more or less directly bearing on the Arts, and are probably difficult to obtain out of the localities in which they were produced, I thought it desirable to purchase not only those of recent date on current sale, but also to collect and to gather information respecting those of earlier period not so easily to be obtained. This pursuit furnished me with a certain amount of occupation in each locality and the result is rather a numerous series of scarce and interesting books acquired at little cost'. Both statements such as these and the range of the acquisitions themselves demonstrate clearly how systematic was Robinson's approach. It is perhaps this quality especially that distinguishes his collecting activities from those of earlier English visitors to the peninsula. No doubt his avowed aim of acquiring 'as complete and varied collection of objects of Spanish Art of Characteristic national types as could be obtained' was intended to appeal to Cole's view of the collections at South Kensington as being representative of all styles, materials and types of manufacture. Nonetheless, it seems that his two visits to Spain, and the acquisitions that resulted, reflect a new and wider awareness of Spanish art as far as the English were concerned. Even though Robinson's bold aims remained only partially achieved, the Spanish sculpture purchased by him for the Museum amply justifies his claim that 'more than one specimen will be deemed worthy to rank with the more remarkable and valuable objects from other sources, previously added to the collection'.

An earlier version of this paper was given at the 1984 Conference of the Association of Art Historians and I am grateful for the comments made then, particularly those of Hugh Brigstocke and Enriqueta Frankfort, who drew my attention to the figure of Cano on the Albert Memorial, and also to Anthony Radcliffe who provided information on the Berruguete prophet.

1 *Art Referee's Reports*, 18 April 1871.

2 Closely related works by Mena include a bust in the Dreifaltigkeitskirche, Vienna, for which see H. Aurenhammer in *Alte und neue Kunst*, 1954, p.111.

3 J. Pope-Hennessy and R. Lightbown, *Catalogue of Italian Sculpture in the Victoria and Albert Museum*, London, 1964, I, p.x.

4 Undated quotations below are from this account in *J. C. Robinson's Reports*, Other letters cited by date are from vol.197.

5 Cf. M. Baxandall, *German wood statuettes 1500-1800*, London. Both the provenance of the V&A pair and the presence of Italian inscriptions on closely related examples at Woburn Abbey and in another private collection suggest that the origin of these pieces deserves reconsideration.

6 For Robinson's contribution in this field see C. Oman, *The Golden Age of Spanish Silver 1400-1665*, London, 1968.

7 T. Martyn, *The English Connoisseur*, London, 1766, I, p.94.

8 For examples remaining in Granada see O. Diaz in *Cuadernos de arte*, IV-VI, 1931-41, p.103, and in *Goya*, XIV , 1956, p.76.

9 See A. Braham, *El Greco to Goya: the taste for Spanish painting in Britain and Ireland* (National Gallery exhibition catalogue), London, 1981.

10 The probable position of the V&A prophet was on one side of the original tabernacle, which was apparently replaced by a larger Baroque tabernacle that dislodged the figures on each side. For a hypothetical construction of the *retablo* see J. C. Aznar, *Alonso Berruguete*, Madrid, 1980.

Patrice Bellanger

expert c.n.e.

sculptures - tableaux
XVIIᵉ et XVIIIᵉ siècles

198 boulevard Saint-Germain 75007 Paris

Tél. 544.19.15

Terre cuite par Joseph-Charles MARIN (1759–1834)
GANYMEDE
circa 1800
Hauteur: 31 centimètres

Contributors

Malcolm Baker is an Assistant Keeper in the Department of Sculpture where he is responsible for European sculpture (other than Italian) between 1400 and 1900. He prepared the sculpture section of the Rococo exhibition and is working on a catalogue of the Museum's baroque ivories.

Stephen Bayley was educated at Manchester University and Liverpool School of Architecture. He taught History and Theory of Art at the Open University and at the University of Kent. He is the author of *In Good Shape* (1979), *The Albert Memorial* (1981) and *Harley Earl and the Dream Machine* (1983). Since 1978 he has been working with (Sir) Terence Conran on making a new 'museum' of design, at present happily located in the old boilerhouse yard of the V&A.

Mrs. Bonython is the author of 'King Cole', published by the Museum in 1982.

Anthony Burton was Assistant Keeper in the V&A Library for ten years, after which he transferred to an administrative post in the Directorate, also acting as Assistant Secretary to the Advisory Council 1979–83. In 1981 he became Keeper of the V&A's branch museum at Bethnal Green, with a brief to develop it as the V&A's Museum of Childhood.

Craig Clunas studied Chinese language and literature at Cambridge and at Peking Languages Institute 1972–1977. He was awarded a Ph.D. in Chinese and Mongolian Literature, London University 1983. He joined the Far Eastern Department in 1979. His special research interests include Chinese lacquer, furniture and carving of the late imperial period, as well as Chinese export art.

Frances Collard works in the Department of Furniture and Woodwork where she is responsible for the archive of information on the history of furniture and of interior decoration. This article is based on material collected for her book, *Regency Furniture*, which is to be published in the autumn.

Joe Earle joined the Museum in 1974 and is now Keeper of the Far Eastern Department. He spent two months in Japan last autumn as a Japan Foundation Fellow. His present chief preoccupations are a book on Japanese lacquer for the V&A Far Eastern Series and the new gallery of Japanese art which it is hoped to open in 1986.

Nicola Gentle studied Fine Art at Winchester School of Art. She joined the V&A Museum in 1978 as a conservator at the Textile Workshop, Osterley Park House. In 1981 she was awarded a Fellowship by the Churchill Memorial Trust to study textile conservation in the Netherlands, Belgium and Switzerland.

Phillipa Glanville, F.S.A., Assistant Keeper in the Metalwork Department, is preparing the catalogue of the early modern English silver in the Museum. She has written on Tudor goldsmiths' work and has a long-standing interest in the history of collecting, a subject discussed in her forthcoming book, *Silver in England*.

Jean Hamilton is Senior Research Assistant of the Department of Prints and Drawings. She is responsible for the Museum's collection of wallpapers. Publications include *Wallpapers, a history and illustrated catalogue of the collection in the Victoria and Albert Museum* (jointly with C. C. Oman), Sotheby Publications, 1982; *An Introduction to Wallpaper*, H.M.S.O., 1983, and various articles in the *Connoisseur* and other periodicals. She is currently preparing a publication on the Museum's collection of European decorative papers.

John Hardy is Assistant Keeper in the Department of Furniture and Woodwork and has responsibility for the collections of eighteenth century furniture; he is also involved in the administration of Osterley Park House.

Mark Haworth-Booth read English at Cambridge and then Fine Art at the University of Edinburgh, joining the V&A in 1970. He has looked after the Museum's photograph collection in Prints and Drawings and Photographs since 1977. His major publications to date are *E. McKnight Kauffer: A Designer and his Public* (1979) and *The Golden Age of British Photography* (1984).

Simon Jervis joined the Department of Furniture and Woodwork at the Victoria and Albert Museum in 1966, and is now the Department's Deputy Keeper. His interests extend beyond furniture to the history of interior decoration, architecture, design and ornament. His books include *Victorian Furniture* (1968), *Printed Furniture Designs before 1650* (1974), *Woodwork of Winchester Cathedral* (1976), *High Victorian Design* (1983) and the *Penguin Dictionary of Design and Designers* (1984). He has published many articles in *Apollo*, the *Burlington Magazine*, *Connoisseur*, *Country Life*, *Furniture History* and other magazines.

Rose Kerr graduated in Chinese Art and Archaeology from the School of Oriental and African Studies, University of London. She studied one year in Peking, then worked for two years at the Percival David Foundation of Chinese Art, and is now Assistant Keeper in Far Eastern Department. She tries to return to China every couple of years to keep her hand in, her most recent trip in April 1984 enabling her to make extensive purchases of contemporary material for the museum.

Donald King, F.S.A., former Keeper of the Department of Textiles and Dress, is President of the Centre International d'Étude des Textiles Anciens and of the Textile Conservation Centre. He has helped organise various Arts Council exhibitions, including *Opus Anglicanum, The Arts of Islam* and *The Eastern Carpet in the Western World*.

Michael Maclagan, F.S.A.; F.R.Hist.S., has a special connection with the V&A being the son of Sir Eric Maclagan, a past Director of the Museum. Since 1980 he has been Richmond Herald of Arms, after a long career at Oxford University, where he was a Fellow of Trinity College. He is the author of many books and articles on historical subjects.

John Murdoch is the Deputy Keeper in charge of the Department of Paintings. He is the author of works on seventeenth century British portraiture, and on the tradition of landscape painting from the seventeenth to the nineteenth century. He is the author of the catalogue that accompanies this autumn's major exhibition, *The Discovery of the Lake District, a Northern Arcadia and its Uses*.

Charles Newton is a Research Assistant in the Department of Prints and Drawings. His particular interest is the collection of topographical material, especially Middle Eastern subjects. He is organising an exhibition of the work of the artist Amadeo, 5th Count Preziosi, who lived and painted in nineteenth century Istanbul.

Anthony North, F.S.A., joined the Museum in 1964 and works as a Research Assistant in the Department of Metalwork. He has written books and articles on arms, armour, base metalwork and Islamic metalwork.

Anna Somers Cocks, F.S.A., the editor, was Assistant Keeper in Metalwork Department, and is now in the Department of Ceramics and Glass. She is the author of *The Victoria & Albert Museum: the making of the Collection* (1980) and co-author of *Renaissance Jewels, Gold Boxes and Objets de Vertu from the Thyssen-Bornemisza Collection* (1984).

Marjorie Trusted is Senior Museum Assistant in the Department of Metalwork. She recently published an article on amber in *Pantheon*, and has just completed a catalogue of the ambers in the Victoria and Albert Museum, due to be published at the end of 1984.

Wartski

ESTABLISHED 1865

14 GRAFTON STREET, LONDON W1

TELEPHONE: 493 1141/2/3

An English eighteenth century, shaped gold box with panels of mother of pearl engraved with wavy lines and applied with chased gold sprays of flowers and butterflies, c. 1740. 6.8 cm.

A Fabergé gold miniature frame in the form of a daisy enamelled shaded white, the aperture set with rose diamonds. 3.5 cm. diameter.

Fabergé spray of lily of the valley, the rose diamond set pearl flowers issuing from chased gold stems with a single reeded nephrite leaf; contained in a crystal vase with *trompe l'oeil* water. 3.5 cm. From the Collection of Queen Helen of Rumania.

An enamelled gold *boîte à mouches*, the inner panels enamelled translucent royal blue over a sunburst *guilloché* ground, further decorated with gold scrolling *paillons*, the *sablé* borders set with half pearls between green enamelled leaves, the interior compartments divided by a sable brush; the lid fitted with the original mirror. By Jean Joseph Barrière, Paris 1787. 6 cm.

A demantoid garnet and diamond set brooch in the form of a lizard with ruby eyes.

An eighteenth century diamond, emerald and ruby set flower brooch.

A jewelled papal cameo by Santarelli of Pope Pius VII, the gold mount profusely set with rose diamonds and the gem set reverse shows the blind heathen in the presence of the light of Christ. Italian c. 1826. 6.3 cm.

THE FRIENDS OF THE V&A

AIMS

To help in the work and activities of the Victoria and Albert Museum and in particular:

To purchase works of art

To maintain a lively exhibition programme

To expand the Museum's training schemes and research projects

To contribute towards the cost of refurbishing the galleries

PRIVILEGES

1. Free and immediate entry to all paying exhibitions at the Museum and to Ham House, Osterley Park, and Apsley House (Bethnal Green has no entry charges).
   The membership normally admits husband/wife or other guest and Friend's children under 16.

2. Special Evening Private Views

3. Advance information on Museum activities.

4. Discounts on selected catalogues and other publications, and purchases in the Craft Shop.

5. Visits abroad and in this country, accompanied by staff from departments of the Museum.

6. Social occasions at the Museum, Ham House, Apsley House and Osterley Park.

MEMBERSHIP

Membership Fee
£15 annually

Special Fee
£10 annually
(for pensioners and those working full time in UK museums)

Corporate Fee
£100 or more annually
(with transferable membership cards)

Benefactor
£1,000 annually
A Benefactor may specify which department or project of the Museum should receive his gift

For further details and application form, please apply to:
Friends' Office
Victoria and Albert Museum
South Kensington
London SW7 2RL
01-589 4040

Index of Advertisers